Strangers like Angels

Strangers like Angels

WITH A DEVIL OR TWO TO BOOT

To ~~████████~~,

Sending you this gift that you may rejoice with us and celebrate that God is still searching and calling His lost sheep.

Alec & Jan Forman

Blessings

Alec Jan

29th October 2014

Matador
9 Priory Business Park
Kibworth Beauchamp
Leicestershire LE8 0RX, UK
Tel: (+44) 116 279 2299
Fax: (+44) 116 279 2277
Email: books@troubador.co.uk
Web: www.troubador.co.uk/matador

ISBN 978-1783063-628

British Library Cataloguing in Publication Data.
A catalogue record for this book is available from the British Library.

Typeset in Minion Pro by Troubador Publishing Ltd
Printed and bound in the UK by TJ International, Padstow, Cornwall

Matador is an imprint of Troubador Publishing Ltd

Sweethearts, Jan and Alec, 1972.

David, Paul and Margaret
May you be richly blessed
So glad we are family

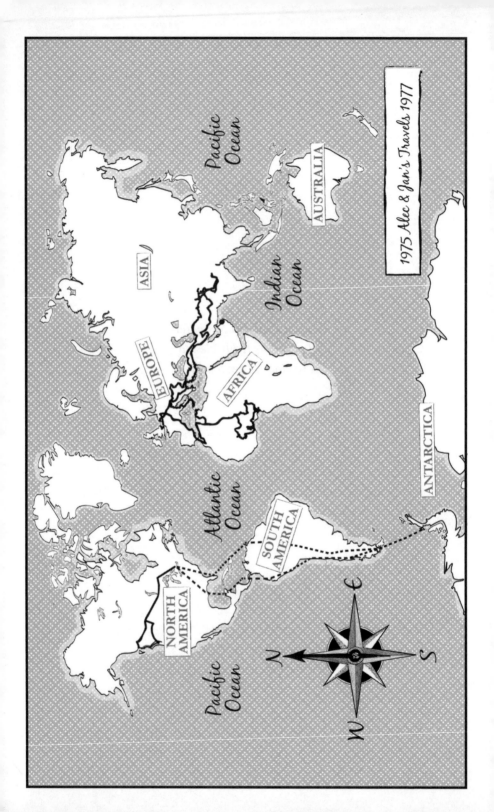

Contents

Before

South

North

East

West

After

Appendix

Acknowledgements

Before

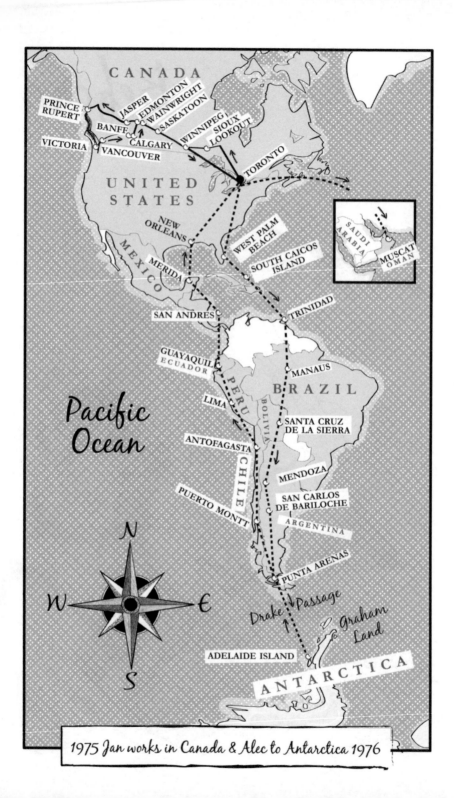

1975 Jan works in Canada & Alec to Antarctica 1976

Midnight Terror

Canada

BANG-BANG-BANG!

Blood-curdling screams echoed through the building. We instantly crouched low and looked at each other in shock.

'What the hell is going on?' cried Sue. 'It sounds like doors smashing to the ground.'

'No, it's gunfire!' I gasped.

BANG-BANG-BANG! The shots sounded closer.

'Hide!' screamed Ingrid.

'But where?' I panicked as I sped to softly close the washroom door, wishing there was a key in the lock.

Escape!

I dashed to open the sash window, but it was firmly sealed from the last paint job. Just as well as we were three floors up.

I looked to the curtained showers and the bloody scene from *Psycho* flashed before my eyes.

'Quick. Over here,' Cathy mouthed in a muted yell, wildly waving to us to come. She was standing by two enormous roll-top Victorian bathtubs, which stood on clawed feet and were covered with heavy

3

wooden boards. Ingrid ran to assist Cathy in raising one board whilst Sue and I went to the second bath and uncovered it.

Cathy and Ingrid, in their slinky nightwear, slid into their bath easily. But for us two, dressed in our jeans, bulky parkas and heavy hiking boots, it was a real challenge. We clambered into the bath awkwardly, entwining our tall bodies in order to pull the board down on top of us. It lay lopsided, but it had to do.

The building became chillingly quiet.

We gripped one another's hands and held our breath, lying in fear of becoming a bloody pulp at any second. Our ears strained to detect any sound of the sniper approaching. My heart thumped so hard that I felt sure the killer would be able to hear it, like a ticking time bomb. I whispered a sigh and breathed again. My tongue felt like a dry flannel. Was this really happening?

Less than an hour earlier...
Sue and I were in downtown Vancouver. We supped beer whilst eating a bowl of Irish stew and listening to a funky folk band, unaware that trouble was brewing. The Harp and Heather pub hummed with raucous merrymakers and cigarette smoke filled the air. A week before we had left Wainwright, Alberta, where we both nursed at the General Hospital. My six-month contract was almost up, so I'd decided to take a holiday to explore British Columbia with Sue, who also hailed from England.

'Drink up,' I cried as I glanced at my watch and saw it was close to the 1 a.m. hostel curfew. We left the bar with only minutes to spare to the next bus and ran through the well-lit streets to the bus stop. A couple of guys I recognized from the Jericho Hostel were waiting there and I was glad we weren't the only ones cutting it fine. The bus arrived and we boarded for the twenty-minute ride, then jumped off and sprinted back to the hostel.

Too late!

Locked out on a cold and wintry night, we scouted around the impregnable building. Suddenly one of the guys spied a way of entry two storeys up and he shimmied up the drainpipe to gain access through an open window. He ran downstairs and unlocked the basement back door, and we slipped inside. Sue and I quietly climbed the stairs to the girls' third floor.

First to the washroom, where we met two young American women, scantily clad in flimsy nightdresses. Desperate for the loo, I dashed into a cubicle and chatted from the other side of the door, as did Sue in another. We introduced ourselves, and Cathy and Ingrid eagerly told us about their travels so far. Having bussed up from California, they planned to take a flight to West Berlin and begin a tour of Europe. I came out to wash my hands at the basin and told the girls about when I'd lived in Germany. The great wine fests, medieval towns and castles, a trip to St. Tropez in France, seeing the luxury yachts of the rich and…

BANG-BANG-BANG!

Quivering, I lay there, waiting and wondering in the silence. I thought of my man, my lover, how incredibly far away he was. My eyes welled up and tears trickled down my cheeks. After six months of wedded bliss in England, we had travelled to Toronto to begin our planned individual adventures. We hugged and kissed at the railway station on the 27th September, three days after my birthday. I alone then boarded the train for the forty-eight-hour journey across Canada to Wainright.

A few days later my Alec, an aircraft engineer, set off from Toronto with Bert, the pilot, in a de Havilland Twin Otter aircraft, to fly south over the Americas to Antarctica. Along with Giles and Slim, who flew in the second Twin Otter, the four men made up the British Antarctic Survey (BAS) aviation team. En route, they stayed overnight at many exotic locations such as South Caicos Island, Trinidad, Manaus in Brazil, Santa Cruz in Bolivia and Mendoza in Argentina.

The long-haul flights took them over the turquoise seascape that surrounds the Caribbean Islands. They saw the vast, forbidding Brazilian jungle with the Amazon River snaking its way through the tropical lush-green vista. They flew south, following the majestic snow-capped Andes mountain range to Punta Arenas in Chile, on the western shore of the Strait of Magellan. With the promise of fine weather, the two planes then flew across Drake's Passage, the formidable expanse of ocean between Cape Horn and the Antarctic continent.

Images of my blond, blue-eyed Alec flickered in my mind. He had been away for five months and in four weeks we were to be reunited back in Toronto. Or would we?

Before I left my room at the nurses' accommodation in Wainwright, I'd placed on my bedside table a farewell love letter to Alec. I'm unsure what had prompted me to write such a letter, but I wanted Alec to know of my unfailing and constant love and adoration of him in case for some reason I died on my trip. God forbid, I felt as if my day of doom had actually come.

Terrified – my guts churned, my skin felt hot, then chilled. I squeezed Sue's hand and she squeezed mine back. It was very quiet. I heard no sirens. Was no one coming to take care of the wounded – or dead? Sue and I, both nurses, could have helped, but where was the gunman?

I wondered who would notify my family if I didn't survive the ordeal. My parents had advised against hitchhiking on the trip. But we had been in no danger from the truckers who gave us a ride from town to town in the Rockies. But now…now!

'Do you think it's safe?' murmured Ingrid from the other bath. A beam of light from the ceiling bulb enabled me to see my watch and I realized we had been hiding in the dirty, cramped, old baths for forty-five minutes. Listening for harmless noises, I heard voices and the movement of people on the floor below. They were orderly sounds, so we agreed to take a chance.

Quietly we raised the wooden boards and stealthily climbed out of the baths. My body felt numb and tingly from being so cramped, but I was very much alive. I carefully opened the washroom door, just a crack, enough to peer out and survey the scene. Seated on the stairs, crouched over, was a young guy who beckoned us to come across the landing.

'Keep down below the windows. He may still be outside.'

Despite his caution, I glanced quickly as I passed by the window. The headlights of emergency vehicles that encircled the building floodlit the hostel. Police were crouched down, guns at the ready, as they took cover behind their vehicles to monitor the situation.

I sat down on the stairs amongst the frightened hostellers. Everyone was talking in whispers as we looked down into the stairwell. One of the injured guys was carried out on a stretcher. His friends recognized his blood-streaked face as he turned his head. His gaze was stunned.

Several armed policemen searched the hostel and it was not long before the press arrived. Reporters from national newspapers and television stations were hungry for any information. They photographed everything from the bloodstained walls to the huddle of folk on the stairs.

The officer in charge ordered us all to go down to the basement canteen. We did as instructed and a babble of noise rose out of the fearful silence. We each wrote a statement detailing what we had seen, heard or experienced before or during the ordeal.

Unbelievably some folk had managed to sleep through the entire incident. They sauntered dreamily into the canteen, wrapped in their blankets, bleary-eyed and confused.

A roll call was taken and everyone accounted for, except one: the young man identified as the gunman. The hours dragged on and the thought of venturing upstairs to our beds in the dead of night appealed to no one. So we gathered together in small groups and talked about all manner of things. But every so often someone reverted back to that fateful hour. It was strange to witness many young, macho men expressing their fear, terror and emotional pain. The rawness and shock of the frightening experience had made them feel vulnerable, open and needing to talk.

'Coffee, anyone?' A hostel employee had put the kettle on. The hot drinks were most welcome.

I sipped the sweet, steaming coffee and munched on a piece of hot, buttered toast. My mind pieced the whole story together as I listened to each witness's contribution to the bewildering puzzle.

The gunman, an eighteen-year-old from Toronto, had been staying all winter in the youth hostel. His roommates considered him quiet with no weird traits – until that night. During the evening he'd been out drinking with several of the hostellers in a nearby bar. Drunk and belligerent, he spieled a tale of woe and how depressed he felt, like he existed within a dead body. He spoke of war and bloodshed; of the automatic rifle and ammunition he had in his dormitory locker. He picked a fight with a guy who ended up with a black eye. Everyone became weary of his unsociable behaviour, so they began to leave.

The young man was clearly disturbed, but since he was drunk at the time, no one believed he really had a weapon. He returned to the hostel in his inebriated, depressed state. There he changed into military attire and hid himself, fully armed, outside in the hostel grounds.

(It dawned on me that he must have watched Sue and I and the guys gain entry into the building. A shiver ran up my back.)

At 1.20 a.m., he blasted his way through the locked front door and dramatically reappeared in his dormitory. He fired a barrage of bullets at his roommates, who dived for cover. One naked guy turned and jumped out of the window, and several others followed suit. Those who had been asleep on the bunk beds had no way of escape, as the gunman fired indiscriminately in all directions. Five young men were seriously wounded and one had a bullet pierce his lung. It was only a short time before he ran out of ammunition. Immediately he turned tail and ran down to the basement, out the door and into the darkness.

The only available telephone had been in the pathway of danger, so it wasn't until the gunman had fled that the alarm was raised for the emergency services to come.

Fortunately, not long after that, the gunman was detained. Having gained access to an ammunition store, he had unintentionally disturbed the owner, who reacted quickly and fired a blank cartridge into the air. The loud, unexpected bang confused the crazed young man long enough for the storekeeper to make a citizen's arrest of the thief, caught red-handed. His lethal frenzy was, thankfully, over.

As the night slipped away and morning came, many of us departed from the hostel heavily weighed down with our backpacks and disturbing memories of the night before. We had all met as total strangers, yet we parted that day having shared an experience none of us would ever forget.

For Sue and me, our holiday continued for a few more days as we journeyed back to Wainwright via Banff, Calgary and Edmonton. I eagerly looked forward to returning to the hospital, to see if any letters had arrived from Alec. The post was delivered and collected at Adelaide Island in Antarctica, by the Royal Research Ship *Bransfield*. During our six months apart, the ship would have gone to the base just two to three times, depending on the ice conditions. Alec's letters would give me great comfort after the unexpected nightmare in Vancouver and I longed to tear up that ominous love letter I had so mysteriously written to him.

Forever Yours

Antarctica

We two nurses eventually arrived safely back in Wainwright, Alberta.

'Thanks for everything, Sue. It was a great trip.'

'Yes, with lots of crazy memories,' Sue replied. 'Have a good journey tomorrow. When will Alec arrive in Toronto?'

'I'm not sure. The last telex message said that he was expected to arrive a month later than the original plan. So I'll just have to twiddle my thumbs whilst I wait around in the city.'

'Oh, too bad.'

'Well, maybe I'll have news in the post,' I said hopefully, giving her a hug. 'Bye for now.'

'Bye.'

I entered the nurses' accommodation and was rewarded with a wad of letters in my mailbox, a couple from Mum and Dad and a dozen from Alec. I ran up the stairs to my cosy room, dropped the backpack to the floor and settled on my bed to open the first letter.

British Antarctic Survey
Adelaide Island, Antarctica
3rd January 1976

My Dearest, Darling Jan,

Well, Bert, our intrepid polar pilot of RAF vintage, and I made it back here to Adelaide Island for New Year, after a week of delays at the US station, McMurdo. The main delay was with the weather, of course.

When we did leave, at 3.30 a.m. on 29th December, the weather was perfect and the light was bright in the land of the midnight sun. We flew away from McMurdo in our trusty Twin Otter, climbed out over Black Island, Minna Bluff, passed Mount Discovery, Royal Society Range, out across a corner of the Ross Ice Shelf, then into the mountains again. Flew up the Beardmore Glacier, a giant ice river fed by two glaciers from the main polar ice cap. Some beautiful rock formations: layers of varying colours – blues, greys, browns – and outcrops of strange shapes. Antarctica is truly a breathtaking and beautiful continent of the world that few people are privileged to see. At the top of Beardmore, the ice cap proper begins, a limitless white wilderness.

A further two hours' flight brought us to the bottom of the world. A speck at first appeared on the horizon, which slowly formed into recognizable shapes as we drew nearer to the South Pole.

The Americans have recently completed a new base at the Pole, a massive dome with three arch-shaped buildings. On landing, the chaps at the Pole Station offered us refreshments, which included fresh cherries with stalks on, would you believe! Our plane was then refuelled to absolute maximum capacity for the nine-and-a-half-hour flight to our British main base on Adelaide Island.

To prove I have been to the South Pole, Bert gripped the occasion, using my camera. He took a photo of me standing beside the red and white barber's pole topped with a silver ball. A rainbow of colour surrounded me as the fourteen flags of the Antarctic Treaty Nations flapped in the breeze. It was incredible to know that the ice was 9,000 feet thick at that point.

I made a pre-flight inspection of the aircraft and noted in the maintenance logbook that there was a hydraulic leak from the nose undercarriage. But we were safe to continue the flight, unfortunately over cloud all the way until the familiar mountains of the peninsula began to appear on the horizon, as the sun shone through and the air cleared. Having fixed our position over Fossil Bluff, we were only an hour-and-a-half from Adelaide, where we eventually arrived at 4 a.m. on 29th December. Yes, thirty minutes since leaving McMurdo, at 3.30 a.m. having spent sixteen hours en route. Very confusing! Flying into the sun near the Pole, time stands still.

After breakfast my mate Slim and I started preparing the new nose undercarriage for the aircraft. This project kept us occupied for three days. There was no loss in flying time, as the weather hasn't been fit here or anywhere else. Howling winds, rough seas and snow falling in blizzards. Not fit for a penguin to be out in this weather, let alone us two.

New Year's Eve dinner was a welcome reward. Base doctor being the waiter for the occasion. Everyone was dressed up posh after taking his weekly shower. Jackets and ties were the order of the day – well, we are British, when all is said and done; got to do things proper!

The menu was as follows:
Sherry to start
Asparagus and shrimp cocktail
Mushroom soup
Roast turkey with all the trimmings
Accompanied by the best Mosel wine

Christmas pudding with brandy sauce
Cheese and biscuits
Coffee and liqueurs
The base cook did us proud and we all mucked in with the washing-up, before the Scots came in complete with tartan kilts, playing bagpipes and offering their traditional black bun.
Spiffing what!
Trust all the letters and the tape I sent via McMurdo have arrived. Looking forward to receiving yours when the ship calls into the base in two weeks. It's only ten more weeks before we'll be together. As each day passes, I long to see you more and more, my Darling. 'I love you' never seems enough for my feelings for you, but I do, more than I can say,

Forever
Your Alec.
xxxxx

Aaahhh, I felt all warm and snuggly inside as I quickly opened the second letter…

British Antarctic Survey
Lassitter Coast
Southern Graham Land
Antarctica
7th January 1976

My Dearest, Darling Jan,

I am writing this while camping on the east coast with the surveyors. Outside we have a regular jamboree, four tents and two planes. To do the surveying more quickly it was decided to send the two aircraft. A good idea except the weather decided otherwise, so now we have two aircraft here doing nothing! Still, they may as well do nothing here rather than at Adelaide, where we have no fuel until the ship arrives.

I will now tell you what I've done since my last letter. Slim and I were kept busy: he was packing up some old-type aircraft oil to send back to the UK whilst I was making a special spanner for use on the aircraft. I enjoyed this task very much as it required a lot of careful measuring, fitting and precision filing. It was very satisfying to see the finished article work, having been that Saturday morning just a rusty piece of angle iron, lying on the rack outside the wooden garage.

Sunday morning was bright – fresh and clear skies at Adelaide – so we air-tested the plane after the nose undercarriage change and refuelled her, ready to go exploring. That day I was acting cook, giving our regular chef his one-day off for the week. A large tin of stewing steak, two tins of broad beans, two tins of carrots and a dash of Marmite to add flavour, and there you have it. Oh, and of course opening a packet of soup and measuring out seven pints of water was the hardest bit.

After lunch, Slim, Bert and I flew off with half-a-ton of dried dog food to Fossil Bluff, where we refuelled, and then on to Ailleen Depot. There we met up with Giles, our other pilot with the second plane. Also waiting were four surveyors and thirty-six husky dogs. Having refuelled again with fuel stored in metal drums there, we all flew on to our present location to set up camp for the night. After pitching the tent, I prepared our meal, whilst Bert tied the aircraft down. Giles and Slim joined Bert and me in our tent for dinner.

Later: I am now sitting outside the tent on a beautiful evening surrounded by numerous small mountains, which are across a very gentle valley that curves around us on three sides. Earlier I walked up the fourth side, an easy slope to a small peak on which the survey station, a pile of rocks, stands. Looking around the scene in the quietness – not a sound, perfect silence – I marvelled at the sparkling rocks and a small pool of water kept liquid by the sun warming the rocks. Growing under the water were very simple plants. Nature is incredible. How can a plant survive in such hostile conditions?

I spent quite a while just sitting and thinking of you, my Darling, wishing you could be beside me so I could put my arm around you and feel you close, sharing this wonderful experience. But all my life is shared with you, Jan, in my thoughts. Wherever I go, you are with me in my heart.

Well, my love, as it's getting late and we are possibly up at six in the morning, I will finish here.

Next day: The weather has deteriorated: we are now in 'whiteout' conditions. This is where the cloud at the right height and thickness diffuses the light passing through it, causing the ground horizon to blend in with the sky and you can't see unevenness on the ground. At its worst you tend to trip over because you lose depth perception of the snow beneath your feet. The whiteout here is so complete that the top of the rocky peak nearby, looks as if it's suspended in space.

So whilst we wait out the whiteout, life consists of eating, writing to you, my love, and reading. This evening we will listen to the news on BBC World Service. What a sorry state the outside world is in – the usual strikes, wars and hijackings. I'm sure you and I should live on a desert island, you know!

However, since we fell in love, problems never seem so bad, knowing you love me and I have you to love and care for. Nothing else is as important to me as you, my Darling. Several times a day I look through the photos I have with me of you and am reminded of what a wonderful wife I have. The laws of chance were indeed kind in bringing us together. I love you, Darling Jan.

Looks as if Giles and Slim are setting off back to Adelaide
after dinner, so I will have to close here. I look forward to receiving
your letters and I hope mine have all been reaching you.
Always remember, I love you.
Forever
Your Alec.
xxxxx

I took a break to attend to supper and bath time. As I climbed into bed I saw that farewell letter I'd written to Alec. I ripped it up and threw it into the bin with great gusto. Blissfully I continued to read all of Alec's precious letters before falling asleep, dreaming of our first embrace when we would meet again.

The following morning, I completed my packing and went across to the hospital to say goodbye to the staff, before going to the train station. As luck would have it, the train was twenty minutes late. Lucky, because as I sat there, the postman found me and handed me a telegram with wonderful news. Clear skies over Drake Passage had given Alec and Bert the chance to fly out earlier from the Antarctic, leaving Adelaide Island on 5th March. Bearing in mind the long-haul flights through the Americas, their expected arrival in Toronto was 14th March. I was so thrilled to know that Alec was arriving sooner than expected that I called Sue, from a public telephone box, to share the great news.

The overnight train arrived and I boarded it for the journey east to Winnipeg, to visit with friends for a couple of days, before I travelled in an executive jet from Winnipeg to Toronto. I felt quite underdressed in my jeans and parka jacket, whilst the businessmen wore smart suits and the women glamorous fur coats.

I rested up after my travels and enjoyed the hospitality of good friends Charlie and Connie at their home in Richmond Hill. Charlie was the product support manager at de Havilland and had been a great encouragement to the BAS aviation team over many years. They made me feel so at home, and Connie and I had some fun shopping trips in downtown Toronto.

The long-awaited day finally arrived. After breakfast I had a bubble bath and dressed before going to the local hairdresser's for a wash, cut and set. Back to Charlie and Connie's to pack, put on my make-up and a mist of perfume. For the finishing touch Connie lent me a full-length, auburn fur coat with a white silk scarf. Only the sunglasses were missing. I walked out into the cold, snowy day and took a bus, a subway train and another bus to Downsview.

The snowfall had escalated into a blizzard by the time Bert and Alec were flying overhead. Downsview airport had closed and they were diverted ten miles to Toronto International Airport and landed mid-afternoon. They parked the plane there, and Alec battened down all the hatches and tied and secured the propellers. Unfortunately the ladder he climbed slipped, and he fell ten feet from the level of the high wings. He was so lucky he didn't leave the airport in an ambulance.

It was half-past-six by the time a taxi brought them to the de Havilland office, where I had been patiently waiting for my man. With a twinkle in his eye, Alec beamed a great smile from his bearded face, framed by his long, windblown blond hair. He enveloped me in a bear hug and I melted into his arms. My explorer had returned, and oh what a night we had, wining and dining in a luxury hotel and enjoying the delights of being together again!

Bedouin Wedding

Sultanate of Oman

Over breakfast the next morning Alec mentioned that BAS were leasing one of the Twin Otters out for the summer. Taylor Woodrow Towell, a construction company, was hiring the plane to support their work in the Middle East.

'They're looking for a crew to ferry the plane from Canada to the Sultanate of Oman and to stay there for five months. It's accompanied, so Giles is going as the pilot and taking his girlfriend, Vonni, along. They asked if I would like to go as the engineer.'

'Really… so I could come too?' I asked.

'Well, if we went, it would delay our journey.'

'Yes, but it's a great opportunity – we should go.'

Still holding on to our dream to take a journey by vehicle, just the two of us, to far and distant lands. The dream we had planned and saved for since we met in 1972 would have to be postponed. But it was too good a job offer to turn down, and the location would be fascinating to visit.

Alec made contact with the BAS office in England that very morning, and within a month we found ourselves dwelling in the fancy new Ruwi Hotel in Muscat, the capital city of Oman. Alec drove out to the airport each day to keep the plane in tip-top condition. I landed myself a job with the same company working in the medical clinic, caring for Omani, Indian and Pakistani labourers. They were building houses, hotels and the Sultan Qaboos bin Said's new palace in the rapidly developing city. Being a Muslim country, Friday was the weekly day off work, when we regularly took a company car out to explore the interior of Oman.

Friday, the thirteenth of August, was just such a day when we left the city and journeyed out into the hot, dry countryside. We drove through an extensive valley where the road followed alongside the winding wadi, a dry riverbed susceptible to flash flooding during the seasonal rains. Villages were built here and there, shaded within their own oasis of palm trees. The road climbed out of the valley up over a mountain pass, rolling up and down, curving sharply to the right and then to the left, cutting through the commanding, rugged landscape. We noticed tiny settlements tucked alongside the majestic mountains. Men were riding their fully laden donkeys, trotting along centuries-old narrow tracks.

We drove from the mountain pass into another rolling valley with a continual change of vegetation. By another wadi, dark green trees and shrubs grew, contrasting with the grey gravel terrain. In other areas we saw spiky, coarse grass, which provided dry fodder for roaming camels. The mountains hauntingly overshadowed the scene.

At the next village we stopped for petrol, which was pumped from a forty-five-gallon drum into metal gallon jugs and then poured into our car's petrol tank. The toxic fumes of the fuel hung in the heat of the breezeless day. The attendant wiped his hands on an oily rag before he took the payment, and stuffed the rial notes into the inner breast pocket of his grubby dishdash robe. Looking down the street, I saw a man leading his camel to drink water drawn from a well. A new, gaudy metal sign displayed nearby, tempted the locals to try the latest soda drink on sale.

Back on the tarmac road, our journey continued for some distance along the valley. Round lookout turrets were strategically positioned high in the formidable mountains. We drove on and on until the tarmac road petered out to a rutted, earth track. The mountains and the valleys were left far behind and before us was a vast desert plateau, sparsely vegetated with hardy shrubs. Far across towards the horizon lay the golden dunes of the shimmering, silky Wahiba Sands.

Journeying on towards the village of Al Gabi, we discovered a special event was taking place. Many men, women and children, all dressed in their best clothes, walked along together. Six of the men rhythmically danced in a line to the beat of a drum, leading the people towards the festivities.

We parked the car close to other trucks and Land-Rovers. Immediately a crowd of children swarmed around us. Brown faces and hands pressed against the windows as they peered in to see the white strangers. Carefully we extracted ourselves from the car and stood and stared at the children, as they stood and stared at us.

Young boys dressed like miniature men, wearing long dishdash tunics of many colours. Cashmere cloth in vivid pink or orange and embellished with embroidery, was wound in turbans around their heads. They each had a small curved, kunjar knife encased in a metal sheath that hung on their richly decorated belts. One lad had a bandolier filled with rifle cartridges around his waist. Each boy carried a simple stick as they mimicked their fathers with their sturdy goat sticks.

The pretty young girls wore colourful dresses over baggy, cotton trousers and were adorned with heavy silver jewellery: necklaces, anklets, bracelets and earrings. Two girls had eight large silver rings pierced through the curve of each ear.

A group of men walked over to our car. One could speak a little

English and he kindly invited us to join in the wedding festivities. A central arena was bordered on three sides by palm frond shelters. The men from the bride's family sat under one and the men of the groom's family sat beneath the opposite shelter. The women of the two families were under the adjoining structure. We sat with the men as inquisitive, unreserved lads crowded around, pestering us to repeatedly shake hands, until a man reprimanded them. They retreated, but remained close enough to stare at us intently.

Coffee and dates were served to the men and they ensured we had plenty too. The people from the Wahiba Bedouins and the Al Gabi villagers welcomed our presence. Alec enquired where the bride and groom were. With a glint in his eye and laughter in his voice, one of the men said, 'Oh, they're hiding!'

In the centre of the arena a master of ceremonies guided the two groups of male dancers, which represented each family, into their movements. Men beat drums and chanted as the eyes of the audience watched the simple, repetitive steps of the performers as they moved around the arena. They passed under the shade of the shelters amongst the guests. An unearthly trance held everyone in its grip. The atmosphere was high and bewitching as everyone became intoxicated with the festivities.

Sprightly lads, handsome, swarthy young men and wizened old hunters all participated enthusiastically with the rhythmical dancing. Their chanting voices rang through the air as they complimented each other's family on their good qualities and wished good fortune for the bride and groom. Then in the centre of the arena the entertainers leapt into the air and threw their sticks and caught them. With gung-ho they raised their rifles and kunjars. There were mock sword fights using heavy, long steel swords and wooden shields held by each swordsman. Every man at the wedding carried a weapon: a well-armed force could be mustered at a moment's notice from that band of warriors.

We were invited to follow a young man to a nearby palm frond hut where we joined in the wedding feast. I was the only woman present amongst the Bedouin as we sat down together on the floor. Shafts of light fell on the bearded men, old in their looks but with eyes of youthful exuberance that expressed good humour as they exchanged tribal tales in their mother tongue. They were masters of the desert, and the hard life and extremes of temperature had sculpted their rugged faces.

A communal tray of piping-hot rice and goat meat was placed down on the grass matting and the men gestured for us to eat. The soft, tender skin of my hand was unaccustomed to scooping up such hot food. The feast had been prepared outside the hut, in giant iron cauldrons over wood fires. Stirred with a large shovel, it was inevitable that sand blew in, giving the meal a strange gritty texture. Sweet halwa and coffee were served after the meal before we left to make room for other guests and returned to the arena. The dancing was in full swing and impish boys were throwing perfume over everyone, intoxicating the air with an exotic fragrance.

Leaving Alec sitting in the shade with the men, I crossed over to the women's shelter to greet them and their children. Several stood to welcome me. The Bedouin women's eyes communicated warmly through the slits of their full-facial, black, cloth masks. They were totally dressed in black, unlike the unmasked village women, who were radiant in their colourful cotton robes. Each lady displayed the wealth of her family by her heavy adornment of gold and silver jewellery.

Time was drawing on and we had to leave the celebration to make the return journey to Muscat before dusk. Back at the hotel, we took a refreshing shower and dressed smartly for dinner. As we sat in the modern hotel restaurant, enjoying our evening meal of smoked salmon with lemon zest, slices of tomatoes decorated with fresh mint leaves and boiled buttered potatoes, we pondered over the wedding. It had been another remarkable experience, rubbing shoulders with the people of the Sultanate of Oman.

Alec and I first met in Germany whilst both serving in the British Army. He had previously been posted to Hong Kong and travelled from there to Singapore, Bali and out to Australia. From Germany Alec served a few months in Northern Ireland, before being seconded to the British Antarctic Survey team. My nursing and midwifery career took me from Germany to Canada and back to England.

Our adventures in Oman added fuel to our wanderlust and the generous salaries doubled our savings of the previous four years. We returned to England in the autumn ready to activate our long-planned dream: to travel in our own vehicle, at our own pace, and explore many countries and cultures. It would take at least a year, but could be longer if we found work along the way. Our planned route was to drive through Europe, ferry across to Africa, overland to Kenya, ship to India and drive back to England.

When Alec and I first dated, he said to me, 'When I reach my sixties, I don't want to look back and regret not having done something with my life. I want to travel and see the world.'

How fortunate was I to have met a man who was hungry for adventure, eager to make things happen and longed to share all that with me!

On 20th September 1976 we purchased a 1971, Series 3, long-wheel-base, blue-and-cream Land-Rover from Alec's Uncle Geoff. Because the vehicle had begun its working life on the farm, hauling pigs and potatoes, it took us three days to flush out the pong. Over several months, whilst we lodged with Alec's parents in Newton Regis, Warwickshire, Alec converted the Land-Rover to become our very first home.

To guard against extremes of weather on our journey, Alec first insulated the interior aluminium walls, doors and floor. An elevating roof was constructed and fitted, which allowed us to stand upright in the back between the kitchen cupboards on the left and the wooden bench-cum-bed on the right. You could sit on the bench and open the drop-down, hinged, horizontal cupboard door as a nifty mini-dining table. As you climbed into the Land-Rover through the back doorway, on the left there was a small wooden box seat discreetly hiding the chemical toilet. Blinds were installed fore and aft of the living quarters for privacy at night, plus small fluorescent strip-lighting. A charcoal filter was plumbed into the worktop, to have safe drinking water pumped from the water storage tank down in the bilges.

My contribution in transforming the Land-Rover into a comfy mobile home was to sew soft brown fabric covers for the foam bench cushions. I also made a long, zipped tube of fabric to store our bedding. It hung along the right side of the interior, providing a headrest for the bench seat. The fabric of the bedding bag was a jazzy pattern of yellow, brown and white that added a cheerful splash of colour to the decor.

A second auxiliary petrol tank was fitted under the driver's seat. The roof rack that extended out over the bonnet of the vehicle carried the large wooden storage box custom-made by my dad in Brentwood, Essex. Two frames, carrying three empty petrol jerry cans in each, were slotted between either side of the box and the upright edge of the roof rack. A further six jerry cans stood side-by-side behind the wooden box. Metal sand ladders were also bolted along the outer sides of the rack. Alec mounted a capstan winch on the front bumper and we had two spare wheels, one on the bonnet and the other on the back door, which made it very heavy to open and close. Padlocks secured everything in place to deter pilfering and bolts were fitted on the inside of each door to keep intruders out as we slept.

On the administration side, I made several trips in and out of London to apply for visas, which involved going from one embassy to the next, delivering and collecting our passports. A Carnet de

Passage for the Land-Rover and International Driving Licences were ordered from the Automobile Association, foreign currencies bought and vaccinations received. We spent a lot of time and money purchasing supplies such as vehicle spare parts, maps, a compass, dried food, medications, a mosquito net, toilet rolls and kitchen equipment including two primus stoves, one that burned paraffin and one petrol. I made two blue leather pouches with cords to go around our necks. These were used to carry our passports and some cash. Traveller's cheques and foreign hard cash were hidden behind wooden panels inside the Land-Rover, to spread our funds out in several secure places. Referring to the advice from experts on overland travel, such as Trailfinders, we endeavoured to be as well prepared as we could be.

At the beginning of February 1977, all our lists were checked off, the ferry was booked, the Land-Rover was ready and there was nothing more to do. The time had come to realize our dream!

South

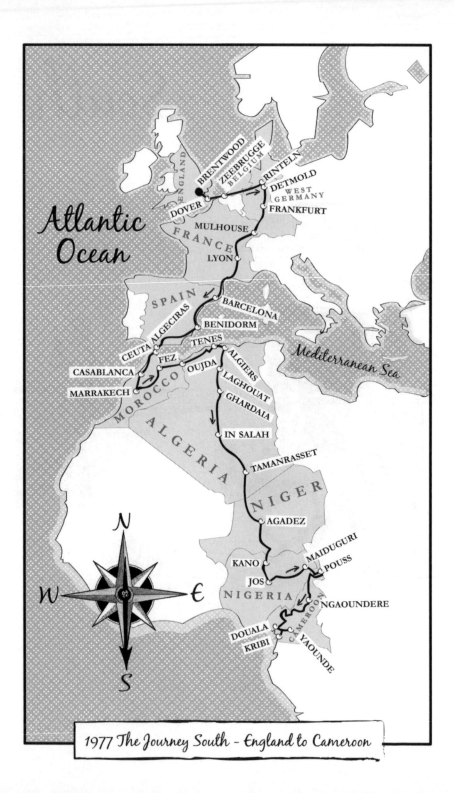

1977 The Journey South - England to Cameroon

Venturing Forth

4th to 18th February 1977
England – Belgium – Holland – Germany – France – Spain

Although the night ferry crossing from Dover to Zeebrugge was calm, we both slept restlessly: quiet and deep in thought as to what lay ahead, disbelieving that our journey had actually begun. It was hard saying goodbye to our families and they must have been concerned as to what we were letting ourselves in for. My being twenty-five and Alec twenty-nine, driving off into the unknown rather than settling down to pursue our careers, create a home and have children. Our parents had been such an encouragement and had hidden their emotions during those tense moments of last-minute preparations.

As we were leaving my teary-eyed Mum placed a medallion in my hands. It was a large, cobalt-blue, flat stone in a pewter setting on a chain. Inscribed on the back: '*Keep Safe*'. Along with the necklace, she gave me a tiny oval picture of Jesus, blanket stitched with red thread around its edge. 'For good luck,' she said as I tucked it into my leather passport pouch. Mum's way of sending her love and protection with us.

*

'Oh my goodness, what's in this tea?' I spluttered as the spiked, hot tea hit the back of my throat. Mum must have put a tot of whisky in it. She had said, 'Something to warm your cockles,' as she handed over the flask when we left Brentwood.

We had driven a few miles out of Zeebrugge before stopping by the roadside for breakfast. It was half-past-six and dawn was breaking. The tea washed down the jam sandwiches Mum had packed for us.

Wasting no time, we eagerly set off again, taking turns to drive the Land-Rover on a dull and dreary day, zipping through Belgium, Holland and into Germany.

'There's a bratty stand over there,' Alec noticed and pulled alongside the fast food vendor at our first key destination, Rinteln, not far from Hannover in northern Germany. '*Zwei Bratwürste mit Brot und Senf, bitte,*' Alec requested in his best German, from what he had learnt while we were both stationed in Germany, five years previously.

'Mmmmm, tastes as good as I remember,' said Alec, munching away.

I tucked into my sausage in a bread roll with equal relish.

'We should go to the campsite by the town's lake, the Doktorsee, to stay for the weekend,' Alec said as he wiped traces of mustard from his ginger beard.

We parked by the Doktorsee and sorted ourselves out. Alec extended the roof in the back and I put the kettle on the paraffin cooker.

'Oo-er, it's going to take some time getting used to these fumes!' I exclaimed as I screwed up my eyes and coughed a little.

As we drank our freshly brewed cup of tea, a couple come across from a nearby caravan, introduced themselves and kindly invited us to dinner. Tony was a dental technician with the Royal Army Medical

Corps and was married to Hanna. He worked at the British Military Hospital there in Rinteln.

'More beer, Alec?' Tony asked as we sat in their smart caravan, feeling pleasantly satisfied after a delicious beef curry and rice supper, enjoyed with a glass of Sekt. 'So if you're on your way to Africa, how come you're over here in Rinteln? Not exactly a direct route, is it?'

'Well, this is where Jan and I met almost five years ago,' explained Alec. 'My mate Slim and I were stationed in Detmold with the Royal Electrical and Mechanical Engineers. Slim would always come up here to see his girlfriend, Jill. She had nursed him back to health in England, after he broke his neck going through the sunroof of his car when he rolled it. Fortunately for him no lasting damage, so he returned to Detmold and his girl was posted to Rinteln. One night he suggested I might like to come along on one of his nights out to the NAAFI Social Club at the hospital, as there were plenty more nice nurses there.'

'Yes, and that evening,' I chipped in, 'I went across to the NAAFI straight after my shift, to give a message to someone. That person wasn't there, but Jill was and she introduced me to Slim and Alec. Jill suggested that I might like to go down town for a drink with them all. Eyeing Alec, I thought, *Wow, he's tall and good-looking – why not?* I dashed back to my room for a quick bath, dressed to impress and was back within an hour.

At the end of the evening Alec asked me out and I was ecstatic! Tricia, my fun nursing chum, was tickled pink when I told her the news after she returned from home leave in England. So much for the awkward blind dates she'd always arranged for me.'

Alec rounded off the story: 'Yes, so as this is the place where we met, we decided it had to be included in the trip.'

Memories recounted and new memories in the making.

We bade our hosts goodnight and climbed into the Land-Rover. We were very tired and ready for our first night's sleep in our new home. Lying snuggled close together in our thirty-nine-inch-wide bed, we soon drifted off.

The next day we had a nostalgic visit around the picturesque town of Rinteln, with its half-timber-framed houses and enchanting market square. Little had changed since I was stationed there for eighteen months with the Queen Alexandra Royal Army Nursing Corps. We sauntered by the Military Hospital and found it was much the same too. A definite 'must do' was having 'kaffee und kuchen' at our favourite café, where we had spent many a leisurely Sunday afternoon. The cakes were as tempting and delectable as we remembered.

On the Monday we drove on to Detmold for Alec to reminisce on his time there, maintaining the helicopters of the Army Air Corps. As the weather was miserable, grey and raining heavily, we only stayed a couple of hours before driving on towards Frankfurt.

Keeping in touch with our families was a key activity on the trip, so whenever we could we took the opportunity to send postcards and letters back home. My dad had fixed a world map to their dining room wall to plot our route, so it was important to let him know the names of the towns that we drove through.

Air Mail

Perpignan, France
15th February 1977

Dear Mum, Dad, David and Paul,

Really enjoying this nomadic lifestyle. Spent four days in Frankfurt with our friends: Bob from the Army and his girlfriend Sabine. On Sunday we drove south to France, crossing the border at Mulhouse then via Besançon to Lons-le-Saunier, where we parked for the night in a car park. Monday, we travelled to Lyon, Valence,

Montpellier, then stayed overnight near Bessan. Driving now between the vineyards of southern France, the snow-capped Pyrenees in the distance. We'll soon be in Spain. From now until 15th March send your letters to Poste Restante, Kano, Nigeria. Hope everyone is well.

Love from Alec and Janice. xxxxx

'What's happened?' I exclaimed.

I had just driven the Land-Rover a short distance away from our camping spot beyond Barcelona and the engine had suddenly quit. Fortunately, Alec twigged he hadn't flipped the switch over to the auxiliary fuel tank that he'd fitted beneath the driver's seat. Problem soon resolved and we rolled on. I drove 100 miles during the first three hours before Alec took the wheel and drove for the rest of the day, a further 228 miles.

'I hope we can take it a little easier once we've reached Africa and not have such long days of driving,' I remarked, as I jotted down in our diary what we were seeing and where we had been.

Amposta was a town set by a river, in a pretty valley surrounded by hills. Cherry trees showed off their delicate adornment of soft pink blossoms in the bright sunlight. Citrus trees covered acres of land and the abundant fruit hung heavy on the branches. We readily stopped and bought delicious oranges and grapefruits from a roadside stall.

At Labrilla, we found a parking place for the night by a small garage and café. I fixed a tasty omelette with bread for supper, and afterwards we popped across to the café for a Coca-Cola. Inside the place was decked out with a television, pinball machines and an open log fire. The long bar was well stocked with booze. Hams and sausages were strung up on high. The barman served two locals with builder-sized sandwiches cut from a gigantic loaf of bread and stuffed full of smoked ham.

*

The next day the weather was glorious and warm as we drove through the spectacular scenery of Sierra de España. Snow-covered mountains enhanced the distant view.

On visiting the town of Baza, Alec drove along the narrow streets until the Land-Rover became trapped in the town square. It was barricaded on one side by a lorry and cars and on the other by two mules pulling a cart. A helpful policeman guided us to turn around and we found a parking space in a nearby alley. We ensured the vehicle was securely locked and slotted the wooden bars Alec had made into the groove at the bottom of the driver and passenger's windows. This prevented the sliding windows being forced open as they could be when just relying on the plastic catch.

It was great to be out walking amongst the locals in the town instead of just driving past. Elderly women were dressed in black, keeping their heavy woollen shawls nestled around their neck and shoulders to ward off the chilly air of the highlands. Browsing around the market, I was tempted by the display of fresh fruit, vegetables, bread and cheeses. But I didn't fancy the meat at all. It looked so vulgar, with the butchered animal bodies, complete with heads, skinned and splayed out on the counters. Flies darted from eye sockets to intestines.

Our supplies replenished, we returned to the Land-Rover by walking across the town square, where a group of schoolgirls skipped in front of the church. Two girls stood a distance apart, held a length of rope and turned it in unison. The other girls waited in line to take their turn to run forward and jump up and over the rope as it swung just above the ground. They chanted a rhyming Spanish skipping song as they played together.

From Baza we drove to Guadix, where we parked and walked up to a vantage point to see the town in the valley below. The droning noise of busy traffic and human activity rose out from the streets with their modern, high-rise flats. Behind us in the distance were houses built into the earth's crust within natural caves along the hillside. Such a curious olde worlde place to live.

As we drove towards and through Granada, industrial smog hung like a mantle over the city. We gladly reached Loja by three that afternoon and stopped on a hill that overlooked the picturesque village. We spent the rest of the day doing a few chores, and a couple of the locals stopped to greet us as they were walking by. They were quietly amused by our living quarters.

On the next day, two weeks after leaving England, we drove the final 113 miles along coastal roads to the Spanish town of Algeciras. We headed straight to the port to purchase the ferry tickets, then to the grocer's to buy food before arriving at the tourist campsite. There we met up with two Australian couples travelling in their Volkswagen Dormobiles. They had been in Morocco for three months and were waiting to go to the Canary Islands.

Alec checked over the Land-Rover to ensure everything was in good order, whilst I did the laundry and prepared the documents we needed for entry into Africa. Alec shaved his beard off, leaving his sideburns, so that his image more closely resembled his passport photo! As we went to bed, we chatted excitedly of the adventures to come.

Total distance driven = 2,222 miles

Gateway to Africa

19th to 24th February 1977
Morocco

Although we had been travelling across Europe, it was only as we crossed the Strait of Gibraltar to Ceuta on the northern tip of Africa that we really believed our long-planned journey had begun. The ferry crossing took an hour and we were driving through Morocco by ten in the morning. The day was still young.

The well-surfaced road meandered over the hills and down into the valleys. In one field I saw a man dressed in a long, hooded robe made from heavy wool material, coax his pony to pull a simple wooden plough, traversing a steep slope. The pony trod deeply into the soft, squelchy soil as the plough dragged slowly through the earth. The man's son was dressed in a long-sleeved jumper and trousers, sporting a woolly knitted bobble hat, like his father. The lad helped the pony by scampering ahead, clearing debris, jagged rocks, clusters of large stones and broken branches that had fallen from an old tree. A rigorous effort was being made to prepare the soil for cultivation on the difficult hilly terrain.

We journeyed towards Chechaouèn and observed many farming

homesteads, small white houses dotted here and there. Gorse, daisies, cacti and an abundance of wildflowers danced in the gentle breeze on the grassy, green hillsides. It surprised me to see these pastoral scenes, not at all what I had imagined for this introduction to Africa.

'Look, Alec, down in the valley.' I pointed excitedly. 'It looks like a country market.'

'Let's go and explore,' Alec responded.

We parked the Land-Rover a distance away, climbed out and set off walking. It was good to stretch our legs and breathe in the fresh country air. We joined the throng of locals making their way to the market, via a narrow bridge that crossed over the fast-flowing river wending its way along the valley floor.

Before us was an amazing sight: three hundred animals – donkeys, mules and ponies – collected together within an enclosure of wooden wagons and carts. A hubbub of munching, snorting and shuffling rose from the animals as they waited patiently for their owners to finish their shopping. The pungent smell of steaming dung wafted its way across to us.

The backdrop was a row of canvas canopies shading earth pits where farriers worked, trimming and shoeing the ponies' hooves. Holding a red-hot horseshoe with long, stout metal tongs, a farrier pressed the shoe quickly on an upturned hoof. The pony's leg was trapped between his leather-protected thighs. The acrid smell of burning hoof rose up in smoke into the man's ruddy face as he checked the size of the shoe. Chink, chink, chink – the hammer perfectly shaped the hot, molten-iron shoe on the anvil. The shoe was fitted again, and when it was deemed just right, it was plunged into a bucket of cold river water that fizzled as the steam rose, cooling the metal. Afterwards, the farrier nailed the cold shoe onto the pony's hoof before he proceeded to the second one, and so on. Ploughshares were also being re-tipped by the farriers, which altogether produced roaring trade that day.

We walked across to the centre of the covered market stalls and saw displayed multi-coloured clothes, pots and pans, vegetables, fruit and other useful goods.

After an hour we returned to the Land-Rover and drove southwest, leaving the pastoral hillsides behind to see flat coastal plains of green meadows. For our first evening in Africa, we parked alongside the beach, south of Rabat, and enjoyed the salty smell in the breeze coming off the Atlantic Ocean.

We awoke the next morning and listened to the waves rhythmically lapping the seashore and pulling back the sand as the sea drew away. Raising the blind at the back door, we lay in bed, cherishing the scene before us. The morning sun rose slowly above the horizon, giving a golden glow to the expanse of sea. We saw the black silhouettes of two fishermen clothed in long, heavy robes wading through the icy water to lay their net. A successful catch! One man lifted the wriggling fish from the clutches of the net and cradled them in the skirt of his robe to carry them ashore. He gently placed the fish into a woven basket before returning to the sea, hopeful of another catch. Swallows swooped up and down in the sky, snatching insects as they flew. Nearby, on the pastures that edged right up to the beach, a young shepherd and shepherdess encouraged their small flocks of sheep to a patch of good grazing. The melodic sound of a flute rippled through the air, gracing the pastoral scene.

'Come on, Alec, we can't lie here all day if we want to reach Marrakech in good time,' I chivvied us both.

Following the coastal road we soon reached Casablanca, where we stopped for a short visit and checked out the souk. A remarkable selection of European-style menswear was on sale. I noticed that some of the city ladies also wore European clothes beneath their coverall djellabas, complete with hood and veil. They looked very elegant and mysterious in their smart outfits. A few ladies dressed so were enjoying the freedom of riding their mopeds around town.

Leaving the bustling city, we took the main road directly south for 148 miles to mystical Marrakech. We located the well-equipped campsite, memorable for its smelly toilets and local drug dealers calling '*Psssst*' from the other side of the hedge, hoping we were desperate for a fix. There was a young Swiss couple also staying at the campsite in their Land-Rover. We enjoyed a mug of Ovaltine that evening as we chatted together, all four of us, cosy in the back of our vehicle.

The next day we drove into the city centre to an official car park with a guard, who watched over our vehicle as we explored the city. The buildings were made of red clay, the modern structures following the traditional colouring of the old. Two grey horses trotted by pulling a royal-looking open-top carriage. The driver wore a long beige djellaba robe and the traditional red felt Fez hat with a black tassel. The local taxi at your service!

Our first task of the day was to locate where to buy petrol coupons. We walked up and down Mohamed V Street, asking various people if they knew where we should go. Eventually we were directed to the Bank of Morocco, Commerce Exterieur. We bought enough coupons for twenty gallons of petrol, the ten-day allowance for tourists to buy fuel at a reduced price.

From the bank we went to the central market square. Young boys and men constantly badgered us to let them be our guide. Unfortunately they did not take our refusal very graciously and some of the immature lads became spiteful and swore at us.

In the square we joined crowds of onlookers: tourists plus many local young men and children just standing around. Together we watched the street entertainers, storytellers, snake charmers, singers, musicians, dancers and fortunetellers.

A man in his thirties played a tune on a simply made string instrument, sang a song and danced a jig. An audience of local people surrounded him, but as soon as he had completed his short act, he made a beeline through the crowd directly to us. He demanded that we pay two dirhams for taking his photograph, but Alec offered him a few francs for the brevity of his act. The performer became nasty, so we made a hasty retreat into the heart of the souk.

As we recovered from this unwelcome reaction, we settled down to explore the market stalls. There was an array of wares to tempt our pocket: baskets, leather goods, copper utensils, woodwork, carpets, blankets, painted glass and horseshoes. Skeins of vibrantly coloured dyed wool, cotton and silk yarn were hanging to dry on high poles fixed across the narrow alleyways. A few veiled women were standing selling pantaloons along the pathway, keeping a watchful eye out for the police, as they were trading illegally.

We stopped to make a purchase of a decorative, unstuffed pouffe made from camel hide. It would be a useful footstool for a future home.

Venturing along the matrix of alleyways, resplendent with exotic shops, we found it difficult to enjoy looking closely at any item before being harassed by one of the many shopkeepers eager for a sale. Unfortunately the constant pressure to buy spoilt our visit to Marrakech, so we decided to leave.

Glad to be on the road once again, we drove northeast through the countryside, in the foothills of the Atlas Mountains. It took a day-and-a-half to drive 400 miles to Fez, passing by Tamelelt, Tanannt and on towards Bin-el-Ouidane. At the last town there was a vast lake, held in check by the largest hydro-electric dam in Morocco, which was built in 1953. The Bin-el-Ouidane Dam was a strategic and vital structure kept under visible military guard. The road was built on the crest of the dam, with the lake to one side and a deep gorge to the other. Fir trees grew up towards the sky, their roots hidden away within the steep sides of the gorge. The road continued down to open out onto a cultivated plateau, where groves of orange trees flourished in the red earth, watered from narrow irrigation channels. From there it climbed to 3,800 feet where we found a place to stop for the night, beyond El-Borj, north of Khenifra.

The following day at eight, the temperature had dropped significantly to 48° Fahrenheit. Driving north of Azrou, a town with European-style houses, we found ourselves in snow-covered, forested mountains at 5,800 feet. Heavy snow fell that morning and the wipers worked hard to keep the windscreen clear. The heater was on full, but my feet felt cold and numb.

As we left the mountains and snow behind and journeyed to the city of Fez, the land became barren and rocky. Fortunately the temperature rose in our favour too.

On arrival, having parked and securely locked the Land-Rover, Alec and I walked towards the old city, passing by the impressive entrance to the palace grounds. Tiny coloured ceramic tiles adorned the massive walls. Twenty-five-foot-high brass doors hung in the magnificent gateway and two workmen were busy cleaning the brass. We ventured along a nearby street of open-fronted shops, their wares spilled over into the thoroughfare. Open sacks of good-quality maize, flour, spices and dates were displayed. In a covered food hall, fresh meat, fish, fruit and vegetables were on sale. Live chickens, rabbits and pigeons waited innocently in cages, not knowing they could be someone's supper that night.

A young man approached Alec and asked to be our guide. He was not the first to hustle us that day and Alec's answer remained the same: 'No, thank you, we don't need a guide as we prefer to explore the city on our own.'

Not ready to give up that easily, he then introduced us to another guy, a student who wanted to show us around. Now it was his turn to annoyingly badger us. To no avail, the student was very persistent and chattered on in reasonable English. He seemed quite knowledgeable, so eventually Alec gave me the eye and we agreed to have him along. No mention of money; he just wanted to practise his English!

We followed the route of the River Fez, that the city was built around, walking through a park with beautiful floral gardens, palm trees and cascading fountains. At the time we were there, the university town housed three hundred and fifty thousand people within the old city walls. An unused fourteenth-century university building was tucked in amongst the shops. Arabian craftsmanship was apparent on the wooden doors, the detailed ceramic-tiled walls and the coloured glass windows. It had surely once been a beautiful building, but it was in desperate need of restoration.

Into the souk, where craftsmen carved tables, wooden chess sets and candlesticks; others made yarn belts, blankets and carpets. A young lad speedily created a design on a copper plate. He used a hammer, tapping on a small metal tool with a patterned end.

Walking down the street, we passed one shop with hundreds of rolls of fabric. Countless djellaba robes for men and women were being made and sold by the tailors. In another shop the leather craftsmen made pointed, slip-on goatskin shoes in various bright colours.

The student guide directed us to go inside a house of carpets. The interior walls were again adorned with tiny, decorative ceramic tiles. We were each provided a seat and given a glass of mint tea in readiness for the owner to begin his sales pitch. Handmade carpets of all sizes were rolled out before our feet. The quality of the carpets was excellent, with richly coloured wool – ruby red, indigo blue, emerald green – woven into elaborate patterns. Through a doorway, I could see three young girls, about seven years old, concentrating and working hard, weaving intricate designs as their fingers rippled over the carpet loom. Unfortunately for the merchant, he made no sale with us that day, despite his aspiring banter and quality carpets.

Our guide led us into a second carpet shop, then a shop selling copper plates and another with fabrics. Each time we were given a place to sit and a glass of mint tea, and then the sales patter began. We soon realized what was happening when we noticed the original young man, who had introduced us to this student guide, was actually following us, trying to be inconspicuous.

'These chaps are working together,' I said under my breath to Alec. 'I bet if we bought something, the guy following would claim commission from the shopkeeper.'

No wonder we were encountering such a heavy sales push.

We continued to meander through the crowded walkways between the stalls and shops. A young boy pushed his way through the crowd, leading his heavily burdened grey mule. A crate of bottles of Coca-Cola hung from straps on either side of the animal's back. The strong mule faithfully followed the lad.

Visiting Fez, you can be sure not to miss the rank stench from the tannery. We saw young boys with their skin stained burgundy, chocolate brown or purple. Their task was to tread down the camel, cow, goat and sheep skins soaking in the pools of dye in round, earthen pits. As we walked along a high perimeter pathway around the tannery, the scene below looked like a gigantic honeycomb.

For four hours we wandered the streets of Fez, fascinated by a kaleidoscope of visual and audible stimuli, not to mention the tangible smells. As we returned to our Land-Rover we stopped to buy bread and cakes from an open stall. We said goodbye and thanks to the two Moroccans and gave them a token tip, but they were not impressed.

We drove out of town to seek a suitable place for the night and parked in a pleasant valley near to Bab-Marzouka. Preparing for the following day's journey, Alec perused the map that evening, checking the route into Algeria.

Total distance driven = 3,071 miles

Mediterranean Repose

25th to 27th February 1977
Algeria

Dear Mum, Dad, David and Paul,

Today we are calling a rest day, as we seem to have been going non-stop since we left England. I didn't realize that our days would be so full, but we spend at least eight to ten hours driving for miles, seeing many changes of scenery. Or we walk leisurely around the local markets, observing the people and their lifestyles. At the end of each day we cook a meal, I write a little in the diary, maybe play Scrabble, and then it's time for bed. We feel shattered – it must be from living outdoors. One good thing: our bed might only be thirty-nine-inches wide, but it's cosy and comfortable so we always sleep well.

We've only stayed three nights at campsites; the rest we've

parked at a suitable place alongside the road, usually away from the villages. It's a good feeling to have a different view every night, on a hill overlooking a gorge and the distant hills, or parked in a green valley where the shepherds come by in the morning, taking their flocks to graze.

Last night we parked on a deserted beach, and the sunset was quite magical. But this morning at six, we were woken by the sound of lorries and a digger loading sand. It looked as if they were going to be there all day, so we packed up and drove a few miles to where we're parked now on a grassy bank, beside the Mediterranean Sea, which is so blue and calm. It's a lovely, warm day and the washing is drying on our mini-clothes horse that is standing on the grass. I'm sitting on a blanket outside and Alec is reading a book in the Land-Rover. The only unpleasant thing is the pesky thunderflies. A while ago, two young boys and their goats came near to investigate us, but apart from that, and the occasional vehicle going along the road, the day is very peaceful.

I drive for up to three hours a day at the moment and Alec drives for five hours or more. We help each other with the chores and preparing our meals. Breakfast has consisted of one of the following: Scotch pancakes, muesli, porridge or tasty scrambled egg made with the dried egg powder I bought in London. Dried fruit soaked overnight is great in the morning too, and we also drink the flavoured water that the fruit has been soaking in. At lunchtime we have soup, prepared at breakfast and kept in the thermos flask, which is one of the most useful things we have. Local bread is delicious and cheap. Oranges too, so we eat a couple of those a day. Our evening meals we cook in the pressure cooker as much as possible and every evening our menu improves. Hungarian goulash, apple fritters and custard last night. Tonight we plan to have meat, potatoes, carrots and peas, followed by pancakes and lemon juice.

Toilet rolls are lasting well: still on the first one, nineteen to go. The main problem with washing our clothes is the water. It's amazing the amount you need to do the rinsing, so it's little and often. We air the clothes by using the Land-Rover fan heaters as we're driving along.

Well, that's all from me today, as Alec would like to add his musings. Hope you're all well. Remember to send letters by 15th March to POSTE RESTANTE, KANO, NIGERIA.

Love from
Janice.
xxxxx

Dear All,

It's now my turn to write something. My goodness it feels as if we've been away for months but it's actually only three weeks. We are still adjusting to living in the confines of the Land-Rover. For instance, the first night manoeuvring the sections of the bed into position was a ten-minute balancing act, but now we have a system that is very swift indeed. Bed out and made with sheets, duvet and all, in less than a minute.

We've started using the charcoal water purifier. After an initial problem of getting more water in the cupboard and spraying up on the ceiling than in the cups, it now works fine. Everything seems to be staying in one piece, including the extendible roof, despite the efforts of Algerian roads. The surfaces are so bumpy and they don't go more than twenty yards in a straight line.

Mechanically the Land-Rover seems to be okay. The oil leak is cured for the moment and fuel consumption is averaging fifteen miles to the gallon. Had some strange readings from the water and oil temperature gauges, so today I took the thermostat out. I had planned to do this anyway to keep the temperature down in the desert. However, upon removing the thermostat I found underneath *it enough large curls of metal swarf to fill a matchbox. That couldn't have been helping the cooling at all.*

We should have every confidence in our Rover for the journey. At the campsite in Marrakech we parked next to a Swiss couple and they were going to cross the Western Sahara in a Land-Rover that was twenty-three years old!

Tomorrow we'll drive on to Algiers and visit the British Consul there, to see if there is any reason why we shouldn't continue our journey south. We haven't heard or read any news for over two weeks. All the people along our route so far have been very friendly. One has quite a tired arm by the end of the day with all the waving. Also, along the roadside are many things for sale – like oranges, flowers and asparagus. Yesterday a young lad tried to sell us eggs at eighteen pence each! He dropped to two for the same price as we drove off, but even that was too much.

Well, it's time for dinner now, so I will close.

Love from Alec.

xxxxx

As it was, when we drove from the coast into Algiers there was no way we were going to find the British Consul, with all the signs being in Arabic and congested traffic everywhere. Fortunately we were able to follow the signs that showed a picture of a plane, directing us to the airport. After some hassle there, we changed a few traveller's cheques into the local currency. We hoped it would be sufficient to pay for all the petrol we needed from Algiers to Agadez in Niger. There was the 'small' matter of traversing the Sahara Desert that we added into the calculation, plus emergency contingency funds.

We stopped at a garage where two young lads were very helpful as they filled our petrol tanks and topped up our water supply. We also bought what we hope is paraffin for the cooker. Leaving the frantic city behind, we headed south through the Atlas Mountains, driving along a winding road through a lush, forested gorge.

It seems as soon as children can walk they are put to work here. We saw a scrap of a girl, couldn't have been much older than four – there she was alone, watching over a small herd of goats!

Total distance driven = 3,727 miles

A Local Welcome

27th February to 1st March 1977
Algeria

Ten miles south of Medea in Algeria, having driven two hours from the capital, we parked for the night on a grassy, triangular plot of land that bordered a curve on the mountain road. A radiant golden sunset silhouetted the jagged outline of the Atlas range. It was not long after we had set up camp that there was a knock at our back door.

'*Bonjour, Monsieur et Madame.*'

'Hello,' said Alec as he pushed open the heavy door and saw a young lad standing there.

'*Je m'appelle Ali,*' he introduced himself. '*Comment allez vous? Où allez-vous? Je vis là-bas dans la vallée à la ferme.*'

'Steady on, I don't understand. *Non compri,*' Alec replied.

Conversation stopped and the friendly boy went away.

'Alec, would you like rice with the fresh fish we bought today?' I enquired.

'Sure, and some of that crusty bread we found at Medea?'

'Okay.'

I prepared the meal as Alec studied the Michelin map for North Africa. He reviewed and marked the 200 miles driven that day and tracked the route ahead.

'We should make it to Laghouat tomorrow.'

'Do you reckon?' I responded. 'How soon will we reach the Sahara Desert?'

'Several days yet, but there are a few interesting towns to explore on the way.'

Dinner was ready to eat.

'Open the door, Alec, and let the steam out, please. Phew! The cooker soon heats it up in here.'

When Alec pushed the door open he was surprised to see the young lad had returned with an older teenager. They said nothing, just handed him a dish of freshly cooked fish and a basket of bread. We gasped in astonishment.

'But our dinner is ready to eat. What shall we do?' I puzzled. 'We can't eat both meals. We'll have to give it back.'

'But they might be offended!' Alec commented.

The lads stood by the door and quizzically watched as Alec and I tried to be diplomatic. We were frustrated at not being able to explain our predicament in their language.

'We'll just have to return it,' I decided. 'Think of their family: they may have little for themselves if they've shared out their meal with us too.'

I showed them our cooked meal and tried to make it plain why we had to return their food. Their cheery faces turned glum as they received back the laden dish and basket.

'Au revoir. Merci,' Alec and I chorused together as they walked away into the darkness. We had been looking forward to our dinner, but every mouthful then seemed tasteless and hard to swallow.

Our meal progressed in silence and our hearts were heavy at our unwelcome response. The first real contact with the local people and we'd goofed.

'Coffee?'

Alec nodded.

TAP, TAP, TAP.

Not again! Our visitors had returned. This time they presented us with coffee. They handed to Alec an engraved copper tray raised on four tiny legs. On it was black coffee in a thermos flask with sugar lumps nestled in a flowery dish, plus two tiny china cups and saucers.

'*Merci, merci!*' I gratefully smiled and invited them to climb inside the Land-Rover, as we moved along our bench seat to give them room to sit.

The lads joined us hesitantly, but stayed for an hour. We drank their coffee and they drank ours. Communication was possible using a pencil and paper to draw pictures for one another and our French dictionary came in handy too. As they learnt something about us, we learnt much about them.

The handsome lads looked young for their age. The eldest was eighteen years old, a car mechanic at Medea, whilst the youngest, Ali, was a fourteen-year-old schoolboy. Seven siblings, all told. Their father worked in the oil fields near Sidi-Bel Abbes and drove a Land-Rover too. An older brother was in the police force. Their disabled mother remained at home, which was just across the road. We even discovered they had a television powered by a car battery.

They left smiling and we were relieved to have been given a second chance. To top it all, we'd even made plans to meet again the following day.

We were up by six, and we ate breakfast, washed and dressed before the lads appeared promptly at eight. They climbed into the back of our Land-Rover and we left our campsite. Ali directed Alec to drive through their village, Beni-Chocoa, to a cooperative farm. There we saw a variety of farm machinery and tractors, plus a well-used and maintained combine harvester. There were substantial barns, one housing several fine Hereford bulls, a cow and twin calves. The labour-intensive farm was set in a rich green valley sprinkled with beautiful wildflowers. I sat down on a grassy bank to enjoy the country scene and made a daisy chain, while Alec wandered around with the lads.

'Jan, it's time to go,' called Alec. 'The lads want to take us to their home.'

'Okay – coming.'

We returned to the location of the previous night, and turned left off the tarmac road and down the earth track to a one-storey house nestled in a depression on the side of the hill. Entering through the doorway, we stood in the courtyard. Grapevines clung to the inner walls. Ali introduced us to his mother, his aunt, his older sister and two younger ones. There were no men around as they must have been away at work. We were welcomed into the aunt's bedroom and given chairs to sit on.

Coffee was served – hot, steaming, black – an intensive flavour.

I looked around the pink-washed room. Hanging on the wall, in a place of honour, was a framed photo of Houari Boumedienne, the Algerian President. The room was modestly furnished with a large wardrobe, a bed, a dressing table, blankets and a couple of bulging suitcases. Perfumes and soaps were arranged on a table. A two-month-old baby girl slept peacefully in a swinging metal crib.

The lads proudly showed us treasures their father had made: picture frames, caskets and model houses made of shells, crystals and matchsticks. Their mother could only shuffle about with the aid of a stick. She sat down on a wooden chair, studied us intently and smiled.

Ali's older sister came in and presented us with lunch: two bowls of couscous ladled with sour milk. We took the bowls and spoons and tentatively tried the food.

'An acquired taste,' I mouthed to Alec and he nodded.

We willingly ate the strange food until we could eat no more, as she had given us such generous helpings. With our lack of French, our conversation dried up and it was time to take our leave.

Preparing to go, we thanked the family for their generosity and they requested gifts from England. I gave a necklace to the sister, a tin of sweets for the youngsters, three marbles to Ali and a felt-tip pen for his older brother. Smiles all around in appreciation for the simplest of gifts. We bade them farewell and drove on south towards the Sahara Desert.

Leaving the Atlas Mountains far behind, we went across the Haut Plateau, where the land was flat for mile upon mile. Far off to the west, we could see an extensive lake with the surrounding land beautifully carpeted with white, orange, yellow and mauve flowers. The earth looked sandy and was strewn with rocks and cultivated with fir trees, many of which had died.

'Look way in the distance, Alec. Can you see the Bedouin camp over there?'

'Yes, and there's a shepherd with his sheep. Say, Jan, you'd better start making detailed notes of the land that we pass through, just to keep a record in case we go off course,' suggested Alec. 'Write down the mileage and what you see around at that stage. It will prepare us for when we have no marked road to follow.'

'Alright, I'll jot it down in the diary as we go along,' I replied.

3,810 miles – *rolling plateau, crossed a dry riverbed, sparse vegetation on distant rocky hills.*

3,830 miles – *plateau of rough, rugged land, a herd of camels, few horses, donkeys and cows were grazing. First sand dunes spotted on the horizon.*

3,850 miles – *rolling hills, clumps of tall mauve flowers bending in the breeze.*

3,855 miles – *Djelfa; a topsy-turvy town, nothing much to offer.*

3,902 miles – *plateau surrounded by rocky hills with tussocks of grass. The colours of the landscape have changed from shades of green to grey, and now to brown.*

3,907 miles – *to the west there is an unusual collection of trees growing – an oasis.*

3,911 miles – 25 miles north of Laghouat we camped on the plateau.

Alec studied the landscape using the binoculars.

'I can see another Bedouin encampment way over there.' Alec pointed in the direction and I could just make out the tent.

We settled down for the night and made plans to approach the camp in the morning. We were hopeful of being invited in to visit their tent, as it's customary amongst Muslims to offer hospitality to strangers. We had experienced much of that during our stay in Oman.

The next morning after breakfast, we pulled up a distance away from the tent, noticing the large flock of sheep and goats. Before long a black, bearded man walked over to greet us. He shook Alec's hand firmly, and then clasped his hand to his chest in the cultural way. He beckoned us to follow him.

We entered the tent: a repaired, striped, wool-woven blanket supported by wooden stakes thrust into the ground in a hexagonal shape, with a taller stake in the centre. The interior was divided into two by a blanket wall, the family space on one side, the other section for the young animals. Two lads brought in the lambs and kids and tethered them inside the tent, then took the greater flock away to graze. A tiny white kitten, tied to a post by a long cord, played with the frayed tasseled end. Two donkeys grazed nearby; one was still loaded with green fodder tied to its back that must have been collected early that morning. One of the donkeys brayed with great enthusiasm, welcoming us to the camp. He made me smile!

The man's wife placed a well-worn grey blanket on the ground to the front of the tent and our host invited us to sit down. His wife disappeared behind the blanket wall to reappear with breakfast: goat's milk, coffee, dates and bread. Then she withdrew into the tent.

The other young children, dressed in sparse, tattered clothing, watched from a distance, unsure of us white people. The father tenderly cradled his youngest in the lap of his robes, a cheery baby daughter, who gurgled when he tickled her feet.

It was a surreal moment in time, one in which to take a photograph would have cheapened a rare and treasured experience. So we simply sat and enjoyed this brief encounter in a nomadic family's home. Again, the language barrier meant our verbal conversation was a non-starter, but somehow the man was able to communicate sufficiently to ask if we had any children's clothes. Unfortunately, we didn't, but I found a small towel in the Land-Rover and handed it to the man, hoping it would be useful.

It was time to leave, so we bade the family farewell and drove to the desert town of Laghouat, where we briefly stopped to look around, but there was little of interest on that day. We continued on our journey, crossing the flat gravel desert where dust devils swirled across the ground. Clumps of maroon flowers struggled for survival, their heads just above the gravel. South of Tilrhemt, the straight road changed as it snaked between the rolling hills. Huge rock boulders were strewn about the land. We passed by the palm tree oasis of Berriane. Four Algerian men prayed by the roadside, having parked their truck nearby. A very long camel train was observed far in the distance on the horizon.

We finally arrived at Ghardaia, which was situated in a valley. It had been a long, hot day and we were in need of a pick-me-up, so we went looking for the nearest tearoom. A refreshing treat: we sat beneath the palm frond shelter, sipping sweet mint tea served in small, sticky glasses. We were glad to have reached the day's planned destination.

The actual Sahara Desert crossing was closer now and we would need to make preparations before going on further, so we looked to find the whereabouts of the official campsite for overlanders. We were told at the police station to take the road east towards Ouargla.

We drove in the direction the policeman had indicated and before too long we arrived at the walled camp. Alec honked the horn and the guard inside the compound opened the big metal gates. We entered and joined many overlanders with their vehicles. Four couples from Berlin were travelling in two well-equipped trucks that even included welding equipment. A couple of the guys worked on their ex-military motorbikes, ready for a rip-roaring ride in the desert.

We found a space alongside a white Ford Dormobile, which was occupied by a New Zealand couple. After supper we invited them into our Land-Rover for the evening. Ian was an electrician and Barbara a veterinary nurse. They were similar in age to us and had spent the previous three years working in London. It was interesting to discover that they had planned the same route as we had and even intended to ship their vehicle from Kenya to India. Such an enjoyable evening spent chatting in our mother tongue.

The 181 mile drive during the day, along with the emotional impact of visiting with the Algerians, meant we were glad when Ian and Barbara decided to leave and go to bed in their van.

It was an unusually noisy night with the locals partying in the nearby compounds. We took a while to settle, but eventually we succumbed to the deep slumber of the weary.

Total distance driven = 4,066 miles

Crossing the Sahara

2nd to 7th March 1977
Algeria

'More tea?' I asked, as we finished up our breakfast of yummy Scotch pancakes. Alec passed his mug for a refill from the insulated white plastic teapot, as he checked over the day's route ahead on the map.

'Well, I guess we'll just keep the compass bearing due south once we leave the tarred road. The map shows hardly any trail at all for the desert crossing. Today we must prepare for the long-haul journey. I'll take the jerry cans and their carrying frames off the roof rack and fit them on the sides of the Land-Rover. Plus I must replace the thermostat, as the engine has been running too cold.'

'Okay, I'll do the washing and then restock the cupboards with more dried food from the roof box,' I added. 'Shall we go and explore downtown later? We need to buy bread and also methylated spirit to start up the cooker.'

'Sure, let's get started.'

After the chores were done we walked into Ghardaia, a pleasant town spread out in the valley with housing areas on three hills, each with its own minaret: the tower from which the imam calls the faithful to prayer. In the main square was the market with goods displayed on the ground. Surprisingly for the location, there was a variety of fresh vegetables, including an abundance of carrots, for sale.

Having bought the items we needed, we walked through the back streets, passing many houses. It was refuse collection day and everyone's rubbish was in a variety of containers outside their doors. The dustmen, dressed in blue cotton overalls with hat and gloves, emptied the rubbish into wicker baskets, which were slung either side of their donkeys' backs.

Lots of children were having fun playing in the streets. The girls wore frilly dresses made of gold-threaded material and the boys were clad in the traditional, cool cotton tunics and baggy trousers. It was heartwarming to hear their joyful voices as they played in the sunshine.

After two hours roaming around Ghardaia we walked back to the campsite to collect the Land-Rover. We called in at the garage for fuel and the attendant filled the two petrol tanks and six jerry cans to the brim. Unsurprisingly fuel prices increased the further south one ventured in Algeria.

The tarmac road led us through the gravel desert with multihued sand dunes in the distance, from soft, dull beiges to bright, golden orange as the sun lit up and cast shadows across the landscape. We passed herds of sheep, goats, donkeys and camels. It was hard to see what they survived on with such sparse vegetation.

Reaching El Golea, a palm grove oasis, we stopped to refuel again and top up our water supply while we had the chance. A few irritating lads pestered us for money; one tried to pull off our GB sticker and another threw a stone as we left. We continued on a few miles to be well away from any dwellings and found a great parking spot with a marvellous view of the oasis and two nearby lakes. A vivid crimson sunset was painted in the sky.

We always parked facing our most direct route away in case any emergency situation should arise, such as unwelcome, threatening locals. Not that we'd had any cause to be concerned, as the people were generally very friendly and left us in peace. However, whilst travelling in a strange land we thought it wise to take such precautions. We had read that overlanders were advised to park near to dwellings, but we preferred to be well apart. That way we could be alert to any unusual sounds and take action if necessary. We also cherished the quietness after a full day's drive with the noise of the Land-Rover engine thundering in our ears.

By seven the next morning, exactly one month since leaving England, we drove away from our campsite along a good surfaced road. For hours we went across completely flat, featureless gravel plains – although the land in fact rose 1,000 feet over the 200 miles as we headed into a strong wind, making slow progress. We became hypnotized by the sameness and thought it would never end.

Suddenly we reached the ridge of a 300 feet high escarpment where a panoramic, rugged canyon opened out before us with high, rocky cliffs, cowboy country-type buttes and sand dunes. To top it all we found Ian and Barbara, the New Zealand couple, had already arrived and put the kettle on. I photographed the scene before us, had a cuppa and drank in the majestic vista.

We continued on a further forty miles before we parked for the night on the sand dunes, two miles north of In Salah: the last outpost before we would tackle the desert for real.

In the morning Alec changed the engine oil and did a final pre-desert-crossing check of the Land-Rover. All seemed to be well. Not far from where we were camped, we could see the Berlin trucks stuck in deep sand. They were lapping up the chance to use their winch, sand-ladders, ropes and any other equipment to extract the trapped trucks.

We drove the short distance to the red clay town of In Salah and went on walkabout. There we bumped into an English couple who had driven north from Zambia. Ian and Barbara happened to come by too, so the four of us genned up on what to expect on the route to Nairobi. We made plans with Ian and Barbara to travel together for the first part of the desert crossing.

'Alec, we should top up our water whilst we have the chance,' I mentioned before we left the town.

'I'll take this plastic water jerry can over to that café and see if they'll let me fill it up,' Alec offered. He returned with the jerry can full of water.

'Not sure if that was a good idea or not.'

'Why's that?' I asked.

'The sink in which I had to stand the jerry can under the tap was slick and stinky. I've washed my hands since, but I can't get rid of the smell.'

'Ugh.' I shuddered.

Next we stopped at the sub-prefecture office to inform the police that we were driving south to Tamanrasset. Supposedly they'd send out a search party, if we didn't arrive and report at the destination police station, after the expected period of time it took to travel across the desert.

It was vital to take the maximum amount of fuel on board, so Alec took down the extra six metal jerry cans from behind Dad's box on the roof rack. Once filled, they were stored in the back of the Land-Rover to be used to top up the main fuel tanks as soon as possible. In total we had seventy-five gallons of fuel and twenty gallons of water for the desert crossing. We felt well prepared for the challenge and excited to see how our Land-Rover would perform off road, using all its cross-country capabilities.

At noon we left In Salah, with Ian and Barbara in convoy, as the imam's call to prayer hailed from the mosque. Alec drove, while I kept busy making notes of the changing scenery and landmarks.

146 miles later the tarmac road stopped and the Land-Rover plunged straight into the desert.

'Unbelievable!' I cried. 'You'd have thought there would be some indication of where to go. There's no markers, no cairns, no stakes, just dozens of wheel tracks going every which way through the sand.'

Alec hesitated for a moment, wondering which track to choose, as none was more defined than another. 'Hang on, I'll follow that local Land-Rover bombing along. He should know where he's going.'

Alec headed off in a southeasterly direction, following the cloud of dust chucked up by the stranger's vehicle. Ian and Barbara followed closely in their Dormobile and we added to the many tracks going the same way.

Twenty-five miles on, we were stuck in soft sand, but with a united push our vehicle was soon out. Not long after we called a halt and parked up for the night, just where we were, hoping there would be no nighttime travellers careering across the sand.

Celebrating our arrival in the desert, Barbara served us each a slice of delicious Christmas cake and a mug of hot chocolate.

The next morning, with unknown hazards before us, our two vehicles set off from camp at seven. Much navigational note taking all day, as we drove across difficult terrain.

4,655 miles – compass-bearing 190°, rolling, rocky plain with soft, sandy dips.

4,657 miles – rock hills to east, sand dunes to west, green, patchy grass along sandy dip.

4,658 miles – gravel plain.

4,659 miles – small herd of donkeys heading east, strips of sand and green grass.

4,661 miles – 7.30 a.m., 190°, clump of white rocks, tufts of long brown grass, track gravelly, hills and sand dunes.

4,662 miles – black hill to west near sand dunes, small camel herd to east, stopped to take a few photos.

4,664 miles – 8.00 a.m., 192°, sand dunes to west, rocky hills east.

4,667 miles – white post, cairns, close to hills, seems a definite track, corrugations!

4,671 miles – alongside tarmac road in construction, camp for workers, grass hut restaurant, sign to Tamanrasset.

4,673 miles – 8.30 a.m., 218°, Arak Gorge, now driving on well-defined corrugated track.

4,677 miles – at 8.45 a.m., 216°, sand dune to west, backtracked half-a-mile as we had lost sight of Ian and Barbara, saw they were okay coming along route by hills.

I recorded as much as I could of what we were seeing out of the window, taking compass readings as well, as we rocked and rolled along, driving over bone-shaking corrugated tracks when even your teeth felt as if they could fall out. I raised my hand and ran my fingers over the rivets on the underside of the handmade roof to see if they were still in place. Remarkably they had not been dislodged.

4,687 miles – Algerian boy living in makeshift shelter, cadging cigarettes.

4,691 miles – abandoned, dead Peugeot car.

4,692 miles – spot two men ahead in red Volkswagen van with German registration.

4,696 miles – 10.15 a.m., 148°, stopped to drink water, doing 12 mph – 12 mpg.

4,706 miles – mirage of crystal-clear water seen, great driving across flat, sandy desert.

4,712 miles – 11.30 a.m. construction camp, track of new road – Citroen and Land-Rover rally vehicles going north.

4,722 miles –narrow valley, soft sand track, twisting around scrub vegetation and trees.

'Whoa, looks like they're in trouble,' Alec said, when he saw in the rearview mirror that Ian and Barbara's Dormobile was firmly stuck in the sand. He slowed down and returned to where they were.

'Need a hand?' Alec asked as we pulled alongside.

'Too right, man. It's stuck solid,' Ian replied.

'Stop revving the engine, you're going nowhere. Your back wheels are just spinning,' Alec cautioned.

The belly of the Dormobile was nestled firmly on a wide ridge of sand. It looked like a beginner swimmer doing doggy paddle: a lot of flailing of limbs, but going nowhere. The van was stuck in a sea of sand and needed our help.

'Okay, all hands on deck,' Alec said as he took our shovel out of the back of the Land-Rover. Ian fetched his and they dug out the sand from underneath and in front of all four wheels of the Dormobile. Then they made a slope in front of the vehicle for it to climb up out of its trap. Barbara and I did our bit when the guys needed a breather.

'That should do,' said Alec. 'Now where are your sand ladders?'

Barbara brought their two sand ladders from the back of their van. These were made from angle iron, which had been welded into short, narrow, robust ladders.

Ian climbed back into the driver's seat and put the van into first gear. Alec firmly positioned the ladders in front of the two rear driving wheels.

'Come over here, girls, and be ready to push,' Alec directed.

Barbara and I positioned ourselves at the back of their vehicle. We were poised to quickly retrieve the ladders, as the wheels would drive them down into the sand and we didn't want to lose them.

'Ready?' asked Ian as he turned on the engine.

'Go ahead,' Alec shouted.

We three pushed hard. The wheels moved forwards, on and off the sand ladders, but immediately got stuck again in the gripping sand. Not enough momentum to keep going forward.

'Oh heck, what the devil do we do now!' exclaimed Ian as he jumped out of the van.

'We'll have to use our winch,' Alec decided. 'But first she'll need digging out again.'

We fetched our water bottles and took a good swig of hot fluid. Nothing stayed cool in the desert. The temperature right then was 90°F with no shade. We all wore the traditional Bedouin headdress to help protect our heads and necks from the sun's unrelenting rays. Alec and I were dressed in long-sleeved red velour shirts and bell-bottom blue jeans, with lace-up tan leather shoes to protect our feet from the hot sand. Feeling shattered, but knowing we had to free the Dormobile without delay, we dug the sand away again, then repositioned the ladders at that time behind the rear wheels.

Alec climbed up onto the bonnet of the Land-Rover and stood on the spare wheel. He unlocked the lid of the wooden storage box and reached in for a long hemp rope. Then he jumped down and carried this across to the stricken vehicle, wondering who in their right mind would travel across the wilderness in such a domestic contraption. He attached the rope securely to the chassis, beneath its back doors. Alec walked back a good distance to our Land-Rover with the rest of the rope and wound the other end around the capstan winch.

Meanwhile I got in the driver's seat of our vehicle, ready to turn on the engine and press the accelerator when instructed. Ian was back at the wheel of his van and Barbara stood by watching the sand ladders, ready to retrieve them as soon as their vehicle was out of the way.

'All set,' Alec called.

Thumbs up from everyone.

'Jan, turn the engine on, but don't put it in gear. I'll tell you when to press the accelerator.'

With the engine on, Alec pulled the lever on the winch and it engaged. He indicated to me to accelerate the engine slowly. The capstan turned, pulling on the rope, which became taut. We were all eyes on the van. Slowly, slowly it began to edge its way out of the sand's grip. The power of the engine exerted itself through the rope and suddenly the Dormobile was free.

'Hurray!' we all cheered and clapped.

Back en route for only three miles when Ian and Barbara's vehicle was stuck again. We turned back a second time, only to drive our Land-Rover into deep, soft sand. Fortunately with digging and using the sand ladders both vehicles moved onto firmer ground.

4,736 miles – sign to Tamanrasset 300 kms.

4,737 miles –3.40 p.m., compass bearing 158°, sandy terrain with strange boulders, one with eyes drawn on looks like a bear!

4,741 miles – sandy plain, swell to drive across, just like in the movies.

4,751 miles – red rocky hills ahead.

4,760 miles – 4.50 p.m. arrived at the tomb of Marabout of Moulay Hass and given a free coffee by the guardian; following the local custom we drove three times around the small white building for good luck.

4,767 miles – 5.40 p.m., temperature 80°F, we stopped for the night by some rocky hills.

The hill we parked by glowed golden with the setting sun. Sand was everywhere in the Land-Rover and we looked and felt dirty. There was sand in our hair, eyes, ears and noses, under our fingernails and between our toes. Alec and I had as good a wash as we could, using a small bowl of water, soap and a flannel.

Ian and Barbara, who had parked the other side of the hill, popped around after dinner. We drank Ovaltine and mulled over the day's antics before retiring for a well-earned sleep, having driven 272 miles across the first section of the Sahara. We felt satisfied with our achievement, but not complacent – for who knew what the following day would bring?

*

Alec and I had an early start the next morning when our alarm rang at four. I'd set the clock wrong, but it was just as well as Alec noticed the rear left shock absorber seal was leaking oil. Three hours later, after he fixed the problem, we departed. Ian and Barbara followed on behind us and within two miles we saw a sign to Tamanrasset, 250 kilometres. We made a mental calculation of how far that was in miles to gauge on our British Land-Rover's mileometer. It was good to know that we were following a definite track by the inevitable corrugations that proved many vehicles went that way.

At midday, driving due south at a compass bearing of 180°, we drove with determination through an extensive area of very soft sand. Having negotiated this successfully, we stopped to check where Ian and Barbara were at that point. With binoculars Alec spotted them way back in the distance, taking a different route. Strange that they hadn't mentioned they might go it alone and we hadn't seen any flashing headlights from them at all.

> 4,830 miles – *no sign of mapped tarmac road, twisting and turning along sandy tracks.*
>
> 4,833 miles – *sign to Tamanrasset, track cut through grey rocky land and hills.*
>
> 4,841 miles – *good track – old tyres, rubbish, oil drums littering landscape.*
>
> 4,862 miles – *1 p.m., driving south at 190°, passed by road construction vehicles.*
>
> 4,883 miles – *180°, passed lorry full of sheep, sandy track, patchy corrugations.*
>
> 4,891 miles – *took a sandy route off the main track to avoid the torturous corrugations; after 2.5 miles the track petered out so we had to retrace our steps. That was not a good idea!*

4,909 miles – 3.50 p.m., 200° stopped for a snack and drink by a huge, white concrete block with a significant sign – Tamanrasset 45 kms – took a photo.

4,910 miles – yellow mud houses, palm trees, goats and Tuareg Bedouins.

4,923 miles – another small village, this time with large, walled compounds.

4,927 miles – we stopped for the night, parked on very rugged terrain.

Total distance driven = 4,927 miles

The Hoggar Mountains

8th to 14th March 1977
Algeria

'Tamanrasset – we've made it,' I exclaimed out loud with relief and pride, bouncing up and down on my seat in excitement as we drove into the remote desert town.

'Yes, we'd better go first to the police station and let them know we're here,' Alec replied.

Afterwards, we located the campsite, which was pretty pricey, although it did have toilets and showers, albeit rather smelly ones. We were allocated a cute palm frond hut to ourselves. The price included breakfast – coffee, baguette and jam – which we enjoyed before we began our chores. Alec cleaned the air cooler, changed the broken shock absorber and completed an overall check of the engine and mechanics. All were hot, greasy and dusty jobs. I completely emptied the inside of the Land-Rover and cleaned out every nook and cranny, which were covered in a fine layer of Saharan sand. Then I washed our clothes, which took all afternoon using my small bowl and bucket.

The campsite was definitely the place to meet up with overlanders. The Berlin group was already there. Safari travel group

'Encounter Overland', with their big truck and twenty some venturesome tourists, had made camp. The Land-Rover parked next to ours had two American guys, two Englishmen and a young Australian woman travelling together. Lots of folk to chat with as we all exchanged travel adventures and news of the route ahead. We were relieved to see Ian and Barbara drive into the campsite later in the afternoon. Their water hose had sprung a leak en route, so they had to do an emergency repair in the desert.

We worked until dark and then had dinner.

BANG – BANG – BANG!

I nearly dropped my plate of food, as I jumped at the sudden, loud noise.

'Crikey, what was that?' I asked Alec, cowering as I raised my shoulders around my head looking frightfully frightened!

'Sounded like gunfire.'

Nervously we went outside and another traveller told us that the locals were celebrating the Prophet Muhammad's birthday – I breathed normally.

For a little evening entertainment a group of us went into town to see what was happening. Thirty men were gathered, chanting and stepping to the beat of a drum and to the sound of a desert flute. Each man held a rifle. At the end of their dance they fired their rifles in unison, high towards the sky. Flames shot out of the barrels and the smell of gunpowder filled the air. The men moved on to the next crossroads and repeated the sequence again. We sauntered back to camp and went to bed. I could still hear the rifle shots in the distance, but knowing they were for festivity and not for harm enabled me to relax and fall asleep. It had been an exhausting day.

After a restful night, we finished the overhaul of the Land-Rover and gave ourselves a personal wash and brush-up. I felt so much better wearing fresh, clean clothes. Following lunch, we left the campsite and drove west to the nearby Hoggar Mountains.

'We'll have to go back to town again,' said Alec. 'How come it's so badly sign-posted if it's such a well-known place to visit?'

We were going around and around in circles, trying to find the right track. An hour passed and we had made no progress at all. Once again we asked a local person the way we should go.

'Thank goodness we seem to be going in the right direction now,' Alec sighed.

We drove for thirty miles into the Hoggar Mountain range that rose up out of the surrounding flat desert landscape. We reached an escarpment and gazed all around at the 360° panoramic view of the rugged, sandy brown, rocky peaks. In the distance was the table mountain called Akar Akar.

Shortly after making camp, a green Peugeot with German registration plates drove up the track. The driver got out and asked if he and his wife could stay alongside us.

'No problem,' we replied.

They too had made a successful crossing of the Sahara Desert, but in their saloon car!

Their arrival was to our good fortune when they invited us to join them for supper: smoked sausage, cheese, soup, bread and lemon tea – delicious. We sat on conveniently positioned, warm, flat rock boulders and watched the captivating changes of the magnificent vista before us. The orange and red fiery glow of the sun radiantly showed off an ever-changing theatrical light show. Finally the sun slipped away behind the mountain silhouettes and down below the horizon. The black mantle of the night shrouded us in darkness. Nature then gave us another spectacular performance as the illuminated full moon took position high in the sky with a supporting cast of thousands of sparkling stars, as far the naked eye could see. A shooting star gave us an extra thrill… and then another, and another.

Sweet dreams.

We were up at five to see the resplendent sunrise behind the Hoggar

Mountains. After breakfast I made a bread pudding for lunchtime. Our drive that day was into the heart of the inspiring, natural landscape barely touched by man, apart from the stone-strewn earth road. It wound up and down, around the mountains, steep here, bumpy there, and at times the track was even partly washed away. Sturdy yellow flowers, like giant lupins, rose straight out of the ground with no foliage.

Turning one corner we saw for an instant a beautiful, white-feathered eagle with yellow flashes and brown wing tips. It stood by the road chatting to a black crow. Our noisy Land-Rover startled the eagle and it took flight, majestically soaring high into the sky with power and purpose.

We stopped for lunch by an impressive rock formation with a giant boulder balanced at the highest point, threatening to fall at any time. With British panache, Alec set up our camping stove and kettle in the shelter of the rocks and we soon tucked into the bread pudding with a mug of hot tea.

Our specific destination that day was the hermitage on Mount Assekrem. Alec put the Land-Rover into first gear, engaged the four-wheel drive and climbed the steep track. Once there, we parked and walked the final four hundred feet up the mountain to a height of 7,965 feet. At the very top, we reached a plateau with sparse scrub vegetation.

The hermitage, a stone dwelling, was located there. It had been the home of Père Charles de Foucauld, a Catholic hermit. We read in our guide that he was born on 15th September 1858, in Strasbourg, France. He served as an officer of the French Army in North Africa. After returning to France, he had a religious experience and in time became a monk. He was drawn back to North Africa, eventually coming south to Tamanrasset and the Hoggar Mountains, where he built his house. His close neighbours were the nomadic Tuaregs. We saw a few Tuaregs living up there on the mountain as guardians of the hermitage. Père Foucauld was sadly murdered by passing marauders in 1916. He must have made quite an impression amongst the local people to be remembered over sixty years later.

We entered the hermitage and found a passageway that led to a curtained chapel, which was quite delightful. A carved wooden crucifix, illuminated by a burning candle, was displayed on a stone altar. Woven mats and cured animal skins were on the floor. In a back room we saw many books, a number written by the hermit himself. There was a guidebook telling the story of Père Foucauld in several languages. A visitors' book inscribed with the names of travellers from many countries who had come to visit the hermitage now holds our signatures too.

The location high on the mountain was also used as a weather station. Scientific equipment was mounted on a wooden stand, to monitor the changing temperature and precipitation.

We walked back to the Land-Rover and drove off in search of a camping spot for the night, even though it was only mid-afternoon. We wanted to have time to relax and enjoy the dramatic region of the Hoggar Mountains. Alec chose to leave the main route and went along a side-track, but that soon petered out. A German-registered Volkswagen van was parked at the end of the track. Alec looked beyond and saw there was evidence of vehicles going further on, even though much of the track was missing. Our faithful Land-Rover chugged along the uneven, boulder-strewn mountainside, until we found a secluded level area of land on which to park. A spectacular view from 7,600 feet as was indicated on the aviation altimeter mounted on the dashboard. The air felt decidedly chilly.

A cheeky, tiny moula-moula bird welcomed us. Black feathered with a white cap and tail. He was friendly and fearless, hopping around our feet. He flew up to perch on one of the metal cages that protected the rear lights, bobbing his head as he watched us inquisitively. In that area the moula-moula was very common and a favourite of the Tuareg people as the bringer of good news.

*

The next morning our little friend woke us up, as he pitter-pattered on the roof. Then he flew down onto the spare wheel and tapped his beak at the back window, insisting it was time for us to begin our day.

After breakfast we rejoined the main route to continue on the circuit. It took us all morning to meander through the mountain range, and we were rewarded with views of magnificent craggy rock formations. I spied another eagle perched aloft on a natural pillar.

The road took us around yet another corner and a lone boy ran out from under a simple grass-mat shelter. He carried a basket of handmade crafts to sell. We stopped and he passed the basket through my open window. I was happy to buy a small, triangular, yellow leather pouch with a red and green fringe. A short, rounded, black wooden stick with a soft point at one end was nestled within the opening of the pouch. Pulling on the carved flat head of the stick, I found the wood was covered in fine black charcoal. It appeared that I had bought myself the local eyeliner that adorns the eyes of Tuareg babies.

Later along the route we saw several Tuareg men riding their camels and another group brewing tea whilst their camels grazed. Leaving the Hoggar Mountains, we drove down to the desert and were astonished to come across a swimming pool in the middle of nowhere. A group of Algerian men were swimming and they invited us to join them, but we declined. By early afternoon our day's journey ended as we parked up on the sandy plain, a few miles from Tamanrasset, and enjoyed a lazy, relaxing afternoon and evening.

The following morning we drove into the clean town with its well-maintained, terracotta mud houses. The main street had open-fronted shops shaded by an avenue of trees either side of the road. Alec called at the bakery, where he competed with the locals to buy a loaf of bread; it was obviously not cultural to queue. The longest arm with the right money won the prize. As the men jostled each other, I snapped a photo, only to find out later that someone else had had their film confiscated by the police after such a shot.

We nipped to the bank to cash traveller's cheques and then checked out the local camel caravan park. There the nomadic Tuaregs met and traded livestock over a glass of mint tea. Each dressed in long, flowing robes, his head covered by yards of soft cotton fabric wrapped into a turban, revealing only his eyes. The few women we saw around town were dressed in indigo-dyed cloth from head to toe. Their faces were uncovered and unprotected from the harsh desert elements.

'Have you heard? There's no fuel in town and hasn't been for three days,' an American girl came to inform us as we visited the campsite.

'Why? What's the problem?' Alec asked.

'Apparently the petrol tanker has broken down in the desert en route south. It seems it may be two to three more days before it comes,' she replied.

'In that case, Jan, we'd better park near to the petrol station, so we can be ready to roll as soon as the tanker arrives,' suggested Alec.

We found a good spot, having first located a water source to top up our supply. We spent the rest of the day reading and playing Scrabble.

Our Land-Rover was one of twenty-two overlanders' vehicles which were hanging around Tamanrasset, all waiting for fuel.

The following day Ian and Barbara came by and they related the story of their two-day camel trek, which had left them with sore backsides!

As we waited for fuel, I washed a few clothes. Whilst scrubbing our sand-stained socks, I glanced up and saw a marvellous sight coming right alongside our Land-Rover. A Tuareg man and woman were riding together on a camel and leading a train of a dozen camels loaded with firewood, a valuable commodity there in the desert.

Late afternoon Alec drew and coloured a draughts board on the back of the Scrabble box as I made us both a mug of coffee.

A Belgian guy, from another Land-Rover parked nearby, decided to walk across to the petrol station. Next we saw him running back to his vehicle.

'The tanker's in,' Alec shouted. He jumped out the back, slammed the door closed and leapt into the driver's seat. 'Hang on!' he warned me as he turned on the engine.

With my arms I shielded all the loose kitchen stuff on the worktop as Alec careered across the rough ground to get in line. The coffee slopped out of the mugs into the plastic washing-up bowl, where I had quickly placed them.

'Well done, Alec, we're fourth in the queue!'

But we still waited as the tanker pumped the petrol into the underground tanks. Two hours later the queue began to move. The local transport was refuelled alternatively to the overlanders' vehicles. We took on board seventy gallons, as did many other vehicles – even more for the big trucks.

The next morning we broke camp at five to be first at the frontier police office. Another two-hour wait before our exit form was completed and our passports stamped. Then across to customs: currency declaration form checked and, after a quick look in the back of the Land-Rover, the customs officer gave us the clearance to go.

'Finally... we're out of here!' Alec declared as we headed south.

Now we would cross the desert alone, anticipating three long, intensive days of driving to Agadez in Niger.

Total distance driven = 5,080 miles

Family Heartbreak

14th to 23rd March 1977
Niger – Nigeria

On sandy hill by a tree plantation,
North of Danbatta, Nigeria
Wednesday 23rd March 1977

Dear Mum, Dad, David and Paul,

Well, we crossed the Sahara safely and the Land-Rover behaved well. It's amazing how many people are driving through Africa, the majority being on private trips: British, Australian, Swiss, American, French, German, Austrian and so on. There's a sense of instant companionship. Everyone's keen to hear how the others' vehicles are going, what the approaching track is like and of any potential problems. People travelling north, south, east, west – all on various time schedules in all sorts of vehicles, from cars to trucks. One couple was travelling with their young children and another couple even had an Alsatian dog in their red Citroen 2CV car.

Our trip is going very well and we're really enjoying the motoring experience. Alec drives cross-country, while I'm chief navigator, making good use of the compass, maps and binoculars. Journeying over a thousand miles through the desert has provided a continuous change in scenery, and a variety of tracks. The corrugations shake you to bits whilst the soft sand grips hard on the tyres. The dust and sand seeps in everywhere and at times it's been quite cloudy inside the Land-Rover. At the end of each day we shook the cushions and brushed away the surface sand, but in the campsites at Tamanrasset and Agadez we had a major clean-up of the Land-Rover and ourselves. The wooden roof box you made, Dad, is amazingly dustproof!

We have spent many hours wandering through the markets, trying to guess what foods they're selling. Millet is part of the staple diet in Niger. Earlier today, in Zinder market, there were many insects that looked like locusts, although very dead and dried, ready for the cooking pot.

Coming south in Algeria, the houses were built from mud, but on reaching Agadez in Niger there were settlements of round grass huts that looked like giant beehives. Since leaving Agadez, the Tuareg people are lessening while the black Africans are increasing, and the women's dress in particular is becoming more colourful. We are still in desert terrain, but the vegetation, shrubs and trees are on the increase.

We have seen beautiful, colourful birds, especially in Agadez campsite where they hopped around the Land-Rover. A burrow nearby was the home of a family of rats, but they didn't bother us as they kept their distance. The variety of insect life is becoming greater in size and abundance, and we'll soon need to use our mosquito net at night.

Our journey from Algiers has taken us straight south – Laghouat, Ghardaia, El Golea, In Salah, Tamanrasset, In Guezzam, Tegguidda-n-Tessoum, Assaouas, Agadez, Tanout,

Zinder – and our next major stop will be in Kano tomorrow, where we hope to find some letters from you.

We're really pleased we brought all the dried food with us, as there is little to buy apart from a few vegetables, bread and expensive tinned foods. Today we were a little extravagant and bought some fresh fruit as a treat: it cost one pound for seven local fruits, including two small mangoes.

Do hope everyone at home is okay. Practically every day we mention one of you – wondering where Dad has us plotted on the map, where David's going on holiday this year, what Paul is up to and whether you, Mum, are still going to floral art classes. How is cousin Jenny doing with her pregnancy? No doubt Auntie Barbara has been out buying baby clothes.

Well, Alec's writing to his folks, too, and we've got the fan on cooling us. It's sticky and hot with the temperature over 100°F today.

So, that's all for now.

> Fondest love from
> Alec and Janice.

North of Danbatta, Nigeria
Wednesday 23rd March 1977

Dear Mum, Dad, Margaret, Tony and Janet,

Well, we've crossed the first major obstacle on our journey, the Sahara Desert, a tremendous experience in every way. One of the most frightening things about it is seeing at regular intervals the abandoned vehicles of the ones that didn't make it. Although observing some of the vehicles people set out in, it's hardly *surprising they break down. People are proving every day it can be done in a car, but we're glad we have a Land-Rover, which at least is built for the job.*

Approaching Tamanrasset, the terrain was mountainous, most of which we drove through and around across sandy plains. In the Hoggar Mountains near Tamanrasset, we saw several beautiful white eagles with yellow flashes and brown wing tips. To see them soaring through the air, hardly ever flapping their wings but using the air currents of the mountains, was a wonderful sight. We also saw a large flock of storks north of Tamanrasset.

Further south in Niger, there were new birds sighted every day. Some brightly coloured, particularly all shades of blue. In the campsite at Agadez I was sure I'd seen many similar birds before in your aviary, Dad. One in particular was mainly brown with a red head and neck. I have taken a photo for identification on return. Spotted our first vultures today, the real evil-looking variety.

North of Agadez we almost ran over three desert antelopes as they flashed in front of us at about forty miles per hour. Some of the most interesting life we have seen is around the water wells. There you can find gathered up to 100 camels, 500 assorted goats and sheep, and 100 cows with the longest horns you've ever seen. Hauling the water up in skin buckets on the end of long ropes, are pairs of donkeys that are beaten unmercifully by little girls, although the donkeys are oblivious to it. At the wellhead the men carry the skins of water to troughs, and the waiting herds and flocks come forward in turn to drink. How they knew which ones had or hadn't drunk, I really don't know.

Another incident worth a mention happened south of In Guezzam near to the Algeria/Niger border. A Tuareg came galloping on his camel across the terrain as we drove past his herd of fifty or so camels. We stopped as he rode up to us, pulled to a halt and couched his steed, which snarled and grunted as it did so. He dismounted and, after fumbling about with his tasseled leather saddlebag, he came to my window and passed through a brass bowl. The bowl had a liberal coating of sand in the bottom into which he poured, from a goatskin bag, a pint of camel's milk and insisted we drink. Well, what do you do but drink – sand and all!

He then asked by sign language if we had any food for him. First thing we thought of was a packet of ginger biscuits. After he'd fought his way through Jan's several plastic bags the packet was sealed in, he pulled out his prize. The sheer delight on his face was a sight to be seen as he ravenously crunched and swallowed one spicy biscuit after another. He asked for tea, so we gave him a dozen tea bags. On requesting water, he held his bucket, made from a truck tyre inner tube, and I poured in half a gallon of 'eau de vie' until he forbade me from giving him any more.

As we said goodbye and went to drive off, his face was full of anguish and he frantically waved his arms about, then dug his hands into the sand. He kept saying a word we didn't catch at first, but then we realized he was saying 'Sable – Sable', which means sand. Seeing a local truck way in the distance that was going in a slightly different direction, the Tuareg directed us to follow.

Later in Agadez, a fellow overlander told us that he had taken the track that our Tuareg friend had warned us not to go on. This guy's vehicle had finished up in deep, deep sand and he was forced to backtrack fifteen miles to find the correct route. Which is no joke at ten miles to the gallon when every drop of fuel is vital. Our chance desert encounter that day was indeed fortuitous.

Tomorrow, we drive into Kano and hope to pick up our letters from home. Could write reams more of our adventures, but must finish for now.

Love from
Alec and Jan.

xxxxx

Kano, Nigeria
24th March 1977

Dear Mum,

We arrived in Kano yesterday and found your letters no. 2, 3, 4, 5, 7 and 8 at the post office. As you can imagine I was shocked to hear of cousin Michael's death. All of yesterday I was very upset and thought a great deal about the family. When there is so much wickedness in the world, it seems so cruel that those who strive to be good people should suffer so.

One of the photos here in my album has Michael standing with David and Paul. Looking at it now, it's hard to believe that we'll never see his smiling face again.

Thanks, Mum, for writing and sharing all about the funeral service. It must be a great comfort to Uncle George, Auntie Eileen and Ann that many people have been so kind. I have written a letter to let them know that, although we are far away, Alec and I are thinking of them.

Jenny's baby will soon arrive, which will soften the sadness within the family. You're obviously on good terms with everyone now. Silly, senseless thoughts about Alec and I will have surely disappeared, when it's printed on everyone's mind so vividly that life is too precious and everyone should enjoy themselves as much as possible and be helpful and kind to one another.

Well, one can talk and talk but I must finish now, as we'll soon be leaving for Jos.

Love to you all,
Alec and Janice.

xxxx

*

'Alec, the letters are finished and ready to go. Shall we return to the post office?'

We had just finished eating lunch, having found a campsite near to the Central Hotel in Kano. The campsite – well, if you could call it that – was basically a small piece of wasteland between the railway track and a brick-making business. The only other camper was Tim, a South African who'd ridden his motorbike all the way north from his homeland. He was very clued-up and gave us many tips about the route ahead.

It was too far to walk to the post office, so we had to go in the Land-Rover. We found it bewildering to be in a city after the solitude and vast expanse of the desert. Thousands of people were milling around on the streets and in the open markets. There were traffic jams to contend with: hundreds of trucks and minibuses transporting passengers, animals and merchandise. Noise, chaos, uproar and the stink of petrol fumes: pandemonium! We quickly took care of our postal errand and returned to the campsite.

After supper, Alec and I visited the Central Hotel for a beer in the air-conditioned bar.

'I can't get my head around the fact that Michael is really dead,' I shared with Alec.

'How did your Mum say it happened?'

'Apparently he was out working with men from the Water Board. They had two vehicles. When they pulled into a lay-by, Michael got out and went to speak to the driver in the second vehicle. He was leaning with his crossed forearms resting on the edge of the lowered window of the driver's door, relaxed and chatting. Next thing a car came racing along the road, clipped and flipped his body into the air and left him to his fate.'

'Did they catch the swine?' responded Alec.

'I don't know, Mum didn't say. All the family must be devastated.

They'll all feel the loss. I feel bad enough and I've not lived in Brentwood for years.'

'As you wrote in that quick note to your mum, it makes the family's reaction to what we did really pointless and sad,' said Alec.

In 1974, after we had been dating for two years, we decided to get married. Alec had just finished his first six months away in Antarctica and was going to be living for the summer with my family. He was working at the British Antarctic Survey office in London, a commuter train ride away. It would be easier on the family if we could share my tiny bedroom rather than Alec sleeping in the lounge.

'So, Mum, do you think you could be free on Friday the fifth of April?' I asked as she was frying eggs for breakfast.

'Well, I don't know. Friday is the day I pick up my pay packet at work.'

She was a dinner lady at the local junior school. Just in for two hours a day, supervising the children in the playground.

'Well, not even to come to our wedding?'

'Janice!' she exclaimed, almost dropping the fried eggs as she served them onto a brown, oval plate.

Well, much discussion followed. Why the rush? Marrying at the council offices! Don't you want a big wedding in church? Why not wait a month and we can organize it all properly?

My Dad didn't say too much, but I imagine there was a lot said behind closed doors. Dad liked a quiet life, but usually went along with Mum's gaiety and love of people and the extended family.

At Christmas time there was always the big family party on Boxing Day, when we all squeezed into one of the family homes. Playing the flour game, the chocolate game and doing charades. My granddad, Gump, had been the life and soul of the party, leading the songs and joining in the games. After he and Nan died, my Uncle George, Michael's dad, took over as master of ceremonies. He did a great job of telling the stagecoach story, when we were each given various parts of the coach and horses to represent and act out. Everyone acted as Indians by standing up and doing a war cry and jig on the spot. Not forgetting Uncle George leading 'I Am the Music Man', when everyone in two's and three's mimed different instruments. By the end of the song, we had produced a lively band. The bagpipes were always the best.

So with being such a close family, Mum was worried how the family would react about not being invited to the wedding.

'It'll be alright, Mum,' I explained. 'We just want a simple wedding now, just you, Dad, David and Paul, and Alec's immediate family. We'll marry at the registry office. I've already made my outfit: you know, the long purple and gold plaid dress with the deep-purple velvet jacket that I've been sewing. We'll have a reception at the pub next door and then we'll go away on honeymoon for the weekend. If we're still going to be living at home, we don't want a big fuss. We can do something with the family just before we go on our Land-Rover trip, when we'll really be starting married life together. Besides, weddings cost a lot of money and we want to put all our funds into our trip.'

'But we can work out the money, as Dad's been putting some aside. Won't you regret not marrying in white?' Mum cautioned me, even though she knew that white for me would be a lie.

'Can you remember the look on your Aunts' and Uncles' faces on the night before our wedding?' Alec recalled.

'Yes, at each of their homes where we visited that evening, they were thrilled to hear we had become engaged that day and admired my beautiful sapphire and diamond ring. Out came the sherry and they raised their glasses in congratulations.'

'But then we dropped the bombshell that we'd be married the next day at the registry office and the ceremony was only for our immediate family,' Alec continued.

'Yes, and even when we explained why, they didn't get it. Mum tried to cushion their disappointment by organizing a gathering for everyone at home on our wedding day, but of course we'd already left for our honeymoon.'

We had become the black sheep of the extended family that wedding weekend and made my Mum very sad.

In a sombre mood, we left the hotel and walked back to the Land-Rover.

Total distance driven = 6,140 miles

Open Doors

24th to 30th March 1977
Nigeria

In the morning we were fortunately up and dressed and had eaten breakfast before the traders called by. Sellers of doughnuts, bananas, bread; even a Land-Rover salesman came along. Being in Africa we had learnt that life is not controlled by the time on your watch. It's more important to welcome unexpected visitors and graciously pass the time of day. Hence we were surprised when we reached the insurance agent's office to find that he was annoyed at our being thirty minutes late for our nine o'clock appointment. We apologised, rather red-faced. After the necessary paperwork and handing over the required fee, we received the documents to prove that we had third-party vehicle insurance for Nigeria. That was a requirement for every country we visited.

As the insurance office was in downtown Kano, we had earlier gone in our Land-Rover and parked along the street. A gang of teenage lads crowded around Alec as he got out, all wanting to guard our vehicle. He chose one and the rest ran off hopefully to the next car parking down the road.

It was crazy in the market as so many people were out and about, and we could hardly see what was for sale. Traders had their goods spread out on the ground, creating so many obstacles underfoot that I was afraid I would step on something or somebody.

As we walked back to the Land-Rover laden with groceries, the many beggars who sat along the rough pavements pestered us. One old lady, a leper, was holding out a rusty can cradled in her fingerless, gnarled, stubby hands, covered with open sores. Her toeless feet were bound in grubby strips of cloth. The effects of the crippling disease had misshapen her face. I dropped a coin into her can. A pittance, but she was thankful. We went on our way, as we could! Walked away from the poverty and suffering that we saw. We were just passing through – but it tugged at my heartstrings and disturbed my thoughts.

'Now to find fuel,' Alec said as we climbed back into the Land-Rover, having paid the teenage guard for his services. 'I was talking to Tim this morning before we left the campsite and he said there's a fuel crisis here in Nigeria. Apparently it happens every year when the fuel depot at Port Harcourt closes for a one-month vacation.'

Our search for petrol took all afternoon as we criss-crossed the bustling streets to locate garages. We knew when there was fuel by the queue of vehicles at the pumps. Fortunately we only needed to stop at three garages to find enough to fill up. It might have been in short supply, but at forty-three pence a gallon we were not complaining.

Our departure from the city was late and night was fast approaching. It took a long time to find a suitable parking place along the unlit country roads. We normally avoided driving at night because of the hazards en route. There could be farmers walking home along the edge of the road, stray animals wandering about and vehicles with only one rear light working, pretending to be a bicycle. Devilish potholes also lay in wait to jolt and jar your body when the Land-Rover hit one as it trundled along.

'Well, it can't be helped. This will just have to do,' Alec said.

He pulled off the road onto the verge of a ploughed field, glad to turn off the engine. It was a quiet location and no one disturbed us as I prepared supper. We ate, then soon after I'd finished the washing up, we settled for the night. Alec was out for the count as soon as his head touched the pillow. It had been an arduous day, one way or another. A tropical lullaby of singing crickets and croaking frogs sent me off to dreamland.

'What was that?'

I awoke, startled by the sound of sirens. Vehicles screeched to a halt; car doors opened and slammed shut. Headlights glared through our back window, softened by the blind.

'Alec, wake up!'

I frantically shook him, but he pulled the duvet closer around his head, not wanting to be disturbed.

RAT-A-TAT-TAT – a firm knock at our back door.

My heart beat fast! My innards quivered!

I grabbed a sheet to wrap around me, crawled to the end of the bed and unbolted the door. Climbing out of the Land-Rover, I shielded my eyes from the bright lights.

Three black policemen stood before me.

'What's wrong?' asked the officer in charge.

'Nothing. We're trying to sleep.'

'Oh, is that so? And where are you from?'

'England. We had trouble finding fuel, so we were late finding a place to stop for the night.'

'Well, as soon as the sun rises, you'll have to move on.'

'Yes, of course, Officer,' I said, relieved that we could remain until the morning.

I climbed back into the Land-Rover and closed the door as the police cars drove off. Alec snored contentedly. I didn't disturb him but tried to recapture that elusive sleep.

At dawn, we were promptly off and away, hoping to avoid any further encounters with the police.

'It was probably just as well you didn't show your face last night, Alec. That policeman might have become more forthright, demanding to see our documents and maybe hoping for a bribe.'

'Yes, you charmed him away like a dream. Well done.'

Our journey took us through bush land. Fulani herdsmen were walking alongside their long-horned, lean cattle that grazed on the sparse, dry grasses. The track traversed several muddy rivers via wood-plank bridges. The sandy land around the villages was farmed and the sown seeds awaited the rains. The Harmattan wind blew dust down from the Sahara, forming a haze over the landscape.

Village women with ebony skin wore bright, bold-patterned, wraparound, ankle-length skirts with matching tops and headscarves. Babies nestled on their backs, held in place with wide bands of cloth. Young toddlers ran naked, several with big bellies and umbilical hernias. Girls were in ragged dresses, boys in holey shorts and t-shirts. Many men dressed in traditional robes with a pillbox hat, and others were in casual European clothes, particularly the young men.

After 143 miles driving through the bush, we reached Jos, a key destination.

Before we left England, Alec and I had the long-awaited celebration to send us off on our married life together. We even had a service of blessing on our marriage at St. George's church in Brentwood. Call it superstition or whatever, but it seemed a good idea to have God on our side as we prepared to set out into the unknown. All the family was invited, but just my four Aunts came, dressed in their fur coats to ward off the cold, wintry weather. There was still that sting in the tail left over from our exclusive wedding almost three years before.

I wore a glamorous, off-the-shoulder, pleated, floral chiffon, full-length dress in shades of pale peach and apricot. Over the dress, I wore a long 'Wuthering Heights' cape, complete with hood made in heavy chestnut-brown satin. Both were my handiwork, made in between the soft furnishing projects for the Land-Rover.

One of our guests was Mr Millar, my former junior school teacher. He was fascinated by our planned route as outlined on the map displayed at the party. Noticing we would be driving through Nigeria, he said we should look up his old friend Phil, from college days, who lived there with his wife. He wrote down the contact details.

We entered the sprawling town of Jos wondering how we would find the couple.

'Excuse me, do you know where Phil and Mary Osborne live?' I called out to a white lady who was walking along the street in amongst the locals.

'Oh sure. You need to drive straight ahead for two blocks, then turn right, down to the intersection and turn left by the gas station. You'll find their house two hundred yards down on the left, in a walled compound where the mission dispensary is,' instructed the helpful American.

'Cheers.' I waved to her with thanks as Alec drove us on, following her directions.

'Hello? Hello? Is anyone there?' I called, standing before the mosquito-screened door of the little house we assumed to be the Osbornes'.

'Yes? What can we do for you?' replied a grey-haired, stocky man who came to open the door. His wife was in the background, sitting at the kitchen table and peeling potatoes.

'Do you remember Dusty Millar?' I asked.

'Why yes, I do,' he replied quizzically.

'He was my former teacher. When he knew we were driving

through Nigeria, he suggested we might call by and see you. So here we are!' I explained.

We introduced ourselves and they welcomed us into the lounge of their simply furnished home.

'Sit yourselves down over there,' Mary gestured, as she brought in a tray of glasses and a jug of ice-cold, refreshing water.

'Oh what a treat,' I exclaimed. 'Thank you.'

During our conversation, which continued throughout the afternoon, we discovered that Phil and Mary were missionaries. They kindly invited us to stay, although we would sleep in our Land-Rover securely parked in their guarded compound. After a delicious supper of fish and chips we went with them to watch students play a basketball match at Hillcrest Mission School.

Sunday morning, after a scrumptious breakfast of fruit, cereal, fried eggs, bacon, toast and tea, we joined the couple in their Volkswagen Beetle. Phil drove five miles into the surrounding hilly countryside to a mud church that had a mud altar and pews too. Seventeen people were there, all told – men sat on the right, women and children on the left. The elderly had deeply scored marks on their faces, an old, traditional practice. Phil led the service and the congregation sang hymns with no books or any instruments. The service was simple and meaningful even though we could not understand the Hausa language.

Afterwards, we visited a local family who lived in a group of interconnecting, round, thatched mud huts. The only entrance was into the largest hut, where we stooped down to go under the low doorframe. It was dark and cool inside; there were no windows and we could just make out the inhabitants. An elderly man sat on his mud bed, which was raised on mud legs to allow a fire to burn underneath in the cold weather. A young girl sat with a nine-day-old baby tied on her back with a cloth. The baby's mother was out collecting firewood. An older woman was also present. In the centre of the room in the sunken earth were the ashes of a fire from which smoke had blackened the grass roof above.

During the conversation Phil asked the old man if he had thought any more about Christianity. The old man shook his head and declared he still believed in the ways of his ancestors. Phil prayed for the well-being of the family.

Leaving their home, we walked past the mud corn bins and the giant, poisonous cacti hedge that encircled the homestead to ward off roaming animals.

We returned to the Osbornes' comfy house to enjoy a delicious Sunday roast beef dinner with tasty vegetables, followed by Alec's favourite – ice cream and chocolate sauce.

The following day, I took the opportunity to do some washing in luxury. Mary put our dirty clothes into her washing machine. Afterwards, I rinsed them thoroughly, enjoying the abundance of available water, and then pegged the wet clothes on the washing line to dry. After sterilizing our water tanks with Milton tablets to stop algae growing, I gave the interior of the Land-Rover a general clean and sort-out. Meanwhile, Alec did an overall maintenance check.

At four in the afternoon, Phil and Mary took us on a fun outing to a recently opened safari park where we saw pygmy hippopotami, elephants, leopards and monkeys.

Relaxing in the evening, we quizzed Phil and Mary about their life as missionaries. 'Whatever we do, be it educational, agricultural or medical, it's a means of sharing the gospel with the local people,' said Phil.

'What do you mean by gospel?' I enquired, not being very familiar with that term, even though I had attended Sunday school as a child, likewise Alec.

'Gospel – well, in a nutshell, it's telling about the coming of Jesus Christ and how he died for us sinners and rose again,' Phil replied.

'In believing in Jesus Christ as your Lord and Saviour, you can go to heaven.'

'Yes, it's true. I know I'm going to heaven,' Mary exclaimed with confidence.

'How can she say that?' I questioned as we lay in bed that night, mosquito net well tucked in under the bed's foam cushions to keep the buzzing bugs out and away from sucking our blood. 'What arrogance,' I continued. 'Okay, she's been doing good for umpteen years, but my life's been pretty good too, caring for people. How can she be so sure?'

'Yes, you can hope that you do enough good to weigh the scales down against the bad stuff you might do,' Alec responded. 'How can anyone even know if there is a heaven and hell?'

'Exactly! Not sure I agree with them trying to convert the local people. Why don't they leave them in peace with their own beliefs?' I said. 'Surely it's cultural that people believe what their family has always believed in.'

Puzzled and somewhat miffed, we drifted off to sleep.

Following an interesting four-day stay it was time to continue our journey. After another delicious lunch at Mary and Phil's table, we prepared to leave.

'We'd like you to take this Bible with you,' said Phil, as he handed us a copy of *The Living Bible*. 'Maybe you can discover something new if you're willing to take the time to read what it says. It's a modern paraphrased edition.'

'Oh thanks, and thanks too for such a great time and all the wonderful meals,' we said as we each gave Phil and Mary a hug.

'Goodbye and God bless,' they called out and waved as we left the mission compound.

It felt good to be back on the road again with new adventures before us. We took the route northwest towards Maiduguri, en route to

Cameroon. The narrow tarmac road was in a desperate state, full of potholes and rough edges. Only really enough room for one vehicle, so it was quite hairy when another vehicle came towards us. Overturned trucks were left abandoned down the banks of the road. Alec drove with total concentration and I kept quiet.

KERPLUNK!

'Oh no,' said Alec, 'that sounded like a rear spring breaking. I was afraid that might happen. I need to pull over.'

Fortunately there was a level piece of rough land to drive onto.

'Let's have a cup of tea,' I suggested, feeling rather tense and tired after sixty miles of driving along the hazardous road.

'Good idea,' Alec replied, as he looked beneath the vehicle at the broken leaf spring.

Sitting quietly together in the back of the Land-Rover, we sipped the hot tea, with a dash of sugar in to lift our spirits, and Alec hatched a plan.

'I reckon we should backtrack and return to Jos. At least we know there are mechanics and spare parts there, whereas we have no idea what's ahead at Maiduguri.'

Alec turned the Land-Rover around and retraced the route back.

'Hey, watch out!' shouted Alec as a local Land-Rover suddenly overtook us at breakneck speed, towards a corner too. 'Crazy fools!'

WHAM – CRASH!

'Yikes – they've hit a huge boulder!' I cried. 'Quick, let's see how badly injured they are.'

Alec drove quickly to the scene of the accident and I jumped out to find three dazed Nigerians emerging from the rammed Land-Rover. Two of the men had streams of blood trickling down their faces. I grabbed clean tea towels to use as dressings and had the men put pressure on their wounds as they all clambered into the back of our vehicle.

'Wimpey Camp, Wimpey Camp,' one of the men kept repeating and pointing ahead.

Alec drove on as fast as he dared whilst nursing the broken spring.

After thirty-five miles we came to the Wimpey Construction Camp.

'Oh no. What have we here!' exclaimed the British site manager.

'We came across one of your Land-Rovers wrapped around a boulder and brought your injured men here,' I explained, as someone else quickly summed up the situation and took the injured men to hospital in the camp ambulance.

'And what about the Land-Rover?' he asked.

'Oh, that's a write-off,' Alec replied, as he bent down to check the state of our rear springs.

'Damn! That's the third new one written off in a month,' the manager declared. 'But, hey – what's up with yours?'

'Broken spring.'

'Say no more. Take your Land-Rover around to our workshop, and my mechanics can fix it overnight. Our air-conditioned guest room is vacant. I hear there's roast duck on the menu for supper and drinks are on the house. It's movie night too, on the big screen.'

Alec and I looked in astonishment at each another.

'Okay, sounds great – thanks,' responded Alec.

It was a terrific night, all round.

We were up at six for a delicious, full English breakfast with the contractors before they started work in the cool of the early morning. When we collected the Land-Rover our jaws dropped as we discovered they had fitted brand new suspension – complete rear springs with shock absorbers on both sides. The still-serviceable parts that were removed we took along with us. Bearing in mind the country's fuel crisis, they generously topped up the vehicle with free petrol too. Then, as an extra-special touch, we spied the words:

WIMPEY, JOS – BAUCHI ROAD

sign-painted in black on the side of Dad's wooden box up on the roof rack. What a unique souvenir!

Total distance driven = 6,478 miles

North

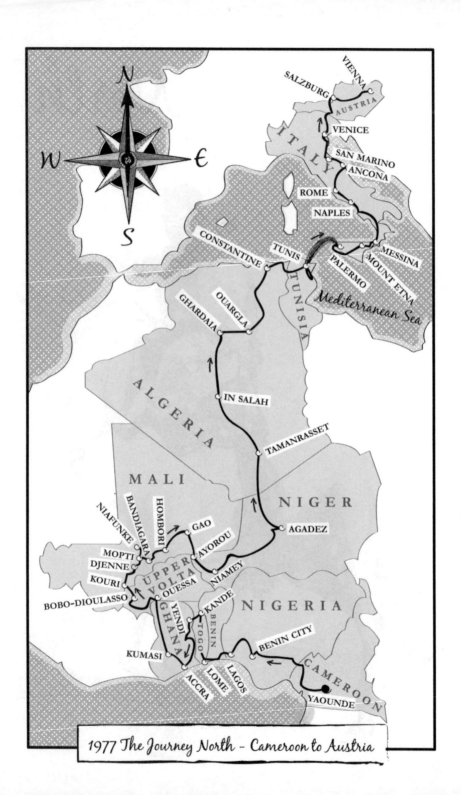

1977 The Journey North - Cameroon to Austria

Rerouted

31st March to 16th May 1977
Cameroon – Nigeria

Benin City, Nigeria
Tuesday 3rd May 1977

Dear Mum, Dad, David and Paul,

Hope you're all well. It was lovely to receive your four letters at Yaoundé in Cameroon. Glad you had a happy birthday Mum. Great to hear that friends Rosslyn and Brian now have a baby they've named Gavin, brother to Laura. Congratulate them from us if you see them, as I sent their postcard before I knew. Sounds as if you've visited Auntie Florrie in Barningham often; hope she received our postcard. You really have been gadding about: visiting the Great Aunts at Clacton, going to London and so on. How's the new washing machine going, Mum?

Since leaving Nigeria and travelling into Cameroon we've been to Mora, Maroua, Pouss, Garoua, Ngaoundéré, Foumban,

99

Bafoussam, Douala, Kribi, Yaoundé, Kumba, then back into Nigeria to Enugu, Benin City and now we're en route for Lagos. Dad, you'll probably need to look in the big atlas to find some of these locations.

Apart from the interesting scenic changes from dry bush to green forest, the fertile highlands, then dense jungle, we've also seen many types of homes made from mud, wood, bamboo, grass, palm fronds and bricks. Whatever is available the locals use creatively.

Our latest treat has been tropical fruit and vegetables – pineapples, papaya, bananas, avocados and corn on the cob – costing just a few pence. Yam, a root vegetable, their equivalent of potato, is quite good; in fact, Alec says he prefers it. They grow rice too, so yesterday we bought what we hope is a good long grain. The first bag we got I had to throw away as it was crawling with beasties after a few days.

The climate in the jungle is very hot and humid, and it's quite a problem with our bedding being very damp in the morning after we've been sweating all night. Drying the washing is a nightmare too! The clothes take so long to dry that in the end they smell as if they need washing all over again.

We also feel hot and bothered sleeping under the mosquito net to avoid the nightly raid of insects, moths and various midges. On a positive note, in the jungle we were thrilled to see swarms of giant, iridescent turquoise butterflies.

Fortunately we spent four relaxing days in Douala. There we stayed in the large air-conditioned house of a young French couple, Michel and Colette, whom we'd met in northern Cameroon. They are math's teachers and were still on their Easter break when we arrived. It was even better than staying in a hotel, with excellent meals prepared by their cook, who kindly did all our laundry too. Alec was able to do maintenance on the vehicle in the relative comfort of their driveway. Embarrassingly, our

French hosts beat us repeatedly at Scrabble even though it was in English. Tucking into snacks and drinks whilst we played, we tried eating olives for the first time – definitely an acquired taste.

From Douala, we drove south through the jungle to Kribi, renowned for its sandy, palm-tree beaches. We had our lunch by the waterfalls where the river cascades into the sea. Next stop was Yaoundé, the capital, where we went to the British Embassy, dressed clean and smart. We asked for news of Zaire, as we had heard there was rebel fighting, but they said we'd have no problem entering as we have already obtained a visa in London. But the Kenya–Tanzania border was still closed. Although there was a chance we could have reached Kenya, providing we found fuel in Zaire, which at present is improbable, we decided to avoid trouble and visit the countries in West Africa. After all, wherever we go is new and exciting.

So now, providing we can obtain visas en route, we plan to visit Benin, Togo, Ghana, Upper Volta, Mali, Niger, Algeria, Tunisia, Sicily, Italy and so on, east to India. Crossing the Sahara a second time will be quite a challenge, as it will be exceedingly hot.

I thought I'd give you a glimpse from our diary of a typical day during our time in Cameroon.

5TH APRIL 1977 – OUR 3RD WEDDING ANNIVERSARY

Our morning antics were observed by six boys and two women, who seemed fascinated in watching us have breakfast, wash the dishes, wash ourselves, Alec shaving and us dressing. Afterwards we packed up and set off along the rough dirt track to Mora, where we stopped at a local hotel for a refreshing, cold lemon drink. Then we took the good tarmac road to Maroua, but en route the dust clouds created by the seasonal Harmattan wind obscured the hills. In the dry riverbed, men were digging holes deep down in their quest to find water. At Maroua we were hassled by the local lads wanting to guide us around, guard our vehicle or such like. Went to the bank to change money and it took quite a while.

As soon as we left the town area the road began to deteriorate to corrugated dirt tracks through avenues of trees. We saw rabbits running on the rolling plains with a few rocky hills in the distance. A great eagle stood by the roadside and then began to run along, flapping its huge wings for take-off. After passing the village of Guirvidig, the landscape changed to very flat, dried marshland. People were living in round, thatched mud huts.

At the village of Pouss it was market day, and there a man was selling handmade hunting arrows. Vultures and ducks were pottering around, looking for tasty titbits. The women were very tall, some with short, wiry, curly black hair, others with shaved heads. Many had piercings adorned with chunky bone or wooden jewellery. Just as we were leaving, a young attractive Fulani couple came and asked us to take their photo. They were dressed in their tribal clothes and the girl's face was heavily tattooed.

From Pouss, we were able to drive on the dry, stony dirt track alongside the River Lagone. We passed many women walking home from market wearing their brightly coloured – blues, reds, yellows and greens – bold-patterned tops with wraparound skirts. They were balancing heavily loaded gourd bowls on their heads as they gracefully walked along. A couple of the women were smoking pipes.

Found a lovely spot to camp by the river – lads

were fishing at the riverside and a dugout canoe was being punted along. We were delighted to see so many birds, flocks of crested cranes and storks, and the occasional eagle. Distant drumming and singing gave a mystical effect to the otherwise peaceful evening.

We often spend time in the evenings reading The Living Bible that Mr Millar's missionary friends gave to us in Jos. We've been reading it most evenings, as this version is as easy to read as a newspaper. We've been thinking and wondering about our own beliefs, which for Alec and I were disappearing. It's good for us to take this opportunity of time and travel to study the Bible and reconsider what it has to say.

So now, unexpectedly, we find ourselves back in Nigeria. We've just spent the past two days in Benin City staying at an Irish couple's home. Tony and Sarah travelled from London to Cape Town, South Africa, two years ago with their young son. Tony met us at a garage in the town, where we were looking for water, and he invited us to stay. As he is returning to England on a business trip this week, he offered to take our films and post them. So you'll soon receive 2 cine films, 3 films of 36 slides and a film of 20 slides. You're welcome to look through the slides and let us know if the results are good.

Remember to post all letters from now until 22nd May to POSTE RESTANTE, NIAMEY, NIGER.

Fondest love,
Alec and Janice
xxxxx

Twelve days later…

Dear Mum, Dad, David and Paul,

Hope you are all well. We are fine. Since the letter we posted in Lagos, we have visited the coastline of Benin, travelled from south to north of Togo and back south through Ghana to Accra. Our route has been Ikeja into Benin, Porto Novo, Cotonou, into Togo, Lomé, Palimé, Sokodé, Lama-Kara, Kandé, across to Ghana Yendi, Kpandu and Akosombo Dam to Accra.

At Ikeja, near Lagos, we stayed in the home of an English family with two young sons, friends of the Irish couple Tony and Sarah we had stayed with in Benin City. Another Tony and his wife Maggie, they had previously crossed the Sahara in a VW Beetle. This Tony is an aircraft engineer with Bristow Helicopters, so he and Alec had plenty to chat about. We visited the airport several times and spoke to the Dutch company Aero-Contractors, which has Twin Otters. Alec enquired about job openings.

On the Sunday we went to Tarka beach with the family, which included a thirty-minute boat ride through Lagos harbour.

The day after, we set off to the country of Benin, but chose not to stay there overnight, as it was compulsory for visitors to pay and stay in a hotel. It was forbidden to stay in one's campervan. I guess they needed the money, but we chose to drive straight on through to Togo.

We were very impressed with Togo and vote it as one of the best-run countries we've seen so far. Everywhere was so clean and fresh, and the country's wealth was distributed evenly throughout the country. There seemed a great community spirit and everyone looked happy. The coastline was beautiful: golden beaches and coconut palms. Unfortunately the sea appeared only fit for surfing, too rough for swimming.

At one coastal village early in the morning, the locals were playing drums and rattles, singing and dancing. We went over to see them and they welcomed us to watch. One lady invited me to join in, so I had a go at dancing Togo style! We found out just before we left that the occasion was in honour of a woman who had died.

The scenery around Kandé in northern Togo was beautiful. Low, rolling hills, distinctive houses and a wonderful market we visited late afternoon. Most of the people there were in high spirits from the local homebrew on sale. The smell of beer was overpowering.

At another market we bought our best bargain yet when we stopped to buy some mangoes. As the lady didn't speak French I gave her twenty-five CFA francs, equivalent to sixpence, and held open a plastic carrier bag. We thought she was never going to stop putting the mangoes in. Forty-four mangoes! I made three pounds of jam and we had fresh mangoes for lunch and dinner for the next three days.

Our reception in Ghana wasn't very friendly. Over the twenty miles leading from the border we were stopped eight times by the police or army to check our particulars. We have since found out the reason: apparently a lot of smuggling goes on in the area.

The drive down along and across Lake Volta was pleasant, crossing by ferry in one place and a floating pontoon bridge in another. We spent an hour helping to clear a load of plastic pipes that had fallen off a lorry onto the ferry. The driver then kindly paid for our ferry crossing.

Our Land-Rover continues to serve us well as a home, and for transport – not just for us, but for locals as well. They clap their hands when they see us driving towards them, indicating they would like a ride. It's fun having them in the back, and if there are two women they chat away in delight, laughing and enjoying their good fortune at not having to wait around for the overcrowded local transport.

We've been grateful for our winch too, as we've been able to help out in some tricky situations. We see evidence of many accidents, with abandoned, smashed vehicles lying in ditches. Turning one corner back in Cameroon, we found an overturned Land-Rover that had fallen off the wet, muddy road. Apparently the driver had swerved when a bird swooped towards his windscreen. A Frenchman who worked there was trying to pull the vehicle out with a rope, but it needed our winch to pull the weight of that Land-Rover. Fortunately the expatriate was able to take the shocked and bruised passengers to the nearest hospital.

We are now leaving Accra to head north to Upper Volta and Mali. We are hoping to see some interesting crafts and folklore at Kumasi, which is supposed to be the place to visit in Ghana. We have been lucky to stay at the Taylor Woodrow Towell guesthouse for the past few days, taking advantage of our working for the company last summer in Oman. It was lovely to cook in a big, open kitchen once again. They had a steward there who would have done all our cooking, washing and so on, but I didn't trouble him. Our stay in the air-conditioned guesthouse coincided nicely with Alec's birthday yesterday and we went for lunch at the Continental Hotel to celebrate.

Letters should next be sent by return to POSTE RESTANTE, TAMANRASSET, ALGERIA.

Well, that's all for now.

Fondest love,
Alec and Janice
xxxxx

Total distance driven – 11,953 miles

Cultural Clash

17th to 22nd May 1977
Ghana – former Upper Volta – Mali

'How do they do that?'

'What?' asked Alec.

'Those women over there, walking along with Singer sewing machines balanced on their heads. How do they do it?' I marvelled at their strength and ability to achieve such a feat.

'Well, you even see tiny tots carrying small bowls on their head,' replied Alec. 'I guess it's their way of life.'

We wandered around Kumasi market and saw men making leather sandals, women selling snails, baskets, clay pots and handmade soap etc., always something different on offer. The sound of music drew us towards a gathering of people. Looking over the spectators' shoulders, I saw three disabled men sitting on a piece of sacking on the dirt, playing simple, traditional, handmade instruments as they sang a folk song. Small coins thrown into the middle of the group by the onlookers were gratefully received.

This sparked a discussion between Alec and I as we walked back to the Land-Rover.

'The poverty doesn't improve, does it, Alec? Sure, there are rich people here in Africa, but the majority are poor. What were we reading recently in that Bible, about Jesus telling a good rich man to sell all he had and give the money to the poor? Then another part said if you have two coats, give one to the poor, and if you have extra food, give it away to those who are hungry. How does that work out? In our Land-Rover we have far more to eat and wear than what we need for one day. What are we supposed to do – give the rest away?'

'No, that wouldn't make any sense, would it? What would the locals do with our dried food like the egg powder?' Alec replied. 'We might have more clothing than we need here, but once we're back in cold climes we're going to be glad of our jackets.'

'I wonder what they think of us driving around in our rugged Land-Rover with all its mod cons,' I pondered. 'They would think it bizarre if they knew we had a chemical toilet hidden under the back seat.'

'Wouldn't be without that, for sure. It's been a boon to us when we've been in a town, or when an audience has stood outside, waiting for our door to open early in the morning.'

'Exactly. But what do many villagers have?' I pondered. 'A hole in the ground, if they're lucky.'

'Yes, it makes your brain hurt, trying to fathom it all out. Remember those four teenage girls in Cameroon who came to chat one evening?'

'Oh, the girls who loved the Ovaltine drinks I made for them.'

'Yes. Remember what they said when they left – "We will pray for you tonight. Will you pray for us?"' Alec recalled. 'They must think every white person is a Christian.'

'Yes, but when did we last pray? After what Mary and Phil shared with us in Jos, do we know what being a Christian really means?'

Arriving at the Land-Rover, we were happy to set aside those knotted thoughts and move on with the day as we drove northwards through the rolling green forests. At Techiman, there was no fuel at the main gas stations – only at a hand pump operated by a private individual who topped up our petrol tanks.

We were not far along the road again before we had to halt at a police checkpoint.

'Where are you going?' asked the pleasant policeman.

'Timbuktu,' we replied, and not in jest.

The policeman shook Alec's hand and waved us on.

North of Wenchi there were fewer trees as the countryside became flat and small cattle grazed on stubbly grass. We crossed the Black Volta River by the Black Bamboi ferry and continued driving along a dirt road. The architecture had changed to rectangular, flat-roofed mud houses with walls connecting each building. Some of the houses were, unusually, two storeys high.

Another police check, then a military check. They wanted to see our passports, vehicle carnet and international driving licence documents, the usual thing. We were given a letter to deliver at the border; nothing to do with us – we were just providing a local mail service.

Farmers worked on the wet fields as pools of water lay on the land where wild white irises flourished. The weather was cloudy, hot and humid, and I felt clammy and weary. As the miles went on by, the vegetation continued to change. The further north we drove, the smaller the trees became with little leaves; there were many bushes and the grass was long, thin and brown.

At Babile market we stopped for a break. Plenty of locally grown produce was for sale, including frothy homebrew beer in clay pots. A crescendo of babbling noise hovered over the market. The beer must have been flowing since dawn. Men carried dried goatskin bags with leather straps tying the legs together, hanging on their shoulders. A lady sat on a tiny wooden stool frying doughnuts in sizzling oil. Her pot-bellied, naked toddler stood close to her side, with flies clustered around his infected, yellow-crusted eyes.

A man flagged us down for a ride and asked to get out at Lawra.

Then a policeman had a ride to Nandom. We became a welcome bus service. Next we stopped and I helped an old lady climb into the back of the Land-Rover along with her walking stick and fully laden basket. She rode with us to Hamile, excitedly chattering away at her good fortune.

It took us three hours to cross the border from Ghana into Upper Volta. The officials were enjoying a long siesta as we waited along with many other local vehicles. It was exceedingly hot and our patience was tested. Officialdom complete, we drove on past several villages to be well away from the border crossing, before we found a place to park for the night.

The air was oven hot and humid. Flies bugged us incessantly. What a night! There was a humdinger of a tropical storm: claps of thunder loud enough to wake the dead, white lightning streaked across the black sky with torrential rain beating on the raised roof. It was a real test of Alec's handiwork: not even a dribble of water seeped through the hinges.

'See who's out there?' I asked Alec, having heard an undertone of voices.

Alec raised the blind. 'Oh it's just the morning gawpers. Four lads standing in a row – each with a dibber spade hanging over his shoulder. I expect they're already supposed to be working in the fields.'

The lads chuckled as they ran off.

We were excited to be on the road again in a new land with a new currency, different languages and new experiences to be had. The people were out working on the land. Bare-breasted young maidens toiled alongside the older women, who had small metal discs in their upper lips. Their homes were fort-like with many clay pots standing outside. Beautiful water lilies floated on a still pond.

'Look – monkeys!' I said, as a pack of light-brown monkeys scampered off into the bush.

'These are the worst roads yet,' exclaimed Alec, as the Land-Rover traversed the rough road like a cross-country rally drive and we were thrown about the cab.

We arrived at Banfora, a pleasant town with some modern shops and buildings and a large market with plenty of imported goods. We bought fuel and changed money at the garage before enjoying a refreshing cold beer at a local hotel.

Moving on, we passed by sugar cane plantations and sugar cane was for sale at roadside stalls. Gangly teenage lads sauntered along chewing on the sweet treat. We stopped to buy several huge mangoes also on sale. We both ate one straightaway, enjoying the delicious, firm orange flesh as the sticky juice dripped down our chins and wrists.

Taking the main route to Bobo-Dioulasso, the road was much improved as we drove parallel to the railway line. We watched out for the donkeys, pulling heavily laden carts along the road. Lads were playing football barefoot on some scrubland at the village of Darsalamey, a common sight as we drove through West Africa. The youngsters and their footie, how they love that game. We found an overnight parking place a few miles outside of Bobo and enjoyed a good night's sleep.

We felt a bit of a buzz the following morning, as we were to visit the second largest town in Upper Volta, Bobo-Dioulasso. Quickly we washed, dressed in fresh clothes and ate breakfast before we drove into town and parked the Land-Rover. All ready for the big explore.

Brilliant – very French! Delicious fresh baguettes were too inviting to resist. We tore off chunks and munched away as we walked across to a fantastic two-storey market. Plenty of meat, fish, veggies, spices and imported goods. Enamel bowls contained thick, shiny golden peanut butter to buy by the spoonful and plopped into the customer's own dish. Sniffing the mix of aromas was a heady experience. Pungent dried fish heads battled with soft, sweet guavas.

There were stacks of beautiful, brightly coloured, folded batches of batik fabric – too many to choose from. Women dressed in fabulous outfits, complete with cloth headdresses, all made of the same fabric. Giant clay pots were on sale to take home and store water. Weavers busily weaved away alongside the busy street, with the traffic going by whisking up the dust from the gutters.

We were tempted to buy several souvenirs from the variety on sale: miniature brass figurines of musicians and dancers, a batik cloth picture and a gourd spoon with a pattern burned in as a decoration. We also found some interesting glass beads, like tiny sticks of multi-coloured seaside candy rock.

We soaked up the lively, bustling, noisy atmosphere of the vibrant town where everyone gathered. They came into market on overloaded bâchées: converted, small pick-up trucks with a metal frame and canopy on the back and bench seats within. Big transport lorries carried passengers way up on top of the battened-down merchandise. Others arrived on mopeds and bicycles galore.

As we drove away we went through yet another military checkpoint. The excellent tarmac road went alongside well-irrigated rice fields and mud house villages. There were piles of firewood for sale along the roadside.

Our stay in Upper Volta was kept short, as we were keen to drive on into Mali. We had no problem at the Upper Volta border control, so drove on through no man's land and arrived at the customs mud hut in Mali, at a place called Kouri.

'*Bienvenue!*' welcomed the customs officer. He gestured for us to sit down on the string-strung metal chairs under the grass-mat canopy outside his office.

A young lad was busy making the tea, which was quite the ceremony. A small blue enamel teapot was nestled on the red-hot charcoal fire burning in a special metal cooker on the ground. Gunpowder tea and a handful of fresh mint leaves boiled away in the water. At least ten heaped spoons of sugar were added, causing the water to bubble over, splashing and hissing on the coals. The lad poured the tea from a height, aiming the flow of steaming liquid into small glasses on a metal tray. All poured out, he then tipped all the tea from the glasses back into the teapot and put it back on the fire again. The tea hubbled, bubbled, hissed and splurt!

The customs officer stamped our carnet for the Land-Rover and handed it back with a broad smile, his white teeth shining brightly against his jet-black skin.

'*Dutè?*' he offered, instructing his young helper to pour and serve.

One hour in all we sat there, as we enjoyed three glasses of tea in total. After each emptying, the teapot was refilled with water, making the tea weaker with each brew. The first glass hit the back of your throat like a double shot of whisky, the second was smoother like sherry and the third glass was pure nectar.

Welcome to Mali!

Total distance driven = 12,915 miles

Day by Day in Mali

22nd to 26th May 1977
Mali

On our first night in Mali we parked in the bush, north of Téné. We had a restless sleep, what with the heat and distant sounds of festivities: beating of drums and singing all night long.

Feeling rather tired in the morning, we set off on our journey north along a tarmac road, passing friendly locals who waved to us as we went by. There were many beautiful birds and hawks to be seen. Sheep and goats grazed alongside big, humped cattle – spectacular, lean beasts with striking, long horns. Elegant, slim white birds known as cattle egrets strutted along the ridge of the cows' backs, looking for tasty ticks and dozy flies.

We turned to the left along a manmade dirt track built up high above the level ground. The flat, prairie-like land was very dry with long brown grasses and scattered trees. Grey mud villages were located by the track every two to three miles. Anthills, shaped like giant brown toadstools, decorated the landscape, creating a village of their own.

We arrived at a river, where the Land-Rover was transported

across on the pontoon ferry that was manned by five strong men. One had a headache and asked me for medicine. I gave him two paracetamol from our well-stocked medical box and he smiled. It was still some distance to Djenné, the historic mud town that we were driving to. Three women with a boy and a baby requested a ride there and we willingly obliged.

Djenné, what a place! Built around its famous, twelfth-century, vast, majestic mud mosque. Walking along the narrow streets between the thick mud walls of connecting houses with arched tunnels was like a biblical flashback. Carved wooden doors and windows added interest to the architectural design. The locals could sleep on mats in the cool of the night up on the flat rooftops, which had rounded-wall boundaries.

The fascinating open market stood before the mosque. It was animated with the sound of the local people, who walked so tall and regally. The men wore loose, flowing robes known as boubous, handmade leather sandals, and carried tasseled leather bags. Upon their heads many had big, wide-rimmed sun hats made from basket weave and strengthened and decorated with coloured leather binding. There was a long chinstrap to keep the hat tightly on the head or slung back off their shoulders. We couldn't resist those hats and promptly bought one each.

The attractive women were adorned in flowing robes and their hair was tightly braided with beads threaded in. They wore their finest jewellery, including nose rings and huge gold earrings, showing off their family wealth, surprisingly worn on a busy market day as they worked.

I approached one group of ladies and asked if I might try to carry the bundle of firewood that they were carrying on their heads. They placed a doughnut-shaped wad of cloth on top of my hair. Then I tried to transfer the bundle of wood carried by one lady onto my head, but it was far too heavy for me. The women laughed at my wimpy effort and so did I.

Leaving the fabled town behind, we drove back across the elevated dirt track and took the tarmac road north to Mopti, an enthralling town set on the banks of the Niger River. There were many modern town buildings designed in a style appropriate for the setting. The local lads soon appeared, asking to guard our Land-Rover and give us a tour. We chose one to guard whilst we went and explored the riverside market alone.

The overwhelming odour of piles of dried fish lying on the ground masked any other smells. Gourds, clay pots, grass mats and baskets with a few fly-covered, overripe mangoes were on sale. We bought a complete cured sheepskin to fill with water as the locals did, to be tied to the side of our Land-Rover on the jerry can rack. Apparently the water would begin to slowly seep out through the skin and then evaporate, cooling the greater amount of water still within – ready for a refreshing wash at the end of a day's drive.

Leaving the bustling market, we meandered across to the boats pulled up by the riverside and then to see others being built on the beach. Huge, long, wide boats, some with grass-woven canopies fitted on a wooden framework over the central part of the boat. We enquired as to the cost of a new boat, having a wild, romantic dream of another journey one day: to travel from the source of the Niger River in Guinea up in a crescent through Mali, Niger and onwards as it flows south through Nigeria into the Atlantic Ocean. Three hundred and twelve pounds to buy a boat and it could be built in fifteen days.

Meanwhile, back to reality: we went to the bank and waited an hour to exchange money. At the next town of Severé we refuelled and topped up with water, filling the sheepskin bag as well. It was five in the afternoon and as we headed north the skin leaked copiously, more than we thought it should.

We branched off at Konna, taking a dirt track that followed the telephone line. Shortly afterwards, we stopped for the night, right

Argy-bargy amongst
the Adelie penguins.

Alec at the geographic South Pole.

Campsite above the clouds. Antarctica. 1976

British Antarctic Survey

A surveyor with Alec & Bert, the pilot, enjoy a mug of soup with sardines & hardtack biscuits.

BY AIR MAIL
PAR AVION

Mrs J.B. S
Nurser
Wau

ADELAIDE
ISLAND

Alec tops up the engine oil on the Twin Otter aircraft.

Alec and Jan together at Niagara Falls.
Canada. 1976

Bedouin wedding celebrations in full swing.

Sultanate of Oman. Summer 1976.

Citrus fruit, nuts and garlic on sale. Spain 16/2/1977

Local traffic in Marrakech. Morocco 21/2/1977

Scouting ahead across Plateau du Tademait Canyon. Algeria 4/3/1977

Rescuing Ian and Barbara's Dormobile in the Sahara Desert. Algeria 6/3/1977

Put the kettle on!
Hoggar Mountains, Algeria. 10/3/1977

Bone shaking corrugated track in the Sahara Desert.
Algeria 7/6/1977

An 'angel' directs our route.
Niger 16/3/1977

Tuaregs drawing water at Tchin-Garagen. Niger 22/3/1977

Flame of the Forest tree, Rey Bouba.
Cameroon 10/4/77

Crowded market in Kano. Nigeria 25/3/1977

Jan admires a feather hat for sale in Bafou r
Cameroon 18/

So what's happening across the river? Cameroon 10/4/1977

Fulani sweethearts at Pouss market. Cameroon 5/4/1977

A typical rainforest track.
Cameroon 29/4/1977

Alec rescues a stranger's Land-Rover, using our winch.
Cameroon 30/4/1977

Market day by the mud mosque of Djenne. Mali 23/5/1977

Nomadic family ask for water in front of
their home, north of Tessoum. Niger 5/6/1977

Jan being a tourist in Piazza Navona, Rome. Italy 9/7/1977

'Do I hear the sound of music in the Alps?'
Austria 19/7/1977

Nigel, Helen, Ross & Alexandra in Vienna. Austria 6/8/1977

Alec & Jan leave Vienna for Hungary.
Austria 6/8/1977

out in the middle of nowhere. It felt so hot that we slept with the Land-Rover doors and windows wide open to allow the air to blow through for a cooler night.

The following morning we were up at five and away by six, following the telephone poles and choosing the best dirt tracks. The terrain was flat with stretches of patchy green grass; other areas had bare sandy earth with a few scattered trees and bushes. There were remarkable purple flowers that had pushed up through the earth's dry crust in the recent rain.

We were charmed by the beauty of the colourful birds that we encountered on the journey through Mali and the fascinating variety of lizards that skedaddled hither and thither. Often in the villages we saw them run along the mud walls. Becoming aware that it was being watched, one lithe lizard froze and played statue. Holding his bright orange head pertly, with one foreleg and the diagonal leg behind raised, his other two feet suckered to the wall, he stood perfectly still. Such curious, comical creatures!

Many people were about, walking or riding donkeys, camels and horses. Several mud hut and grass hut villages had distinctive mud mosques with wooden trims.

We passed Korientze, a riverside village where herds of cattle and goats grazed nearby. Two women each held a long wooden pestle to thud in turn into a deep wooden mortar, pounding millet into flour. They sang and clapped in rhythm as they released and caught their pestle. We marvelled to be in the beautiful and mysterious land of Mali with its varied people groups, who mastered the challenges of living there.

The track became indistinct and hard to follow. Flocks of large and small birds were down by the river. We drove past a sandy area with clusters of palm trees and then there was no track at all. We stopped to ask a family the way to Sarabou; their home was an isolated grass hut by the riverside. They pointed the way to go.

We laughed when a squat, hairy, wild black pig decided to race us along the way. What a spunky little chap!

On reaching Sarabou, the track had disappeared again and then a young boy saw that we were lost, so he ran in front of our Land-Rover and went into the shallow river. He beckoned us to follow him and showed us the direction to go through the bush on the other side. We then followed mere donkey tracks and had to repeatedly stop and ask the way from the occasional person we came across.

Near the village of Konga we saw two trucks and a Land-Rover going along the main route, so we gratefully followed behind until we arrived at the large town of Saraferé. Celebrations were going on: women danced, sung, clapped and beat out a fantastic rhythm on their gourds. A man played a wooden flute.

We left the jubilant sounds behind and gave a ride to the postman, along with his mailbags, and found he was heading to where we wanted to go – Niafunké. As we drove down to the river, there were men making bricks from mud and grass mixed with water. The formed bricks were released from the mould and left to dry in the sun.

The river was thirty yards wide and there was no bridge or ferry. I removed my socks and shoes, then waded in to walk across, to see how deep the water was. The riverbed felt smooth and firm under my bare feet and the water lapped against my knees. Alec decided it was not too deep for the Land-Rover and he drove to the other side. I climbed back in and we continued on across the dry, grassy flood plains, sometimes following a track, sometimes not, but guided by the postman.

Unfortunately the next stretch of the river to cross in the Niger Delta was that much deeper and Alec decided it was too risky. If the engine stalled and water was sucked up into the exhaust pipe, we would be marooned without a paddle. Disappointed to not be going to Niafunké or Timbuktu after all, we left the postman to wade across the river, holding the mailbags high above the water.

On our return towards the town of Sarferé, several bâchées passed by, each of these vehicles heavily loaded with passengers in the back and up front in the cab. Live goats and sheep had their feet tied together and lay high up on the roof on top of piles of baggage and merchandise. Live chickens hung upside down with their feet bound and tied along the sides of the bâchées. Their heads dangled and bounced along in the clouds of dust thrown up by the vehicles careering along the earth road.

Arriving at Korientza again, we saw several flocks of sheep with their shepherds. Then we passed a Tuareg riding high on his camel, leading a string of camels loaded with goods that were secured in leather bags. What an enthralling day, and there were more adventures to come.

The next day we drove back to Mopti, giving a ride to two locals whose bus had broken down. On arrival we discovered the bank was closed for two public holidays. Three Tuaregs came across and one spoke to us in fluent English and explained that we could exchange money at the hotel. He was from Gao, our next major destination to the east, and we talked about the route to go there. He advised us on how to take care of the skin water bag we had bought, to prevent it from losing water so fast: sew up any holes, smear the outside with butter and then soak the skin in water before filling it up.

We exchanged French francs into the local Mali francs with a Frenchman at the hotel. Then we filled the tanks with fuel and water before setting out to Koro, where the road climbed up to the impressive Falaise de Bandiagara. We drove to the edge of the escarpment and saw the extensive view of the landscape far below. The red-shale rugged road heading down towards the plains was slippery, steep and uneven, and for some reason the Land-Rover's speedometer cable suddenly snapped.

We passed four men riding on their donkeys and then a man walking alone flagged us down for a ride. Whenever he saw someone he knew, the man had us stop the Land-Rover so that he could greet his friends. At one Peuhl village of grass, igloo-shaped huts with low doorways, we stood nearby and observed the local people's dress and mannerisms and took photos as our hitchhiker chatted away.

The next stop was at a Dogon village where the houses were made from the red earth and were permanent dwellings. This completely different form of housing reflected the lifestyle of the two people groups. The Dogon farmers stayed in one place as they worked the surrounding land. Peuhl, or Fulani people as they are also known, moved with their herds of cattle to find fresh grazing so their temporary homes of grass could be transferred to another location.

Our passenger reached his destination at the village of Madougou, where the Dogon mud houses and Peuhl grass huts were built side-by-side. We checked on the route to Douentza and drove on towards a magnificent rock face where a mud Dogon village was nestled in the depression of the craggy rocks, totally camouflaged. It was only visible as we drove closer and could see the outline of individual huts and the tall, round corn storage bins, also made from mud and standing on legs.

That night we parked on flat farmland with only a few trees here and there. As we prepared to go to bed a herd of donkeys galloped by in a cloud of dust. During the night we heard the sound of voices close by, so we cautiously closed and locked the doors and windows.

We were up at five as the sun rose and found that those voices belonged to fellow travellers who had camped nearby. They were preparing to leave on their donkeys.

As we ate breakfast a man, four women and a boy walked along carrying baskets of manure on their heads to scatter on the adjacent fields. We greeted one another and I gave them a mango.

Soon after, a wonderful old man stopped by – a Dogon farmer wearing a tunic, trousers, jacket and straw hat and carrying a sheepskin bag, a leather shoulder bag, a dibber spade and a forked stick. He looked about eighty years old. He could still remember some English from when he worked for the local authority in Accra, Ghana, in 1935. He spoke the old English sayings of the elderly people in England. He asked me for medicine for his aches and pains and I gave him some paracetamol.

It wasn't until seven-thirty that we finally got away, after several more visitors came by. The dirt track led us through delightful countryside, past little villages with some of the houses built of stone. In the fields there were all ages of Dogon people working on the land. We saw a camel train of thirty camels being led, laden with salt. The Land-Rover clambered gallantly up a boulder-strewn, hilly track past a light tan-and-white monkey playing on a fallen tree. The road east from Douentza was very scenic as we drove across flat bush land, surrounded by rugged mountains.

Alec slowed down when we came across a broken-down truck carrying five men. I gave them some water to drink and Ryvita crackers and jam. A couple of local lads, who suddenly appeared, shared the snack as well.

Driving towards Hombori, across the semi-desert plateau, the bright white sand glared in our eyes and we were glad to have our sunglasses to hand. The temperature was high at 108°F and a hot dusty breeze blew in the open windows as we drove along.

Next we stopped by another broken-down truck that was carrying fifteen men. One wheel had a puncture and they had no means to fix it, so we gave them three big repair patches. We eventually reached Hombori and Fatima's Hand and marvelled at the unique huge rock formations that jutted straight out of the ground.

We continued on eastwards before stopping at a police checkpoint, where some kind lads refilled our yellow plastic jerry can with water from the well. Their bucket was made from a recycled truck tyre inner tube, with a strong wire handle to which was attached a very long rope.

The temperature had risen to 112°F.

Alec drove along the deep, rutted sand track when suddenly the Land-Rover stuck rigid, requiring the spade and sand ladders to the rescue. Children came over from the nearby Peuhl grass huts and tried to entice us to buy woven mats just as we were involved in freeing the Land-Rover!

We stopped in the early evening and parked on a level area of brown, stony ground. Having travelled 230 miles cross-country that day, we were shattered.

Total distance driven = 13,660 miles

Stop the Craziness

26th to 30th May 1977
Mali – Niger

'Why won't it work?' I cried out loud that very same evening as I furiously pumped the paraffin cooker and tried to light it.

'Why didn't we fit a swish camping gas cooker instead of this stupid ol' thing?' I said even louder, hoping to disturb Alec as he studied his beloved maps. Couldn't he hear my frustration as I rattled and banged the tiresome object?

'ALEC! ALEC!' I shouted in fury. 'It's useless!'

He looked up, not at all pleased to be disturbed from his quiet interlude after an exhausting day of driving. As I wept the tears drew lines down my face as they rolled through the dust of the day.

'You should be glad you have such a handy little cooker and don't use firewood and three rocks like the ladies do here,' Alec replied. 'Then you'd have something to complain about.'

'But that's normal for them. A gas cooker would have been so much easier, like some of the other travellers have fitted in their campervans.'

'Oh sure, they're great, until you can't buy a gas refill,' Alec said as he lit the humble cooker with no fuss at all – smart alec!

'What's up, Jan?' he asked as he gently held my shoulders and looked tenderly into my eyes.

'Nothing. Nothing at all,' I replied, dabbing my tears and blowing my nose on a handkerchief.

'Now I know you better than that. Something's wrong.'

'It's okay. You go back to your maps and I'll fix supper,' I whimpered, brushing him aside.

Half-an-hour later, we tucked into a bowl of pasta covered with piping-hot tomato and onion sauce. Then soaked up the remaining juice left on our plate with a dried-up baguette. It was as hard as nails, left over from the bread that we had bought three days earlier in Mopti. With our stomachs filled and feeling well satisfied, we both relaxed.

'So, Jan, are you now going to tell me what's troubling you? It's not like you to get so het up over such a trivial thing.'

'My mind has been so confused lately. Ever since we went to see Phil and Mary in Jos, our journey hasn't been the same. I wish we'd never met them.'

'How do you mean?' asked Alec.

'Well, with all that they said and what we've been reading in the Bible they gave us – it's totally frazzled my mind. I'm constantly thinking about the words Jesus spoke and I can't see how it can make any sense at all.'

'I know what you're saying. I've been wondering the same,' said Alec. 'All that religious stuff was okay when we were children, but what's it got to do with our lives now? We were doing great before, so why consider God at all?'

'I think it's really spoiling our trip. Why should we be bothered with such deep thoughts? I just wanna enjoy our travels and have lots of fun, not be made to feel guilty by what Jesus said. That Bible is messing us up.'

'I'll tell you what,' Alec suggested, 'I'll just hide it away. When we return to England, we could always go and ask a vicar what it means.'

'Good idea!' I said, relieved.

I felt the black, moody cloud dissipate from within me as Alec stashed the Bible away, behind one of the panels in the Land-Rover. Out of sight, out of mind. Sleep came good and easy that night, despite the heat.

The following day we found ourselves driving through a blinding-white sandy wilderness, where we felt far more exposed to the harsh elements than we ever did in the Sahara. The parched landscape was shrouded in a dust cloud. You could tell neither where the sky began nor the earth ended. The odd tree was here and there, roots stretched deep down into the earth seeking water to quench its thirst, clinging to life.

In the distance we saw through the dusty haze a group of Tuaregs beside a waterhole, drawing water for themselves and their animals – toiling for survival.

We stopped to winch out a brand-new Land-Rover that had wedged itself in the deep, rutted, soft sand tracks. It was loaded with sardines, vegetable oils and other food products sent to Mali as part of the World Food Programme, from Holland, Denmark and Norway. The nationals in the vehicle were thirsty, so we gave them some water and they gave us four mangoes in return. It was inconceivable to us that the locals carried so little water, if any, when they embarked on their trans-desert journeys.

Fortunately the remaining twenty miles to Gao were via a well-surfaced road and we arrived at the Niger River in no time at all, only to find there was no sign of the ferry. I felt yucky: boiling hot, dirty and my scalp was coated with sand. My skin had begun to chafe in the extreme conditions, causing heat rash and nasty sores. I was in need of a good soak in a rose-perfumed bubble bath. We were both parched, so took the opportunity to drink plenty of water whilst we hung around.

A young, go-getter lad sporting a watch and heart-shaped

sunglasses offered to go and call the ferry to come, for 1,000 Mali francs. He was onto a right good deal, but as we were not in any rush we didn't take up his offer and he didn't get his big bucks.

After their long siesta, the ferrymen showed up around four in the afternoon. They had us drive onto the flatbed ferry along with another Land-Rover and a lorry. The ferry crossing was quick and we soon arrived in the big desert town of Gao, only to discover a niggling fault on our vehicle.

'Shush! Can you hear that, Jan?' Alec had his ear to the side of the rear left wheel.

'No, what?' I replied.

'Hissing! Sounds like we have a slow puncture.'

To his dismay, Alec discovered a long, sharp thorn had been driven into the tyre. He took a while changing the wheel as darkness fell that evening. I sat on a rock and watched, swooning over Alec's strength and tenacity as he jacked up the Land-Rover to remove the offending wheel. He swapped it for the spare, replaced and tightened the nuts, then lowered and stowed away the jack.

Alec looked across at me and wondered where supper was!

The next day, a Saturday, we had the punctured inner tube repaired at a 'hole in the wall' mechanic's workshop down town. The swarthy mechanic's skin glistened with sweat as he eased the tight inner edge of the rubber wheel onto the metal rim, using long steel levers, and then manually pumped up the tyre, all for a steal.

From Gao we took the only route southeast down to Niamey. The sandy dirt track ran parallel to the river, snaking its way along the semi-desert terrain, past a string of villages built alongside the water's edge. At Ansongo, women were filling their goatskin bags with water from the river. They lifted the heavy bloated skins and straddled them over their donkeys' backs. Other women were bathing or doing their laundry in the easily accessible water. A patchwork of colourful cloths and clothing was stretched out to dry on the riverbank.

At the market the local children badgered us for money, sweets, cigarettes, whatever they could think of. I saw a naked, mad man walking about unself-consciously, his hair matted and neglected, his skin grubby and covered with sores. We bought dried mint leaves for tea, sweets and tins of sardines. The latter always seemed available in the desert markets.

Next we drove out of town for quite a distance and found an isolated place to park. Two wonderful hours of rest followed our lunch and sweet mint tea, during the hottest part of the day at a temperature of 110°F. Feeling much refreshed, we continued on a further eighty miles to Labbezanga to cross the border from Mali into Niger.

Driving onwards for some miles until we saw a huge, formidable dust storm far in the distance. The dark grey wall of dust, several hundred feet high, spread across the horizon and rolled towards us at a considerable speed. As the route was along a totally flat landscape it offered no protection whatsoever. Alec parked the vehicle with its rear end facing into the wind, to shield the engine, as we waited out the impending storm. We looked back through the rearview mirrors and watched it coming in all its might and power, tumbling over and over, picking up spindly bushes along its path. The alarming sound of the wind grew louder and louder as the eerie storm closed in. Suddenly we were engulfed in the dust cloud and day became night. It blew under the back door, forming our own mini-cloud within. The strong wind rocked our fortress as it rushed across the plains.

In the midst of this phenomenon, three Tuareg men mysteriously appeared from nowhere and walked by our Land-Rover. Their turbaned heads bent down into the wind and their flowing robes billowed out behind them as they were going to, who the devil knows where!

Thankfully during the hour-long ordeal we suffered no more

than an extra coating of dust. Alec turned the Land-Rover around and we continued on our journey.

Just ten miles on we were delayed again, when the police flagged us down for no apparent reason at all. We stopped dead in our tracks and handed over our passports and car documents to the officer in charge. He carefully checked through each item, eyeing us as he did so. The vehicle itself then came under scrutiny as he walked around to the back, opened the door, clambered inside and proceeded to search through the cupboards. Rummaging through all our stuff, his attention was drawn to a bag of dirty t-shirts, socks and underwear that warranted a full inspection. What was he hoping to find?

Eventually he climbed out, handed our documents back and waved us on. By then it was getting dark so we quickly drove on to find a place to park for the night, on the banks of the Niger River.

Each day's journey had its own tale to tell and we looked forward every morning to what we would discover and experience on that day. Come Sunday, we still had a further 155 miles to go along the bush roads before we would reach Niamey, the capital of Niger. We made an early start as the peachy, soft sun rose and cast gentle, pastel hues on the arid landscape. A handful of fishermen punted quietly in their pirogues along the calm river, hoping for an early morning catch. Hungry birds pecked in the sand at the water's edge, searching for grubs and insects. Suddenly they took flight, startled by the Land-Rover's noisy engine that stole the tranquility of the dawn.

Our drive soon had us at the town of Ayorou. Yet another customs search, though not quite as thorough as the previous day. Always ready to explore, we tarried a while to appreciate what Ayorou market had to offer. Strategically located on the periphery of the desert, it provided a trading centre for the nomadic and farming communities. Bellowing camels from the north carried merchandise in leather bags on their humped backs. Braying donkeys pulled carts loaded with grain from the south. We watched traders bargain with their customers to agree on a price for their purchase. Salt, clay water pots, gourds, fish, onions, small mangoes, limes, fabrics and jewellery were amongst the array of goods on sale.

The Tuareg women, dressed in indigo cloth, had gold coins plaited into their hair, which accented their unveiled, tanned faces, weathered by the sun. In contrast, their striking men were clothed in flowing robes of a single-coloured, heavy cotton fabric. Yards of soft muslin, very often a deep blue, were wrapped multiple times around their heads to form majestic turbans; only their eyes were exposed to the elements. A couple of trendy, young Tuaregs, who wore sunglasses and carried huge boom boxes in shoulder bags that were made from vivid psychedelic cloth, strolled around the market holding grand umbrellas on high.

The dark-skinned local women wore off-the-shoulder blouses, wraparound skirts and matching headdresses, all made from multi-coloured African prints. Even their babies would be held onto their backs with the fabric of the same print.

Some men in the market were dressed in t-shirts with trousers and the usual flip-flop footwear, suitable for all ages and genders. But many men were dressed in their traditional outfits, tailored from plain bazan or colourful African print fabrics. This outfit consisted of long pyjama-style trousers held up by a drawstring, with a matching tunic with long sleeves. Over this was worn a loose flowing boubou, of which many had elaborate designs of machine embroidery decorating the neckline and front panels.

The market experience thoroughly enjoyed yet again, we returned to the Land-Rover and continued driving south. On reaching the tarmac road there was inevitably more traffic. The terrain gradually changed to the bush, with increased vegetation and leafy trees. We passed villages of round mud huts with tightly layered, thatched, conical roofs.

'I think we should find a camping spot early today, so that we can have a rest this afternoon, then go into Niamey first thing tomorrow,' Alec announced.

We looked for the best place to park. But it took forever, driving mile after mile, searching for an isolated location in order to avoid the inevitable spectators.

'We're getting closer to the capital so we need to park soon,' Alec said as we scanned the bush.

Shortly afterwards, he pulled off the road and brought the Land-Rover to a halt by a very sparsely leafed tree.

'Not much shade for the middle of the day!' I remarked.

'Well, it will have to do,' Alec retorted grumpily.

'Couldn't we just go on a little further? We might find more shade,' I whined.

'What's wrong with here? It'll do just fine.'

I responded with a silent sulk and just sat there.

'Grrrruuh! Okay. Okay. Have your own way,' Alec hollered as he restarted the engine and drove at speed towards the deep ditch that ran alongside the road. We went down, then climbed up in seconds, but heard a resounding wrench from the rear end. The spare wheel mounted on the back door had hit the downward slope hard and bent up the said door.

'Damn, blast and damn again', or words to that effect, came spilling out of Alec's mouth.

The afternoon was spent under the sparsely leafed tree, while Alec repaired the ailing door. I sheepishly made tea to soothe our sensitive spirits. Needless to say, we attracted some local visitors who stood and watched us for some time, before wending their way onwards to wherever they were going.

The following day we drove into Niamey, eager to see if there was any mail waiting for us at the post office. We were richly rewarded with ten letters. We had to pay two pounds to receive them, but what the heck, it was swell to hear from our families. Just what we needed:

a boost of love from home. We went to a local bar, sat and drank cold beer, as we read every word of every page – it was pure joy.

Truly a Red Letter day!

Total distance driven = 14,182 miles

Extreme Challenge

31st May to 10th June 1977
Niger – Algeria

We eventually arrived in the desert town of Agadez after three gruelling days of driving over 600 miles from Niamey with the daily temperature rising.

The road conditions were variable, from good, well-graded dirt roads, to deeply rutted sand tracks – in which, at one point, the Land-Rover became trapped until a passing local truck stopped and a dozen men jumped off and pushed us free. Other dirt roads were seriously corrugated and the jolting Land-Rover threw us up from our seats as the safety belts jarred into our bodies, trying to hold us still. Alec fought to control the jerking steering wheel, pulling this way and that, as the wheels skimmed the hard ridges. If you maintained a speed of forty miles per hour, you'd have a relatively smooth ride until you crossed an irrigation gully cut across the track. Hitting a gully at speed sent the vehicle into the air and it landed with such force that the heavy Land-Rover rammed rigid into the ground. It threw us towards the windscreen and then we would thump back down hard onto our seats.

Clouds of red dust enveloped us from the increase of passing traffic, so by the time we arrived at the Agadez campsite we looked like clowns with reddened hair and faces, had camel thirst and were ready for a cold beer. The pleasant campsite was situated seven miles out of town and boasted clean squat toilets and rigged-up, perforated bucket showers. It had a simple restaurant in secluded gardens with shady trees and a swimming pool full of fluorescent green water.

Busy days at the campsite, as we prepared for the second crossing of the Sahara. The advisory put out by the Automobile Association read that it was extremely unwise to travel in the desert between May and October, due to the heat and difficulties arising in the event of a breakdown. From June onwards, the southern Sahara was subject to violent rains and the roads could become impassable. Well, we had made our decision and were committed to make the crossing at that time.

On Sunday 5th June, we left the campsite at half-past-five. Our thermometer read 89°F. Taking on my role of desert navigator again, I had the compass, diary and pen on hand to record time, mileage and notable features, as we set out to drive the 1,000 miles north across the Sahara. Travelling unaccompanied, we knew this would be a risky drive, pushing ourselves to the limit each day. We registered our intended route at the Agadez police station and were soon out of town.

Initially Alec drove the Land-Rover across the parched flood land that supported a few scattered trees. In leaving early we hoped to take advantage of the sand being firm from the coolness of the night. After driving twenty-nine miles in the first hour, we arrived at Tegguidam-Adra, a village of twenty huts. A small flock of goats gathered by a well to drink the water drawn by their shepherd boy. He waved to us as we passed by.

Although it was a hot day, the air was pleasant on our faces as it breezed through the open windows. Dust kicked up into the back of the Land-Rover, owing to the poorly sealed door following the ditch incident. As we drove across the flat gravel and sand plateau I saw an unusual small plot of fenced farmland that I noted down in the diary, along with the compass bearing as a reference point en route.

We took a break after seventy-seven miles at the small mud desert town of Tegguidda-n-Tessoum. There were many fine-looking Tuaregs who rode proudly on their camels through the streets. They sat on decorative leather-covered, wood-framed saddles that fit snugly over the camel's hump. Naked children with Mohican haircuts came and asked us for pens.

We topped up our water supply, including filling the new goatskin I had purchased the day before in Agadez market. It had been thoroughly treated and prepared to carry water, unlike our first purchase. The headless, swollen, hairy skin with trussed-up legs was stretched out on the side of our Land-Rover, tied with coarse rope to both ends of the jerry can rack.

We continued on for twenty miles across a wide expanse of undulating sandy plains as far as the eye could see. The ground was sparsely covered with pale yellow grass and scattered thorn trees that offered little shade. The temperature had reached 100°F and the sun glared relentlessly.

A totally remote location, yet we came across a tent which was the home for an isolated Bedouin family: a mother, two children and a disabled father with a club foot. Two camels and a couple of goats grazed nearby. The sound of our approaching Land-Rover grabbed their attention and they hailed us to stop. The mother held a two-quart tin by its handle high in the air. They needed water, so we stopped and shared our limited supply.

Not until fifty minutes and fifteen miles later did we actually see anyone else. A small camel train with a Tuareg on the lead camel was way off to the east and three horses grazed not far from the well-defined track. When the track was obvious, metal stakes or forty-five-gallon metal drums marked it well, but when there was a myriad of tracks going all over the place there was not a marker in sight.

At In-Abangharit waterhole there were hundreds of camels gathered with their masters. Hot, steamy camel dung littered the ground and the fresh odour greeted us. A teenager willingly filled up our plastic jerry can with water. We had left the driver and passenger doors of the Land-Rover wide open as we walked about, to stretch our legs and loosen our muscles. On our return we found our tin of sweets had been nicked. Well, if that was all we had stolen from us on the trip, we would be very fortunate indeed.

On the next part of the journey the track took us across the sand dunes. The Land-Rover had averaged twenty-seven miles per hour since we broke camp seven hours before. By midday the temperature had reached 112°F, so we stopped for lunch and a siesta until four, by which time the temperature had risen even further, to 116°F.

We left the sand dunes behind as we continued northwards across the desolate inhospitable, hot gravel plateau, where no vegetation grew at all. After forty miles driving in the wilderness, we came across three children who beckoned us for water. They were dressed in matching woven cotton tunics. The two boys both had a Mohican hairstyle and each wore a leather talisman around his neck. The third child was a young girl whose hair was neatly plaited. There was no sign of any adults, nomadic dwellings or animals in the vicinity. The children did not appear particularly distressed, but of course we gave them a drink and a few Polo mints too. We took a couple of photographs to prove the story to ourselves in the future.

It was unnatural for us to just drive on and leave them there, but our travels in the desert had shown us that all is not what it appears to be. How often we had stopped far away from anybody, only to find someone mysteriously show up out of nowhere.

By six in the evening we arrived at Assamakka, on the Niger frontier, marked by a solitary mud hut office. We had done well to find it in the middle of the desert. A short-wheel-base Land-Rover, driven by Italians, arrived under military escort. Maybe they had unknowingly driven by the border control. After the formalities were complete we took the opportunity to top up with water, but later found it to be contaminated with sewage. I had a restless night worrying about the foul water, even though our water filter could purify it to a pristinely clear and safe fluid to drink. Fortunately we had not added any bad water to the goatskin.

On day two of the Sahara crossing we were up and away from Assamakka by half-past-five. Alec initially followed the poorly defined tracks very carefully as we traversed the barren desert in the half-light. I noticed an outcrop of rocky hills to the west and noted it down.

Later there were deep, sandy ruts and the Land-Rover got stuck solid on the high central ridge. Alec shovelled the sand away from beneath the chassis and freed the vehicle. His grubby shirt clung to his sweaty back as he climbed back in and we drove on.

One hour later we arrived at the isolated mud village of In Guezzam, where the Algerian border officials were stationed. We waited for an hour-and-a-half before the customs and police offices opened. They roughly searched our vehicle, making us feel nervous. Finally we were given permission to go and we both breathed a sigh of relief as we left.

The hard, corrugated sand tracks wound between low, rocky hills to the east and west. We passed several stripped, abandoned vehicles, a visual reminder of the vulnerable and dangerous position we had placed ourselves in, driving across such hostile, unforgiving territory. The track was now running through wide-open, sandy plains with patches of pale green grass and striking purple rocks.

At ten in the morning I checked our direction with the compass. We were headed 322° north, having driven seventy-three miles so far that day, and the temperature was 108°F. The terrain changed to rolling grey gravel plains with distant hills. The rippled road gave such a boneshaker of a ride that Alec drove off the main track to seek relief. Bad mistake – the Land-Rover plunged into deep, soft sand. It took thirty minutes to release the vehicle. Alec first digging then driving, as I pushed the back of the vehicle and retrieved and repositioned the sand ladders, to repeat the whole procedure – all beneath the fierce, blinding sun. By one o'clock, we had driven a further fifty miles and were glad to stop for lunch and a long nap.

Later in the afternoon we continued on along a significantly improved track. Several trucks and jeeps passed us by as they travelled southwards. One truck had broken down and the driver and passengers requested that we stop. Alec lent them a hacksaw blade to repair a puncture. It was used to roughen the surface of the inner tube in preparation for smearing on the glue, to adhere the repair patch. We gave them a gallon of water and they gave us each a glass of sugar-saturated mint tea and fresh dates.

The good track was short lived as we bounced across severe corrugations once again, going alongside gravelly, rolling sands with bordering hills. By seven we took refuge from the exhausting expedition and parked the Land-Rover beside a huge rock, not far off the track. We washed our hands and faces in the cold, blackened water poured from the goatskin.

It was a cool, moonlit night, so after supper we rested for a while outside. We lay flat on our backs on sleeping bags spread on the hard sand and looked up to the star-studded heavens. A tranquil moment of bliss as we relaxed in the quietness and solitude of the desert.

The next morning it took two hours to drive the remaining fifty miles to Tamanrasset, our midway staging post. Arriving by eight, the temperature was pleasant at 86°F. We reported to the customs and police stations and our travel documents were perused and stamped. As part of a malaria control programme they also took our temperatures, which thankfully were normal.

We booked in at the familiar campsite, at a cost of two pounds a night. That hurt after all the free nights, choosing a location wherever we fancied along the trail. Alec set to repairing the rear left spring, which had broken another leaf during the desert crossing. He also patched two of our plastic water jerry cans that had been leaking. I attended to the laundry and sterilised the sewage-contaminated water tanks. We were grateful to be in one location for a while.

It was fascinating to observe who would choose to come on such a safari adventure. There on the campsite was the rugged, macho guy, whom we'd nicknamed the Knight, in his shining white Land-Rover. Perched on the bonnet of his vehicle was his glamorous blond girlfriend, looking every bit a model as she manicured and painted her long nails pillar-box red. We had previously met them on our journey south, at the Agadez campsite. They were well known for rescuing stranded overlanders whose vehicles had broken down in the desert.

At one stage of our journey southwards, we came across a Volkswagen campervan parked in the desert. There beneath the shade of a 'Martini' umbrella was a bikini-clad young woman, lounging on her sunbed. She wore sunglasses to tone down the glare from the glossy magazine she was reading. No one else appeared to be around, so we stopped to see what was going on.

'Oh, my boyfriend got a ride on a truck. He's gone off to Agadez to buy spare parts to fix our van,' she casually responded, as if it was the most natural thing in the world to be sunbathing in the Sahara. We checked to make sure she had enough water and food before we continued on, hoping that her boyfriend would return as planned.

During the evening in Tamanrasset, we chatted with another English couple. Their travel costs had been funded by compensation that the chap had received after a work injury left him lame. On hearing their travel tales, we were thankful that we had made the decision to turn west from Yaoundé in Cameroon and not continue driving east through Zaire towards Kenya. Apparently they had been held up and seriously threatened by drunken Zairian soldiers waving loaded machine guns. Customs officers had aggressively searched their vehicle and the ferrymen charged them an extortionate fee to take them and their vehicle across a river. Their disturbing experience had totally put them off Africa and they couldn't wait to put their feet back on European terra firma. Too bad!

The following day we had a restful lie-in until eight, then got up to enjoy fresh baguette, jam and coffee served by the campsite staff, while we sat on bamboo chairs beneath a palm frond gazebo.

Afterwards, Alec popped into town to organize the third-party vehicle insurance for Algeria, changed money at the bank, bought bread from the bakery and collected letters at the post office. We had a late lunch, then packed and left town by five, having refilled the water and petrol tanks, of course. The air was thick with dust, the wind was blowing and, remarkably, it was gently raining!

Thirty-five miles north of the town, we drove along a corrugated track across rocky, hilly terrain. An Algerian soldier waved us down and asked us for cigarettes, cassettes, souvenirs or whatever we should care to give him. As we had nothing we wished to part with, Alec drove away in haste. Further along there was a group of soldiers working on the new road that would go from Tamanrasset to In Salah. A short while later we passed by several army camps.

Just after eight, having continued for a further sixty-five miles, distancing ourselves from the army, we decided to stop as night was falling.

We were perturbed when two soldiers appeared and gave us some plums. They stood around for ages watching us, obviously expecting something in return. Thankfully they eventually gave up and left. That night we slept with our doors and windows securely locked in case our unwelcome visitors returned.

On day five of the Sahara crossing, at five in the morning, it was still dark as we ate our breakfast. The rumble of several Army trucks driving by shattered the peace. They carried the early shift of soldiers to the construction site, to toil on the new road in the coolness of the dawn.

It was a lovely drive across sandy terrain that morning with scenic, rugged, rocky hills in the distance. Later on the track became rough and ridged with well-defined corrugations, which ironically had become a totally normal surface for us to rattle along. Alec observed that the engine ran much cooler that day, compared to the same hour on previous days.

By half-past-nine we'd driven eighty-four miles and arrived at the familiar, small, sacred white building, Marabout of Moulay Hassan. We drove around it three times again, for good luck. The climate was very pleasant at 90°F by noon, so we kept on going. The route varied from a newly cut track, level and comfortable to drive along, to one that deteriorated into corrugations and then to soft sand.

When our Land-Rover wheels became firmly engulfed in the deep sand we were so thankful that the Italians, whom we'd seen at the Niger frontier, happened to come on by. Following the Samaritan code of desert travellers, they rescued us by winching the Land-Rover out onto firmer ground.

Having enjoyed a cooler day, we were surprised by mid-afternoon when the temperature shot up to 120°F as we arrived at Arak Gorge. There we stopped, ate lunch and took a two-and-a-half-hour break.

At five we set off again, following an easily identifiable corrugated track that ran along the foot of towering cliffs. It took us through beautiful, rugged mountain scenery that was quite different to the sandy route we'd driven along on our journey south. Three-and-a-half hours and forty miles later, we parked for the night by the side of the track.

The sixth and final day of traversing the Sahara seemed short and sweet. We set off at seven in the morning to find the tarmac road and anticipated a heavenly respite from the constant rough ride. After leaving the hills, the track cut through a plateau of firm white sand. Steadily clocking up the miles, we drew closer and closer to our target.

In less than four hours we located the tarmac road and were ecstatic. Our trusty Land-Rover had taken us for a second time safely across the Sahara. Fears of breaking down and being trapped in the unmerciful, desolate desert vanished. We felt tremendous relief and great achievement as we drove the final sixty miles to In Salah. Magnificent golden sand dunes fanned out on either side of the tarmac road, in celebration of the victory won on that day over the mighty Sahara!

By noon we were at a café shack in the town drinking cold sodas. Our thirst quenched, we discussed the ongoing journey. In the coming days we would continue through Algeria to Tunisia and to the edge of the African continent. We were both looking forward to reaching and crossing the Mediterranean Sea to Sicily and beyond. It had been an exhilarating experience exploring West Africa, but we were more than ready for a little European luxury.

Total distance driven = 15,777 miles

Treats Galore

11th June to 11th July 1977
Algeria – Tunisia – Sicily – Italy

We motored north in Algeria on an excellent tarmac road from In Salah to the palm tree oasis of El Golea. There we stopped at the open market and enjoyed the fresh scents of the fruit and vegetables on display: carrots, onions, beetroot, melons, tomatoes, plums, oranges and apples. I chose to buy the plump ruby-red tomatoes and sweet burgundy plums. Tempting wafts of newly baked bread had me eagerly handing over cash for a loaf straight from the oven. Tossing the hot baguette from one hand to the other, I tore off a piece and gave it to Alec.

'Mmmmm… that was worth the drive,' he said, chewing away as we returned to the Land-Rover.

Now that the journey was less taxing, we ventured unhurriedly from place to place over the following days, as we made our way north towards the Mediterranean Sea – from El Golea to Ghardaia and then east to Ouargla and Touggourt, passing Bedouin encampments, camel trains and flames of fire burning high in the air on the oil fields. The days were baking hot with high winds, but the challenge of the environment and climate did not seem as critical then with the relative security of a real road. I guess we reckoned someone would come along at sometime if we broke down. Plus our Land-Rover had proven trustworthy and we were confident in our ability to fix things.

At Biskra we turned east off the main road along the picturesque route through the Aurès mountain range to arrive at an impressive canyon known as the Balconies of Rouffi: a rugged, bare, splayed-out rock face, cut through by the river. Palm trees, pink floral bushes and other lush vegetation grew abundantly along the sweep of the gorge. Naturally camouflaged houses were situated on the terraced cliffs.

At Timgad we stopped to visit the vast ruins of a Roman city, built in AD 100 as a military garrison to defend against marauding Berber tribes. Even in its ruined state it was possible to imagine the former grandeur of the site.

We drove on to Constantine, an imposing, busy industrial city built high on the plateaus either side of a deep gorge. A suspension bridge reached from one side to the other, a masterful engineering achievement above the craggy ravine. As we walked about the city for a couple of hours, we saw hundreds of people and so much traffic. It felt strange, but was a normality we'd need to adjust to. We sat at a street-side café table, delighting in a cold, freshly-pressed lemon drink with a dish of 'haven't had forever', delectable scoops of strawberry, chocolate and vanilla ice cream. Heaven comes at a price, we discovered, when presented with the bill.

In less than 100 miles we finally reached the Mediterranean Sea, a vast expanse of beautiful blueness. We parked and I quickly jumped out of the Land-Rover, took off my shoes and socks, and ran across the golden sandy beach into the shallow water. I raised my hands and shouted 'Yes!' in sheer joy. I smelt the salty air and breathed it in to fill my lungs, right down to my very toes. Meanwhile, Alec stood beside the Land-Rover and planned the route ahead on the map he'd laid out across the bonnet.

We then continued onwards to Annaba, a seaside town situated on the breathtakingly scenic coastline. As it offered no campsite we decided to drive on, until we came to a clearing by the side of the road. Such a pretty little location with a gorgeous display of wildflowers that nodded their colourful heads in the sea breeze. Alec removed the jerry cans and unbolted the racks from both sides of the Land-Rover, to store them up on the roof rack. Along came a dozen cows, udders bulging with milk, being driven along the road going back home. Their tails swished around their rumps, swatting pesky flies. The farmer hailed a greeting. Life was sweet.

On Wednesday 15th June, ten days after leaving Tamanrasset in southern Algeria, we arrived at the next border crossing. The buildings were very posh and sparkly clean and the border officers were efficient at their job, both at the Algerian and Tunisian posts. From there we drove directly south from the delightful coastal town of Tabarka to Ain-Draham and then on to Jendouba. We enjoyed travelling along the roads through rolling farmland where crops of wheat, barley and cheery yellow sunflowers were growing. Cork and olive trees were common in the area too, whilst cattle and sheep grazed on the pastureland. We passed three women dressed in colourful midi-length cotton dresses, fetching water in elegantly crafted terracotta pots with handles like in biblical paintings. At Jendouba, I took a photo of a two-storey white house with sky-blue-painted shutters and window frames. Perched in a huge nest on the roof apex were two gangly storks. Walking by the house was a lad leading his donkey to the water supply, a roadside tap. There he filled two large plastic jerry cans to load on his beast of burden.

Our journey took us east to Tunis, then south to the holiday resort of Sousse. I felt refreshed in Tunisia and I thought it would be the ideal place for a package holiday. It had everything: sun, sea, beaches, modern hotels, plus the fascination of being in Africa. The heady, aromatic spices in the markets and the fragrance of the perfumes and incense in the souks sparked our senses. Delicious foods were available, from freshly caught fish to matured cheese, fruit, vegetables and a choice of olives. In the north, Tunisia had well-cared-for towns and villages for tourists to stay in the hotels, yet it was not far to go for an excursion south into the desert. Luxury and adventure nestled side by side.

A swim in the warm sea felt fabulous, just like being in a luxurious jacuzzi. Our menu took a leap too, when I fixed a scrumptious supper of new potatoes, fresh peas, tomatoes, fish dressed with mushroom sauce, followed by pancakes and oranges.

The following day we drove back to the attractive city of Tunis. What wonderful items to buy in the medina, from kaftans to copper plates, pottery, hand-woven blankets and leatherwear, and there were lots of persuasive stall owners. As we had been buying at least one souvenir from each country that we visited, I decided that a useful brass pestle and mortar would be a fine addition to our treasures.

Alec stopped to have his shoes cleaned by a boy shoe shiner and I walked on to see the stalls of gorgeous, vibrant, fresh flowers for sale, a tantalizing treat I had to forego in our roving home.

Culinary delights tempted us too and we succumbed on several occasions. Following a long walk around Tunis we found a restaurant serving brik a l'oeuf: a national hors d'oeuvre of egg and parsley, parcelled in unleavened bread, fried and served with a slice of lemon. We ordered this dish for each of us, with a basket of bread and a bottle of water, for just sixty pence. Our evening meal later that day was a little more extravagant in cost and local cuisine. For one pound each we enjoyed a bowl of tomato soup, couscous with vegetables, entrecôte steak and chips with a side salad, followed by crème caramel and slices of freshly cut peach.

On that same evening we were to cross the Mediterranean Sea by ferry to travel to Sicily. How exciting was that! After our meal we slowly meandered along the tree-lined main street, back to where the Land-Rover was parked. There was no hurry, as the ferry departure was at ten.

In a timely manner we drove to the port and dealt with formalities at the ticket, passport and customs booths. Alec drove the Land-Rover into the bowels of the vessel and she purred at the prospect of the next adventure. The ferry was only a third full, thus the atmosphere was quiet and calm as passengers prepared for the night crossing. Everywhere on the ferry was clean, well furnished and well organized. We went to our cabin to canoodle and cuddle before being lulled to sleep by the repetitious, deep voice of the powerful engines, as the ferry navigated steadily across the sea.

'Darling, do you have everything?' Alec asked me the next morning as we left our cosy cabin.

'Yes, I hope so. I just remembered to pick up our toothbrushes from the sink.'

'Good, then let's go and find the canteen for some breakfast.'

Alec led the way along the narrow cabin corridor to the central stairway that took us up to the dining area. After a cup of tea and a sweet bun, we sauntered out onto the front deck to watch the approach into Palermo harbour. We stood together, Alec behind me, his arms hugged around my waist as he kissed my neck, shielding me from the gusty breeze blowing off the sea. Many boats moored by the docks bobbed in the wake of the ferry. Some early risers were already enjoying the gentle morning sunlight as they ventured out in their yachts and fishing vessels.

The ferry docked and, once secured, the passengers were told over the tannoy system to proceed to their vehicles. We readily went down to the vehicle deck and climbed into the Land-Rover. My tummy fluttered with butterflies as I anticipated the fun we would have exploring the island of Sicily and the joy of hearing Italian, the language of love.

We were welcomed onto Sicilian soil by the drugs squad team: a golden Labrador dog with his handler. They both climbed into the back of our Land-Rover and checked out the contents of our home. The officer was suspicious of the white flaky substance stored in a small plastic box in our kitchen cupboard. He called the attention of the dog, which had been conscientiously sniffing every nook and cranny. The dog sniffed the contents and immediately looked into his handler's eyes as if to say, 'It's potato powder, you dummy.'

With a restrained chuckle, we happily left the border control behind to find a parking place right at the docks, as the city of Palermo surrounded the harbour. It was just as well we did, as the streets were congested with parked vehicles on the pavements, even double and triple parked. Our first task of the day was to locate an insurance office to buy the Land-Rover third-party insurance to cover Europe. The clerk at the tourist office pointed us in the right direction, having given us maps and brochures for Sicily.

Palermo had many striking buildings, churches, statues and fountains, giving testimony to the architectural styles of the invaders of Sicily over the centuries. We particularly enjoyed looking around the Palatine Chapel built by the Norman conquerors in the eleventh century, within the Saracen Royal Palace. The chapel was embellished inside with richly coloured mosaics of biblical stories, and on the exterior, warriors were depicted.

It was inviting to walk along the pavements of the main shopping streets where glass-fronted shops displayed shoes and clothing in an attractive way, with labels showing fixed prices. Household items and furnishings were for sale, indicating a way of life quite different to what we had become used to. Yes indeed, our Romany lifestyle of little fuss, minimal requirements and free spirit had drawn us away from the western norm.

Our ten days spent exploring Sicily were splendid. From Palermo we drove to Trapani, a fine view of which we had from Ence, a hilltop village nearby. Then to a campsite at Marsala, where we had a thorough 'spring clean' over the next five days. The Land-Rover looked the cleanest clean it had ever been, even having its first wax polish.

We made our way across Sicily and visited Roman and Greek temples and Baroque cathedrals in towns with wonderful Italian names such as Terrasini, Segesta and Taormina. Ancient buildings, but many a busy town also had modern high-rise blocks of flats and great supermarkets. I felt overwhelmed by the abundance and choice of foods and other goods. But I was thrilled to buy two folding camping chairs so that we could sit comfortably outside of our Land-Rover in the evenings.

The charming island had beautiful, rolling hills, lush green vineyards, orange groves and villages perched on hilltops with stunning villas along the craggy coastline. We smiled when along came a traditional Romany cart pulled by a fine bay horse with white plumes fixed on the bridle between its ears. The harness was bedecked with bold-coloured tassels, trimmings and round brass bells, whilst the covered wooden cart was decoratively painted to match. The driver, a stocky elderly man dressed in shirt and trousers with a shabby waistcoat and a flat cap, passed us by jauntily. He was on his way to market to sell his clay pots, which were nestled in wooden crates in the cart.

We arrived and parked at the foot of Mount Etna. The first half of the climb was via a cable car, as the active volcano was over 10,000 feet high. Then we walked four miles to the bright-yellow-hued crater: a seemingly bottomless pit, three hundred yards across, belching forth sulphurous fumes with frightening rumbles from below. Alec had me pose for a photo. There I sat, perched on the distinctly warm, rocky edge of the volcano, with windswept hair and a cautious smile. I tried not to breathe in the smoke and my eyes were smarting. I'd seen all I needed to see, so I led the way back down the old grey lava track, hoping the volcano would not spew up its molten guts before we were safely out of harm's way.

Our last port of call in Sicily was Messina, where we went to visit the main attraction at the cathedral. The bell-tower displayed a huge astronomical mechanical clock. At noon the large statue of a lion roared and a cockerel statue crowed as the ancient legend of the Madonna della Lettera was played out by a dozen figurines.

From Messina we took the ferry for the half-hour crossing to the mainland, Italy. There we followed the western coastal road, initially through the hills, snaking around the tight corners, until it branched out through farmland and orchards of flourishing peach trees. The locals rode mules and donkeys or drove horses and carts. Curiously, when we stopped to buy bread and other supplies, no one ever had any loose change, so they gave us sweets or matches instead.

The unhurried drive along the coastal road took a couple of days before we arrived at Battipaglia, a big town where there were festive lights strung across the main street. It was buzzing with tourist activity, with lots of souvenirs, drinks and ice cream for sale, but it was not until we took the minor road down to the sea that we came across the real action. There were hundreds of cars, overflowing restaurants, beach huts and large, colourful umbrellas shading holidaymakers in the briefest attire, as they sipped sodas whilst lying on striped sunbeds. There was not a patch of sand to claim for our own, so even if we had wished to sit amongst the crowds to eat our lunch, it was impossible. We gladly drove on.

In just a short distance we arrived at Salerno, right on the beachfront, a totally crazy place. The traffic was abominable for us quiet desert travellers. Cars, trucks and scooters were all over the place, overtaking each other, throwing caution to the wind. It was a wonder that we made it through there in one piece.

'Maybe it'll be quieter at Pompeii,' said Alec as he negotiated the traffic as nimbly as he could with our tank of a vehicle going along such narrow streets.

We managed to find a lay-by to stop and eat our lunch beside the main road, en route to our afternoon tourist visit. Along with coachloads of visitors, we saw the fascinating ruins of the ancient

Roman city of Pompeii, destroyed in AD 79 by the molten lava that flowed from the sudden eruption of the volcano Mount Vesuvius. It was an archeological dream as so much of the original city had been carefully exposed. We saw kitchens, courtyards, gardens, frescoes, mosaics, an amphitheatre and even the disturbing form of dead people turned into rock.

We took a quick visit to the main square of the new city with the same name. We wanted to go into the cathedral, but as Alec was wearing shorts he was forbidden to enter.

Not so fortunate in our parking place that evening, being surrounded by passionate lovers in their squeaky cars and piles of rubbish!

Early on Monday morning, the 4th of July, we drove into the frantic city of Naples and tried to find a parking place. It was a nightmare. At one point, after Alec parked next to a public garden area, a weird little Italian man appeared brandishing an open penknife and threatened to call the police. We eventually parked near the docks, paying 1,000 lire (sixty-seven pence) to a man dressed in a white shirt, shorts and socks, with smart tan leather sandals and a dashing Panama hat.

Naples was a busy, noisy city with interesting back alleys lined with old, tall terraced houses. There were flowers and plants on the balconies and laundry was hung out to dry on lines strung across the street. We visited a beautiful domed church and enjoyed seeing the fountains and sculptures that enhanced the city. Naturally we called in at a local restaurant to savour an authentic Napoli pizza with a glass of the local red wine. My taste buds had a party!

That evening we parked at an old quarry that was joyously carpeted with a rainbow of wildflowers. As I cooked supper, a cloud of gnats flew into the Land-Rover and gathered in the upper part of the extended roof. As they flitted around my face I took action by removing the saucepan off the burner, leaving the flames exposed. I switched the fluorescent light off, climbed out of the Land-Rover and closed the door. The insects all yielded to the flames and the coast was clear for me to continue cooking whilst keeping the door firmly closed.

The next day we drove leisurely from Naples to Rome, stopping en route at Cassino, a modern town with expensive clothes and shoe shops. We visited the interesting Abbey of Monte Cassino, but our historical, architectural and arts extravaganza had only just begun.

At Tivoli, the open-air market bustled with traders and customers haggling over prices. Clothes, shoes, handbags and household goods were all on display, and we came across an excellent cheese and ham stall, alongside the usual stalls of fruit and veg.

On arriving at the capital, we found a great campsite on the outskirts with the wonderful luxury of clean, tiled toilets and hot showers.

Over three days we walked for miles around the streets of Rome exploring the Roman Forum, Colosseum and Vatican City with its museum plus St. Peter's Basilica and the Sistine Chapel. The Pantheon, a dome-shaped building, was an incredible, massive structure built nearly two thousand years before as a temple to the gods of ancient Rome, but was consecrated as a Roman Catholic church in the seventh century. We purchased a lovely book of photographs of the city sights with detailed descriptions, a cheaper option than taking slides with our camera.

Whilst in Rome we also went to the British Embassy and applied for new passports. The pages of our original ones were filled up with visas, plus the entry and exit rubber-stamping executed by the African border officials.

We took a romantic evening walk in the city, to visit the famous floodlit Piazza Navona. There were three magnificent fountains over its length, famous for their legendary statues. Around the edge of the square were alfresco cafés and restaurants, where diners enjoyed a glass of wine with their platters of Italian cuisine. Musicians serenaded their ready audience, whilst street performers blew fiery flames into the air from their unblemished mouths. Leather crafts, jewellery and paintings were on sale, whilst talented artists drew portraits of patient clients. It was midnight before we went by bus the five miles back to the campsite.

Leaving Rome, we held on to many treasured memories of the stunning architectural and artistic craftsmanship that we had seen during our stay. We felt well and truly topped up with Italian history and cultural fascinations.

Total distance driven = 18,383 miles

Venice to Vienna

12th to 30th July 1977
Italy – Austria

Vienna, Austria
Saturday 30th July 1977

Dear Mum, Dad, Margaret, Tony and Janet,

Having a restful day today in Vienna woods. After a slow start this morning we drove along the 'Höhenstrasse', a twelve-mile-long, scenic road built during the depression to give employment. It follows the Kahlenberg Range, which overlooks Vienna and has woods and vineyards on its slopes. After a walk in the forest we had lunch and are now in a meadow, sitting on our camping chairs and writing letters. The sun is trying to break through on this hazy day.

Since our last letter we have visited many places. From Rome, we drove towards Ancona via Rieti where we camped by Mount Terminillo, looking out over a beautiful Alpine view. Large herds of horses grazed on the slopes. During the evening we stood outside to listen to the lovely sound of the bells ringing in the church a mile away. The mountain churches are very plain, made of wood with tall, slim spires.

The next day we continued on to Ancona via Polverina, Macerata and Osimo, through picturesque, hilly scenery, and passed many vineyards. In Ancona we looked up Maureen, Jan's neighbour from childhood days in Brentwood. She is married to an Italian cheese maker called Claudis. Jan and I were amazed to be talking to an English girl one moment and to an Italian girl the next, as Maureen was speaking fluently in the two languages with all the actions! That evening we went out with the family for a five-course meal in a country restaurant. Here is the menu:

Handmade spaghetti with sauce
Smoked bacon with sweet melon
Assorted charcoal-grilled meats, including thrush and
*   pigeon, with salad and chips*
Cheesecake made from the mozzarella cheese that Claudis
*   makes (It was an indescribably delicious dessert.)*
Fresh fruit, peaches and bananas, and of course the local
*   wine and plenty of bread*

The next day Maureen came with us to the health centre in Ancona to arrange for us to have cholera vaccination boosters. That was all sorted with no delay as she easily communicated our request to the Italian nurse.

As it happened Maureen's sister, Theresa, was visiting from Brentwood and she willingly hand-carried our exposed films to deliver to Jan's parents.

We said farewell to the family and journeyed from Ancona along the coastal road to Cattolica, then inland to San Marino, a tiny kingdom in the middle of Italy. We saw panoramic views all around from the dramatic castle, as we enjoyed the beautiful, sunny weather in the nineties. The place was crowded with tourists, souvenir stalls and restaurants.

From San Marino we rejoined the coastal road north of Rimini and drove through Ravenna, Comacchio to Chioggia – a miniature Venice with an excellent market of fresh produce. We bought two large fish, which Jan fried in oil, adding olives and herbs for flavour, and served with a mushroom sauce for a delicious supper.

We drove on north the next day to romantic Venice, where we parked in the nearby campsite and went into the city by bus. Venice was enchanting, even with thousands of tourists milling about; it seemed so peaceful without any cars. Spent a most enjoyable two days there. We arrived in the city early and walked across to Piazza San Marco. Looked around the glorious Basilica and Doge's Palace. Went to the top of the famous Campanile bell tower in the Piazza, to gain a wonderful view over the whole city and lagoon. We walked along the narrow streets with their terraced houses and over the quaint bridges that straddle the canals, which were busy with all sorts of boats providing various services: taxi boats, ambulance and police, rubbish collectors and food deliveries etc. A ride on a gondola cost a pricey twelve pounds, so instead we enjoyed a long ride on the waterbus for just sixpence. Chamber orchestras were playing at the cafés in the main square.

We visited the Murano glassmakers. On display there was an elegant glass ornament of four beautiful horses pulling a chariot for sale, but only for a rich man's wallet. In the shop we were fascinated to come across the same beads that we had seen in the market at Bobo-Dioulasso in Upper Volta, the beads that looked like tiny sticks of multi-coloured seaside candy rock. We discovered they were actually Venetian glass and had been used for bartering by the early traders.

During the evening there was an open-air festival of orchestras, bands, majorettes, singing gondolier oarsmen, plus a forty-minute firework display across the islands. Amazing! Must have cost a fortune. We were both wearing our very large Fulani sunhats from Mali, so we could easily find each other if we wandered apart in the crowd.

We arrived in Vienna early last Sunday, booked into the campsite and spent the day doing chores. The next morning we were up early and out of the camp by eight to walk a mile to the tram stop. There we bought a five-day season ticket for two pounds, then rode five miles into the city centre on the very efficient tram system. We located the post office and found only one letter from Jan's folks in Post Restante, which was not surprising as we were a few days early. Then we spent much of the day window-shopping, seeing all the latest fashions. We were tempted by café displays of truly scrumptious looking cakes, but sadly they were beyond our budget.

As we walked through the Stadtpark we saw trees, shrubs, glorious flower beds, pools with ducks and swans, and large green lawns dotted with common pigeons, sparrows and shrieking peacocks in all their splendour. A statue of Johann Sebastian Strauss was strategically placed, reminding all passersby of Vienna's musical heritage. We were thrilled to be there in the park for the daily open-air Strauss concert, played by a ten-piece orchestra. We sat for an hour and listened to the music as the sun was setting, before we caught the tram 'home' again. You would have loved to have been there, Dad.

The next day was a little drizzly but pleasant and so, undeterred, we walked around the Baroque gardens of Belvedere Palace, built in large terraces, with a central fountain with elaborately carved statues, lawns and floral beds. No more mail at the post office, so we had a snack lunch in Judenplatz, where there was an old bus that anyone could try painting – graffiti style. A real artists' haven, as there were also blocks of stone and wood for budding sculptors to shape.

In the afternoon we visited the Spanish Riding School. In the stables, fifty Lipizzaner stallions were housed; all handsome animals standing knee-deep in oat straw in their individual, black-painted, wooden stalls with highly polished brass fittings. Although there were many horses there, the 'Stars' were on tour, so there was no show in the impressive riding hall, but they showed a film of a performance instead.

We walked back to the tram stop through some of the older streets with many interesting shops. We arrived back at the campsite and prepared and ate dinner, before going out again to the 'Prater', Vienna's permanent funfair. Just about all the rides were diabolical – what people will pay to be tortured!

Wednesday morning, at the post office we found three letters – thanks for yours. During that day we went shopping in the city in the morning, then visited the Votivkirche, an imposing Gothic church with twin-spires and radiantly coloured stained-glass windows.

That evening we went to see the operetta 'Wiener Blut' at the theatre of Schönnbrunn Palace. It was the first time I'd worn a jacket and tie since leaving England, and Jan wore a long dark green skirt with her embroidered gypsy blouse for the occasion. We strolled in the beautiful gardens before going into the elaborately decorated theatre for a most enjoyable evening.

On Thursday we went into the city to check at the post office again, but no more mail for us. We looked around car shops, trying to get filters etc. for the Land-Rover for the onward journey. Had lunch in yet another park, the Volksgarten, which was laid out into lots of small gardens and lily ponds. In the afternoon we returned to the magnificent Schönnbrunn Palace to visit the Imperial Apartments. Saw forty-five of the fourteen hundred rooms; all so splendid. An English-speaking guide, who gave us an insight into Austrian history, showed us around.

On Friday, Jan did some more washing while I went into the city to British Leyland suppliers to buy some spare parts: a rubber axle stop to replace the one that split in Africa plus fuel filters. I was going to buy a second spare fan belt until I was told it cost eight pounds compared to one pound thirty pence in England.

We have to wait here now, for a parcel sent by Jan's dad. It contains new filter cartridges for our drinking water that we have to receive before continuing our journey out to India. I hope they turn up by Monday.

Well, that'll be all for now. Hope everyone is keeping as well as we are.

Fondest love from,
Alec and Jan
xxxxx

Vienna, Austria
30th July 1977

Dear Mum, Dad, David and Paul,

Thanks for the three letters we received in Vienna, which I will answer first before telling you our news. Thought you'd be pleased with the letter we sent via Theresa from Italy along with the films. Your summer weather seems rather dismal for the holidaymakers. Since we've been in Austria it's alternated, one sunny day, one cloudy. One morning whilst sightseeing in Vienna it rained. It was the first time in six months that we were actually out in the rain, as although it rained often in the rainforests of Cameroon, we seemed to always be in the Land-Rover.

We were thrilled to hear that cousin Jane and Rhu are adopting a baby boy. How excited they must be! Hope the legalities work out okay and the baby is confirmed as theirs. We have sent them a card of congratulations.

Thanks for telling us all about the Queen's Silver Jubilee celebrations, Mum. I bet your front-room window looked grand, decked out with the Union Jack and the Queen's photo.

From the way you write, I imagine you and Dad enjoyed your day's outing in London, especially the visit to the Grenadier Guards' Regimental Headquarters.

We had a great time travelling through Italy, especially enjoying the food. Pasta was a favourite in every shape and size imaginable. Wine was very affordable and accompanied our evening meals. Our supply of Marmite has lasted well and adds a touch of English flavour to our continental breakfast of bread and jam. The latest goodie we discovered there was a delicious, nutty chocolate spread sold in useful containers like wine glasses and a butter dish. Made of glass with sealed lids, they are a great addition to our kitchenware. Tinned tomatoes were inexpensive, so we stocked up with a few cans.

We were inspired to create our own delicious pizza, simply baked in the frying pan, and were pretty chuffed with the result. Here's the recipe for you, in case you'd like to try making one:

FRYING PAN PIZZA

1 level teaspoon dried yeast, 1 level teaspoon sugar in 1/8-pint hand-hot water. Allow to work for 10 minutes, before mixing into 4oz of flour to make soft dough, adding more hand-hot water as necessary. Roll out into pizza shape to fit the frying pan. Cook at medium heat in pre-heated frying pan with the bottom thinly covered in oil. When brown underneath, turn over and spread a savoury topping on the cooked side and continue heating until all is toasty-hot and baked! Topping suggestions:

tinned tomatoes and a little cheese, anchovies, bacon, olives etc. Enjoy with a glass of Italian red wine and supper is complete.

From Venice we headed directly north through the Dolomite Mountains where the air was so fresh and clean and the grass so green. We crossed the border into Austria at Sillian and from there to Lienz and north to Zell am See, including a visit to the Grossglockner mountain and glacier. Then we drove north to Lofer, a really charming town, and nipped into Germany where we visited Bad Reichenhall, Berchtesgaden and Konigsee. Back into Austria to see Salzburg, Bad Ischl, Bad Aussee, Liezen and Mariazell, and then we eventually arrived here in Vienna.

All one can say is the scenery was magical all the way: mountains, lakes, waterfalls, fast-flowing, crystal-clear rivers giving way to rolling farm and forest land towards Vienna. The adorable, picturesque alpine houses were decorated with window boxes of bright red geraniums.

You asked how our shoes are standing up to the hard wear. Well, our Clarks lace-up shoes are excellent – so comfortable and, after the occasional clean, they look like new. The soles have hardly worn at all. The other day I bought a pair of tan sandals. They're not a perfect fit, but it's a job to find what you want in a foreign country, and they're ideal for me to wear with skirts in Europe. Our clothes are fine and they're staying cleaner for longer, now that we're driving on all tarmac roads.

Thanks, Dad, for taking all that trouble with ordering the water filters. It's good that we have such an efficient base manager, as it would be difficult for us to take care of home matters whilst we are travelling. Thanks for renewing our medical insurance. We weren't surprised to see the premium had gone up. And thanks too for sending the tax form to the accountant – whom I'm sure will deal with it well.

Yes please, let us know the balance of our building society account. Providing we have some money left, we may buy some European foods that you can't buy or are cheaper than in England, on our return home. Is it possible for you to find out from Customs and Excise if there is a limit to bringing in foodstuffs for personal consumption?

Hope the films we sent via Theresa have turned out okay. We were a bit concerned that the temperature was so high when we returned through the Sahara that it might have spoilt our films. You should also receive two other films – one Kodak of Sicily and Italy, the other just a roll of developed Agfar film. The latter photos of Germany and Austria may be rather disappointing as our Olympus Trip 35 camera decided to play up when the aperture control failed. Thankfully this happened whilst in Austria and not in Nepal. We had the camera cleaned at a cost of eight pounds and fifty pence and it's now working okay. But to be sure we have bought a Voigtlander VF 135, which is a nice little camera.

We are now ready to leave Vienna, but keep checking at the post office for the water filters you ordered for us, Dad. Hope the parcel comes soon as we're itching to move on.

The next postal address is: POSTE RESTANTE, ANKARA, TURKEY. Last posting on 15th August 1977.

Fondest love from

Alec and Janice

xxxxx

Total distance driven = 19,456 miles

The Mystery Unfolds

30th July to 2nd August 1977
Austria

'I reckon we should see if we can find somewhere free to park tonight,' Alec announced.

'Why's that?' I asked as I sealed the envelope closed on the final letter written that afternoon.

'Well, who knows when the parcel will actually arrive? And we don't want to keep forking out money at the city campsite if we don't need to.'

As luck would have it we discovered a deserted car park of an abandoned restaurant in the Vienna woods. That same evening we went to a wine fest at the nearby village of Grinzing, where we enjoyed a glass of red wine whilst listening to oompah accordion music and the locals' banter. We slept very well that Saturday night in the dark forest.

'Good morning,' called a young man in jogging gear, who was sitting on the perimeter wall of the car park.

'Oh hello,' replied a bleary-eyed Alec, as he was climbing out of the Land-Rover at seven-thirty the next morning, desperate for a pee.

'So what brings you to Vienna?' asked the chap. 'You look like you've been on a safari.'

'Well yes, we've driven across the Sahara a couple of times, but now we're travelling through Europe before going on to India.'

'Really! Had any trouble with the Land-Rover?'

'Not a lot, just a few punctures, snapped the speed cable and broken rear leaf springs, an age old problem with Land-Rovers.'

'Any trouble getting spare parts?' enquired the inquisitive Englishman.

'Well, I stocked up with all the small stuff, seals, air and oil filters, puncture repair kits etc. before we left England. Then I've had to rely on what we can buy locally for bigger items. At least this vehicle is well used in Africa, so you can buy spare parts.'

'That's true. By the way, my name's Nigel.'

'Oh right – good to meet you. I'm Alec and this is my wife Jan.' Alec introduced me as I clambered out of the Land-Rover, wondering who was outside.

'Well, I'd better get back home as my wife Helen will be wondering where I am. She'll be surprised that I'm even out on a run, as it's not my passion. I just woke up early this morning and felt like going for a run in the woods before breakfast,' Nigel explained. 'I tell you what – would you both like to come to our home tomorrow evening for a meal and meet the family?'

'Well, that's real kind of you, but we're hoping to be off to Hungary first thing, providing our parcel has arrived at the post office,' replied Alec.

'Yes, my Dad ordered and sent out two charcoal cartridges for our drinking water filter. We can't leave for India without them,' I added.

'Oh well, I'll jot down my address and phone number and you can just turn up around five if you're still here,' Nigel offered.

'Thanks,' I said, and I fished out a pen and notebook for him to scribble down his contact details.

'Bye, have a nice day,' I called after the friendly guy, as he ran off down the track.

'Bet you're dying for a cuppa,' I offered Alec when he returned, having relieved himself behind a tree. 'I would have made one earlier, had I known that chap was gonna be gassing for so long.'

'Yes, I wonder what he's doing living in Austria?'

'Maybe we'll find out, if the parcel doesn't turn up tomorrow.'

It was an overcast morning, so we visited the technical museum for a couple of hours. At lunchtime the grey clouds burst and heavy rain fell as thunder rolled around the hills. Despite the wet weather we ventured to the Lainzer Tiergarten: six thousand acres of old royal hunting grounds with fifteen miles of high stone walls around its perimeter. There was space to run and grazing land for many deer, horses and wild pigs.

Early Monday morning the heavens opened again. Rain pelted down onto the roof of our Land-Rover and the chilly air made us quick to wash and dress. The interior soon warmed up from the cooker, as I prepared scrambled eggs on toast and a pot of tea for breakfast. We ate slowly as we read novels, hoping the rain would stop. It didn't – so Alec eventually braved the storm and went outside to change the engine oil. Afterwards, we drove into the city to the post office.

No parcel! The situation was extremely tedious and frustrating.

'Let's go and see where we can buy replacement oil filters,' Alec suggested. 'Plus the water pump is erratic so we could do with a new one.'

It rained and it rained. We didn't stop for lunch, but snacked on biscuits as we continued our search for the spare parts. Bought an electric pump for our drinking water at a camping store, then we headed back to the post office, but still no parcel. By now we were both pretty peeved, and for want of something better to do, we decided to contact Nigel and tell him we would be arriving for supper. Finding a public telephone box, I dialled the number and Helen answered.

'Well, she was pretty friendly and even offered for us to stay the night too,' I shared with Alec. I gave directions from a Vienna city map and he drove us to their home.

'Welcome,' Helen greeted us, as she opened the door. Her bubbly hair framed her fresh face and twinkling eyes. She was as short as we were tall. Two red-haired youngsters peeped around the sides of her full skirt, before they scuttled off down the hallway.

'I'm Helen – so pleased to meet you – and that was Ross and Alexandra, our two treasures. Do come on in out of the rain. What a desperate day. You must be glad to be in the dry,' she said as she took our jackets to hang on the metal hooks in the hallway.

'Here you can stay in our bedroom, as Nigel and I will take the front room.'

'Are you sure?' I asked, surprised that this young woman was ready to let strangers use their master bedroom.

'Oh yes, yes – no problem. In fact it's a whole lot easier for us in the morning, when the children are up and about. You might even get a lie-in,' she reassured. 'Here are some towels. You're welcome to take a bath. There's lots of hot water.'

I don't know if she said that because we smelt, which we probably did, or because we'd come in from the cold.

No matter, I took up the offer and soaked myself in a luxurious, hot bubble bath. The first bath in six months – wow, it beat the briskness of a shower. Heaven! I dressed and joined everyone in the front room only to find that Nigel had returned from work. Greetings were made again as Helen announced that dinner was ready.

All seated around the table, we politely kept our hands in our laps as we waited for the chance to serve ourselves from the laden dishes of roast lamb, potatoes, carrots and green beans.

'Let's give thanks to the Lord for our meal,' Nigel said to the fidgety children, who calmed down and put their palms together in a prayer-like manner. 'Dear Lord, we thank you for this day and especially for our visitors. We pray you will bless our time together and we thank you for this good food, prepared by my wonderful wife. Amen.'

'Amen,' we mumbled, whilst Ross and Alexandra shouted, 'Amen,' and raised their plates ready for Mum to serve them first.

'Hungry scamps!' exclaimed Helen, raising her eyebrows and smiling. 'Do help yourselves to the mint sauce and gravy,' she said as she served us next.

'Care for a glass of wine?' offered Nigel.

We passed our glasses for Nigel to fill and we all settled down to enjoy the delicious meal. We were soon deep in conversation, us sharing stories from our journey and them telling us about their work with a church organization. Helen even told us how she became a Christian. How bizarre it was to find ourselves with missionaries again. Maybe they could explain what that Bible was all about.

The next morning the rain had stopped and Alec and Nigel went into the city to search for the parcel. As it still hadn't been delivered to the post office, they visited the South Station customs office and discovered no record of its arrival. Alec was given free use of their phone to call my dad to ask if the filters had been sent for sure, and he confirmed that they had.

'So what would you like to do or where would you like to go?' asked Helen as she and I cleared the breakfast table.

'Oh, I'm happy just to be here and chat with you,' I replied, so pleased to converse with an English girlfriend. We talked about many things, including Christianity. I told her about our time with the Osbornes in Jos and showed her the Bible they had given to us. Earlier that morning, Alec had retrieved it from behind the panel in the Land-Rover.

We enjoyed a milky coffee for elevenses and had a good chinwag.

Ross and Alexandra kept busy drawing with wax crayons on big sheets of white paper. Their subject was the gigantic safari machine that we had arrived in. They drew it in the desert. Alexandra's had a big yellow sun in one corner and Ross drew a scary lion about to pounce on the Land-Rover.

Alec and Nigel returned for lunch – bread, salami, cheese, stewed plums and custard. Ross and Alexandra then went to bed for an hour's rest, reading and napping, whilst Helen's language helper arrived and Nigel left for his office.

So Alec and I went out for a walk in the warm sunshine to a local park. A few ducks and a black swan skimmed across the calm waters of a large pond. A red squirrel ran up a tree as we sat on the bench beneath. Bees buzzed in and around the purple lavender blossoms and white cabbage butterflies fluttered from flower to flower. The heady smell of freshly mown grass hung in the air.

'So what do you think?' I asked Alec.

'What do I think about what?'

'This Christianity,' I clarified.

'Oh. Why? What do you think?'

'I asked you first.'

'Well, it's odd, how we've met up with this young family and discovered that they really believe too,' Alec replied.

'Yes, I always thought that the Church was just for the milestones in your life – you know, birth, weddings and funerals.'

'It seems Jesus isn't just for children like when we went to Sunday school,' continued Alec.

'It's strange to hear Helen share how Jesus is real and meaningful in her life today,' I pondered.

'Yes, she and Nigel talk of Jesus like he's a personal friend, just like Mary and Phil did,' said Alec.

He took my hand as we stood up and mulled over those thoughts as we strolled back to our host's abode.

We arrived at their flat to find that Heidi, the Austrian language helper, was leaving and Helen had planned to take Ross and Alexandra to the playground. I grabbed the chance for another soothing bubble bath, whilst Alec relaxed in a comfy armchair to read one of their many books.

The quietness vanished the instant the family returned. Everyone's attention was on Nigel, who was groaning and flinching in serious pain. Before he left work, he had accidentally trapped his left thumb when closing the heavy safe door. Ouch!

Nigel lay down on the sofa. I gave him strong painkiller tablets and gently wrapped a tea cloth, with crushed ice within its folds, around his elevated, pulsing thumb.

As it was, we were due to accompany Nigel and Helen to their boss's home for a barbeque that evening. A student called Mike turned up to babysit and the four of us left, taking a salad and dessert to share at the potluck. Nigel put on a brave face all evening, whilst we had fun and enjoyed the gathering along with two other invited couples. We left early at nine-thirty as Nigel was then looking and feeling decidedly rough, being in significant pain from his unfortunate mishap.

Before bedtime Helen made a hot chocolate drink for each of us, then took the opportunity to explain further about Christianity. She gave us a booklet that contained Bible verses and God's plan of salvation. Nigel encouraged us to consider becoming committed Christians. We now realized that being a Christian was more than just a name or the way you have been brought up within your own family. The entire time they talked, I shook like a leaf inside as this topic stirred up my emotions. I felt uneasy, but excited, as if about to leap off a high diving board, not knowing if there was water below to cushion my fall and keep me buoyant.

When Alec and I eventually went to bed we held each other tight and decided that the next day we would pray to God for forgiveness. A calmness and peace enveloped us and we drifted off to sleep.

Total distance driven = 19,546 miles

No Turning Back

3rd to 6th August 1977
Austria – Hungary

After breakfast the next morning Alec and I went to the post office and found there was still no parcel. We were niggled, but we just had to deal with it, so we decided to see what the family's plans were for the day.

After lunch we took the tram with Helen and the children to visit the Stadtpark. We walked around leisurely, as you do with children who are fascinated by things you only give a glance at normally and may not even notice.

For the entire journey, three-year-old Ross tightly carried in his clenched fist a bag of stale bread. At the park we discovered why it was so precious to him. Standing by the pond with his open-toed sandals on the lip of the shore, the water seeped into his beige cotton socks. He soon attracted a noisy, excited, quacking audience, as he tussled with opening the knotted bread bag. He threw morsels of dry crusts to the hungry ducks that paddled towards him, and a few swooped in from the other side of the long pond. The ravenous flock crowded around Ross as he backed away, trying to feed them as quickly as his little hands could grab and drop the bread.

Meanwhile, Helen managed to salvage a chunk of bread for her little girl to feed a large tortoise that was kept in a fenced enclosure nearby. Toddler Alexandra was fascinated to watch the tortoise stretch its head out of its shell house where it had been sleeping. It walked slowly towards her and poked its head through the chain-link fence. Alexandra excitedly, but cautiously offered the bread to the creature, and it opened its gummy mouth and claimed the titbit. Squealing with delight, she quickly withdrew her hands and tucked them into her lap as she crouched down and peered at the tortoise.

'Come, let's go to the swings,' Helen called, and we walked across to the playground.

Ross and Alexandra were eager to go on everything: the swings, the slide, the roundabout and the seesaw. Lots of other children were there too, with their mums and nannies, enjoying a warm, sunny afternoon in the park.

Back at the flat, Helen gave the children a bath, whilst I offered to make pizza and salad for supper. Nigel returned from work, his thumb still giving him gip, especially when he knocked it unintentionally. Ross and Alexandra were well ready for bed after they had eaten, so their dad did the honours of reading their bedtime story.

'So that's the dishes done,' Helen said as she poured the dirty, soapy water down the sink and I hung the damp tea towel over the warm oven rail. 'Do you fancy a cup of tea, Jan? I expect the men will have a beer.'

'Sure, I'd love one.'

The evening continued, the four of us relaxing in the study, talking about every subject under the sun, except for God. I wanted to bring the subject up, but was hesitant.

Nigel excused himself to go to the loo, saying a quick prayer in his mind as he walked along the hallway: *Well, Lord, if you want us to talk more about you, they'd better bring the subject up.*

'Do you think we could read through that little booklet again?' I asked when Nigel returned.

Whoa! That was quick, thought Nigel. *Thank you, Lord.*

Helen went across to her well-loved, roll-top ladies' desk to fetch her Bible. She sat down and opened it, to find another booklet like the one I pulled out from my jeans pocket. We read it together page by page. The quoted Bible verses left us in no doubt that we needed to actively acknowledge God's love for us. Alec and I said the prayer at the end, inviting Jesus to take the throne of our lives, accepting God's gift of forgiveness.

This gift was not because of how good we may or may not be, but because of God's son, Jesus Christ, dying for us on the cross. His willing sacrifice and his blood that was shed made us righteous before God. It was only then that I truly realized that Jesus is alive in heaven and one day we will see him, on our death or when he returns a second time on earth. Eternal truth, a hidden treasure revealed through the scriptures, written down from the Ancient of Days.

At breakfast the next morning Helen said that she and Nigel were thrilled by our decision to become committed Christians. Alec and I were enthralled and blown away by what had transpired. To think of the chain of events that had led us to this point: meeting with my old school teacher's friends in Nigeria and being given a modern edition of the Bible; significantly, the fact that our route was dramatically changed because of rebel fighting in Zaire, so that we returned to Europe at this stage of the journey and did not drive directly across Africa and ship to India; the water filters that were supposed to last for two hundred and fifty gallons instead clogging up after only sixty gallons, making our need imperative to wait in Vienna and receive the parcel from England; and then Nigel's early run that Sunday morning, when he told us the times he had ever gone out jogging you could count on the fingers of one hand. Unbeknown to us, a divine golden thread was woven into our journey, to shine a light on our path.

There was still time to really appreciate and learn from Nigel and Helen's walk with God. That evening they shared the parable Jesus told of a farmer going out in his field to sow seeds and how they all grew differently depending on whether they fell onto rocks, on the path, among the thorns or on good soil. Jesus then related how the seed can be compared with the Word of God and how we receive it, and what can come into our lives to destroy it, or overcrowd it, or hopefully nurture and hold on to it and allow it to grow in our lives.

To help us develop our reawakened faith, Nigel and Helen checked over their bookshelves and gave us a pile of books to read on our travels out east, books on understanding the Bible and about other Christians' lives. Nigel also encouraged us to especially study Romans chapter eight.

In perfect timing, God-ordained it would seem, the parcel arrived at the post office on the Friday. The water filters were finally in our hands and there was nothing to stop us continuing on our journey. Brilliant! That evening we, with all the family, went out for a celebration meal at a local inn. Sitting outside on the terrace, we enjoyed a delicious meal of pork chops, meat roll, green beans, potatoes, bread and wine. It was a wonderful way to finish an unforgettable week. Later, after Ross and Alexandra were tucked up in bed, we spent time together in prayer.

I realized any prayers I may have said in the past were just before an exam or when I'd been really afraid. When you feel alone and vulnerable, you pull on threads, voicing a plea to a distant being who may be able to help in some vague way. But now it was going to be different, as we realized that God is interested in all that we do and wants us to acknowledge him in our decisions and plans, our comings and goings, our ups and our downs. We had begun to explore a whole new spiritual dimension of life.

*

Six months and two days since leaving England, on Saturday 6th August, we set off to drive east to India. A lot of incredible things had already happened on our journey and we were eager to see what else might be around the next corner. We were so looking forward to being back in the Land-Rover, our vehicle by day and our bed by night.

On that last morning I took one more luxurious bath and dressed in clean clothes. Alec and I sat at the table with Nigel, Helen, Ross and Alexandra and ate a bumper breakfast of muesli with yogurt, followed by fried eggs and bacon, then pancakes with maple syrup and coffee.

As we left, we hugged each one of our new friends, thankful for their generous hospitality. We had come for a meal and stayed for almost a week.

'You may think you're on an adventure as you travel in your Land-Rover, but you have just begun the greatest adventure of all – following Christ!' said Nigel. 'Make sure you write every month to tell us how you're doing with reading the Bible and what escapades you're up to.'

'Will do,' Alec and I responded in unison.

'Here's a happy gift,' said Ross, stretching up on his tiptoes to hand me a homemade cake through the open window.

'Thanks so much,' I said, as Helen then held Alexandra up to my window. We clasped hands and bade each other farewell.

'Don't forget to come and see us on your return journey, will you,' Helen reminded us. I could see that our friendship had only just begun.

We drove away, sorry to leave Nigel, Helen and their children, but glad to be on the road again. The Land-Rover chugged along enthusiastically, off to new and distant lands. It wasn't far out of the city of Vienna that we reached the border. After waiting half-an-hour for our visa to be issued, we entered the communist country of Hungary.

Driving through the countryside, we noted that the land was extensively farmed. We overtook horse-drawn carts driven by the locals. Frisky foals trotted freely alongside the harnessed mares, as they became accustomed to the ways of the road.

When we stopped for lunch, a middle-aged Hungarian man came along and passed the time of day. He was visiting his homeland after years of living in Australia. A steam train whistled on by, taking its passengers to their destinations, black smoke puffing up into the blue sky. The main village streets were lined with simple, one-storey grey houses, with fenced gardens of blossoming flowers, vegetables and fruit. Chickens scratched around in the dirt. We saw a pig grunting contentedly, basking in a muddy pool as it enjoyed the warm afternoon sunshine.

In Sopron, we stopped for petrol and called by the supermarket for supplies. The store was grubby and the shop assistants wore short, scruffy white overalls. There was very cheap flour, chocolate and milk for sale. All the Hungarian products were economically packed and reasonably priced: alternatively, anything imported was expensive, as one might expect.

We continued driving on towards Lake Balaton where we decided to camp for the night, alongside the railway tracks. The airflow from the passing trains actually shook the Land-Rover and rocked us to sleep.

Total distance driven = 19,616 miles

East

1977 The Journey East - Austria to Nepal

As It Was Then

7th to 31st August 1977
Hungary – Romania – Bulgaria – Turkey

Ankara, Turkey
Wednesday 31st August 1977

Dear Mum, Dad, David and Paul,

Thank you for your two letters, which we received yesterday; also a letter and card from cousin Jane and Rhu came too. So thrilled that they have been selected to be adoptive parents for baby Rhu. Loved his photo. How kind of Jane's in-laws to invite Auntie Eileen and Uncle George to their home in Scotland. We hope they enjoyed it and it gave them a little respite since Michael's death. We're wondering what happened to the hit-and-run driver – did the police track him down?

Thanks, Dad, for your detailed report of your three-day trip with Mum to Wales; sounded marvellous.

We were sorry to hear on the news that Elvis Presley died, a couple of weeks ago on the 16th August. How sad that his celebrity life led to such a tragic end.

Well, I do hope you've made a pot of tea for yourselves so that you can relax and read this long, newsy letter about what we've been up to lately.

We left Austria and entered Hungary near Sopron, then took the road to Lake Balaton, where we camped for the first night. We drove onto Tihany the next day, a bright Sunday morning, where the local oompah band was playing. That was a jolly welcome! We stopped and bought ice cream cornets that were delicious and really welcome on such a hot day: 90°F.

Afterwards we continued on to Kenese, Polgárdi and Velence, and arrived at the impressive city of Budapest, built on the banks of the busy Danube River. Walking around the main streets, we saw a number of the buildings were being renovated, cleaned and painted. In the city park there were several activities for the city-dwellers, from the boating lake to concrete games tables and benches where many older men were gathered to play chess and cards. For lunch we enjoyed a bowl of delicious Hungarian goulash with a hunk of bread at a workman's café.

We ambled around the city for much of the afternoon before popping into a grocery shop to buy four pints of milk, a loaf of bread, coffee substitute tablets, a bag of semolina, some soft cheese and blue Stilton. It's always an adventure to see what foods are available in each country that we visit.

From Budapest we drove south to Kecskemét, a very attractive country town that you would have enjoyed seeing, Mum – from the charming, civic hall with its painted floral walls, ceilings and stained-glass windows, to decorated houses, gardens, fountains and lively market stalls. I bought a really useful knotted-string bag made in Russia, which scrunches up in my pocket but then stretches out to carry the shopping.

From Hungary we crossed into Romania at Oradea. The border crossing took an hour-and-a-half but we were soon on our way to Sirbi. Hope you're finding all these places on the map, Dad. We had a comic incident later that day, when I tried to buy some milk and the storekeeper had no idea what I wanted, even after me mooing and squatting down to mime milking a cow. What a hoot! The man followed us outside, where his customers gathered to admire our Land-Rover as they tried to fathom out what we needed. Then I tried a smattering of French, which one young man understood. They all roared and said we'd have to wait for the evening milking!

We really liked Romania, such beautiful scenery and friendly people. The journey up to Sighetu Marmetiei and south to Bogdan Vodă to Borsa was one of the most fascinating. People lived in little wood houses, with carved wooden gates. Everyone dressed in traditional clothes. We were invited into the home of one family just to see their handicrafts, embroidery and weaving. I hope the photos come out as we saw some real characters. We also visited the tiny wooden churches where the inner walls and ceilings were completely painted all over with pictures of the saints. The bigger churches at the monasteries at Vatra Moldovitei, Humorului and Voronet were painted with pictures on the inside and outside, visually telling biblical stories.

One evening we were parked by a river near the road to Cimpani, when Alec was able to help out a rather embarrassed Romanian Army officer. He had come to rescue a military truck that was stuck in the river. The officer drove his truck into the water in his rescue attempt and managed to get stuck too. Alec winched the second truck out, but the first truck needed the assistance of a local farmer with his tractor, as it was firmly rooted into the riverbed. The Army officer was extremely thankful that we'd helped him and couldn't get over the fact that our Land-Rover was our very own personal property. We shared our supper with the soldiers – cold pizza, bread pudding and a mug of Ovaltine.

Whilst travelling through Romania we ventured into Transylvania, Dracula's homeland. Spooky? No, it was a delight. We went over a high mountain pass to eventually reach Lake Vidraru and its mighty dam, and we saw spectacular scenery all the way.

Further on at Curtea de Arges we visited a gypsy funfair where nearly everyone was in traditional dress. We went to see the magicians' show in a tent, which was surprisingly good. Many of the roundabouts were chairaplanes operated by hand or powered by old paraffin engines.

On to Bucharest, the capital, where we had the chance to see a fabulous show called 'Romania Rhapsody'. It was a fast-moving performance of dancers and singers in their colourful costumes, with loud, energetic, get-up-and-move music.

From Bucharest we drove to Giurgiu, where we crossed the border via a bridge over the river into Bulgaria. This country seemed to be the most communist out of the three, with posters everywhere of Lenin, red stars and the symbol of the hammer and sickle. As in the other two countries, all farming was collective and we passed many plots of land allocated to the storing of combine harvesters and other farm machinery in large numbers. Sunflowers, tobacco, sugar beet and corn crops were growing. Haymaking was very primitive, using a scythe to cut the grass. In all three communist countries, horses and cattle were also used in the farm work.

We spent a few hours in the capital Sofia, a clean city with minimal traffic. There was a little more variety of goods in the shops, but not a great deal of anything really. If you shop in a communist country, you buy only what you set out to, as nothing is really appealing. Not like in England when you often return home with twice as much as you planned to buy.

From Sofia we went south to visit Rila Monastery: striking historical buildings, where the monks worked as millers, bakers and cooks. We viewed a monk's simple room. The beautifully painted church was overflowing with pilgrims taking gifts to the altar. Shirts, tablecloths, clothes, flowers and money were brought by the mass of people. When the pile became too high a monk gathered the offerings in his arms and carried them to a room on the side. Flowers were taken and put in a sack as fast as they were placed on the altar. The people lit their candles and placed them on the stand, removing a previously lit candle that had not yet finished burning. We couldn't understand what was going on – what happened to all those gifts? It was a very strange and frenzied sight and we were glad to leave.

Leaving the communist lands behind, we drove to Turkey where we spent four days visiting Istanbul, a fabulous city, so colourful, noisy and full of atmosphere. There were hundreds of shops, one street just selling parts for cars, another only plastic containers and yet another street of piping. One shop sold nothing but red plastic dolls, another just beach balls. There were the shoe-shining boys with their shiny brass boxes containing brushes and polish. The Grand Bazaar had streets of jewellery, copperware, rugs, sacks of aromatic spices and dried herbs, sweet shops with scrumptious goodies, good butchers selling pricey meat and shops selling plump green and black olives with delicious cheeses. Open market stalls sold fruit, vegetables, nuts, dried fruit and barbecued fish. Other stalls sold hundreds of cardigans, jumpers, jeans and cotton underwear. Our senses were on a victory run.

We visited the mosques and Topkapi Palace and enjoyed a seven-hour ride on a boat along the Bosphorus, which only cost twenty-five pence each. We had a glass of tea each, at a café on the Galata Bridge where the men smoked hubble-bubble pipes. Many ships were docked in the harbour.

Leaving Istanbul, we crossed the Bosphorus over the

suspension bridge. *We were very aware of leaving Europe and verging towards the wonders of Asia. Our route from Istanbul was via Izmit, Sakarya, Tarakli and Ayas, through hilly scenery that was very similar to the hills of Oman. Ever-changing colours of rocks. The women were dressed in simple peasant style, the men in European clothes.*

We have found the people of Turkey very friendly and helpful. Yesterday we stopped to take a photo and a couple pulled up in their car to ask us if we were okay. Recognising that we were from Britain from our GB sticker, the man said in broken English that he had been to England, staying at Leigh-on Sea. His wife gave us an apple and a bunch of grapes.

Arrived here in Ankara yesterday afternoon – some of the city roads were closed because it was a national holiday, 'Victory Day'. Red Turkish flags flew everywhere. We wandered around the shops and markets, and met two local students in the city park and spoke with them for an hour. Last night we slept in the Land-Rover where it was parked in a street.

I'm just writing this letter before visiting Ankara's museums. We're presently sitting in a café eating some delicious baklava, a nutty, syrupy, flaky pastry enjoyed with a strong espresso coffee.

Well, that's all our news up to date – remember to send the next post by 20th September 1977 to POSTE RESTANTE, LAHORE, PAKISTAN.

Fondest love,
Alec and Janice.
xxxxx

Total distance driven = 22,336 miles

Tales from Turkey

1st to 5th September 1977
Turkey

We had a full and interesting day visiting the Ankara museums of ethnography and archaeology, before leaving the city in the late afternoon to drive towards Balâ. That night we camped on a burnt stubble field. The red glow of the setting sun enriched the impressive view of wide-open farmland with distant hills.

I prepared a scrumptious evening meal combining the culinary delights we had bought in Ankara's city market: fried fish, boiled potatoes, runner beans, slices of lemon, green pepper, tomatoes and olives, followed by fresh figs and hot custard, plus Turkish coffee. Well, my attempt at making it anyway. I used our (purchased for a pound) coffee maker: that being a royal-blue enamel, mini saucepan with a pouring lip and a long, thin handle. I put in plenty of coffee grains and ten spoonfuls of sugar, half-filled with water and stirred before boiling for a few minutes on the cooker. The water became a strong, black syrup that I poured into tiny coffee cups: another recent purchase. The aroma matched its full flavour.

*

The following day we travelled through Balâ, going on passed vast fields, over the Kopnikoy Bridge and on to Bayramözü. Afterwards we crossed over the Hirfanli hydroelectric dam and went alongside the stunning blue Lake Tuz, with its white salt encrusted beaches. Boys along the roadside were selling sunflowers, melons and grapes. They indicated they wanted cigarettes by puffing at their first and second fingers, patting their lips. When we didn't oblige, because we had none, they threw tomatoes at the Land-Rover and one lad threatened to throw a bottle.

At Aksaray, we asked the police the way to the mosque, which we had heard was worth a visit. We followed the police in their Volkswagen car until they became distracted when they stopped to arrest a man. We never did see the mosque!

Taking the road to Nevşehir, we visited the caravansarie of Ağzıkarahan, a thirteenth-century motel for camels and donkeys and their owners. It once provided stables, shops, bedrooms, kitchen, baths and a place of worship.

Out of Nevşehir we took the route towards Avanos and soon the extraordinary valley of Cappadocia was before us. As it was getting late, we needed to find somewhere to park. Alec drove along a dirt track off the main route and stopped close to a stone-block house where a man lived with his two sons. The oldest lad came over to see us – we asked his permission to park there and he assured us that we were most welcome. Later he demonstrated this by giving us four huge bunches of black grapes that he carried in a metal bucket. We shared our supper with him. Alec then went to meet his father who was cutting big blocks from the natural soft rock terrain. He stopped his work and invited Alec to look inside their home.

'We have been so fortunate with the people we have met on our journey, don't you think?' I commented as we later sat together on our bench seat inside the Land-Rover, enjoying a mug of Horlicks.

'Yes, for the most part that's true. It's just the odd shepherd lad along the road who might turn nasty when we don't give him any cigarettes,' replied Alec. 'On another subject, tomorrow we're going to explore Cappadocia. It looks a fascinating place according to the brochures I picked up yesterday at the Ankara tourist office.'

'Oh really? We read about Cappadocia in the Bible just the other day. Let me see if I can find it,' I said as I reached for our precious gift from the Osbornes.

It had become a valuable guide to our daily life as we followed the study notes that Nigel and Helen gave to us called *Search the Scriptures*. When we accepted Jesus Christ as our Lord and Saviour, the Holy Spirit came to dwell within us, to teach and reveal more of God's truth. It's like we had been blind, but now we could truly see and understand so much more, as the misty veil had been removed. Even the world about us – the flowers, the birds, the creatures, the trees and the whole countryside – was visually brighter and clearer than before.

'Oh, here we are, it's at the beginning of Peter[1]: "To the Jewish Christians driven out of Jerusalem and scattered throughout Pontus, Galatia, Cappadocia, Ausia and Bithynia".'

As we fell asleep that night, I wondered what evidence I would see of the historical Christians' presence in the location we planned to explore the following day.

As the sun drew back the curtains on a new day we got up and were ready to leave by seven-thirty. Having said goodbye to the stonemason and his sons, we drove to the town of Avanos. There we parked and enjoyed a walk around the cobbled back streets. We came across a big market where the usual fruit and vegetables were for sale. In addition we saw dried chillies, sunflowers, clay pots, fabrics and even old plastic shoes, which were sold by weight.

---

[1] 1 Peter 1 v. 1 TLB.

At Goreme we visited the rock churches created within caves. At that time the area hadn't developed its full tourist potential and the places of interest mentioned in the brochures had little supervision or maintenance. Sadly some of the wall paintings had been spoilt by graffiti.

We were amazed as we surveyed the valley of Cappadocia, with its toadstool formations of soft rock in shades of pale yellow and pink. It looked just like a landscape in a children's fantasy book, where whimsical creatures dwelt.

At Kaymakli we went down into the underground city. It was seven floors deep with four ventilation shafts open at the surface. Centuries ago, persecuted Christians took refuge in the city, hiding for up to a year from their enemies. As we entered the site, the guard at the entrance informed us that the lights would be switched off after thirty minutes, as it was near to closing time. We had to bend double to wander along the steeply inclined, narrow tunnels until we reached a spacious room and could stand up. From that room there were other low tunnels leading on to other rooms. Some had been used as stables, storage areas and family living spaces. I felt claustrophobic, not knowing how far we would wander deep underground before we should return to the exit. Fortunately we made it before the lights were extinguished.

'My, that was an astonishing feat of architecture. Can you imagine digging it out, let alone living down there? And we only saw a fraction of its vastness,' I said to Alec as we walked back to the Land-Rover, our eyes squinting in the bright sunlight.

'Yes, life down there would have required skilled management, coping with hundreds of people needing food, water and sanitation,' Alec pondered.

'And think of dealing with births, sickness and deaths underground too,' I added. 'What did they do for light? I wonder if they would secretly come out to the surface now and then.'

'Totally mind boggling!' Alec said. 'They must have had a remarkable faith in Jesus Christ to be willing to suffer so!'

Our drive out of the valley went along country tracks by golden-grassed hills, where we were uncertain of the right direction to go. Fortunately we came across a dusty, new white track that eventually led us to the main road. There were bulldozers working on the road, so we stopped to ask a driver the way. He pointed to the right and we drove in that direction through a village and then into a gorge, along the steep, winding road that sloped downwards, going between the soft rocks of various shades of brown. Once we were in the depths of the gorge, we followed the trail between the bright green trees and foliage, and then crossed a shallow stream. We parked for the night next to a graveyard.

Up by six, we enjoyed a bowl of comforting, warm porridge with a mug of tea. We were not the only early risers. A group of men, women and children rode by on a troupe of donkeys. The fluffy brown baby donkeys ran freely alongside their mothers. The women were dressed in brightly coloured dresses, their heads covered with white scarves.

We followed the road along the floor of the gorge, which widened as the route took us through several more villages. There were many abandoned cave homes on the bordering cliffs. At one point the road climbed high up a hill, providing a magnificent view of the remarkable Cappadocia lunar landscape. Sheep nonchalantly grazed on the scrubby fallow grassland. The road descended on gently down the hill, drawing out into flat terrain. Big herds of small brown cattle and goats munched their morning feed.

Ten miles outside of Kayseri we refuelled and topped up our water reserve. A Turk who could speak English came and asked if we would like to go and see his family's carpet business. We declined and he went away. Shortly afterwards he returned with a bleeding finger, wanting first aid. I obliged and washed and bandaged the wound. Soon we found ourselves following him as he drove his car into Kayseri. Random; I thought we had declined his offer. Well, he certainly had an unusual salesman's trick that caught our attention.

Arriving at his little office, we saw he had about fifty carpets in stock, of varying sizes. We let him know that we definitely did not want to buy a carpet, but would be willing to see them. Then the show began.

First he displayed the old, woven carpets of nomadic designs, fifty to eighty years old and not that expensive. The wool had been dyed with natural colours from vegetables, roses, other flowers, grape juice and walnuts. We asked to see the new carpets made by his family and he showed us several exquisite carpets, many using shades of blue and beige. At £130 to £170 each, they were far more than we could afford on our tight travel budget and definitely too large for us to take away.

But one small carpet took our fancy in soft shades of green and orange wool with a nomadic Mucur and Kazak design. Despite the fact that we still didn't want to buy and transport it to India and back, when the price dropped, he won us over. He dropped from 1,700 lira to 1,000 lira, or in other words, from £56 to £33. The deal was done. We had become the proud owners of a gorgeous handmade Turkish carpet from the astute salesman.

We left his office-cum-shop and took a walk in and around the castle in the town – a dramatic backdrop to an excellent bazaar, set within the castle grounds. Lots of appetizing fruit and vegetables were for sale.

After lunch we drove thirty miles west of Sivas, passed by a few villages and enjoyed seeing the autumnal terrain with ploughed fields of dark brown earth, bordered by golden grass and rolling hills in the distance. We found ourselves a splendid elevated parking spot with a panoramic view of delightful scenery to enjoy for the remainder of the afternoon. Once again we became a fascinating curiosity. On this occasion three young lads walking by stopped and observed us for half-an-hour, as we set about our usual evening routine.

*

We travelled on a further 500 miles east over the following two days before entering the Persian Kingdom of Iran.

Total distance driven = 23,204 miles

Travel Cameos

6th to 14th September 1977
Turkey – Iran

'See that snow-capped mountain over there? Well, that's Mount Ararat where Noah's Ark came to rest,' Alec announced on a chilly, clear morning, as he referred to the map he was studying.

'Really? That's amazing,' I said as I handed Alec his second mug of tea. I marvelled at God's ongoing revelation of *His-story*.

'Well, today's another milestone as we'll be crossing into Iran. That'll be the twenty-third country we've visited in eight months,' Alec reported, as he folded the map to be in the right place for me to navigate that day.

Our first port of call was the nearby Ishak Pasha Palace, a great example of Ottoman architecture built in the eighteenth century, high up in the craggy mountains. We explored the striking edifice and climbed the minaret within its high walls. From there we looked out across the vast expanse of grassy plains to the range of mountains on the opposite side. Below was Doğubayazit, the last town on the eastern flank of Turkey.

Later on at the border control, the formalities of the passport and customs officials were dealt with expediently. We drove the short distance to the Iranian border police post and had our passports stamped. After a further two miles we arrived at the customs station. One always felt a little jittery when going through border controls and we had heard that the Iranian border was very hot on drugs. Not that we were carrying any, but you do hear wild stories of drugs being planted on your vehicle without your knowing and we were not looking for any trouble.

We queued along with many other trucks and cars, all waiting for vehicle documentation. An hour later we were still queuing and waiting patiently. The customs officials must have gone off for their lunch, so we had ours too. Afterwards, we walked across and looked at a glass cabinet where the items on display had been used to hide drugs: a gas cylinder, portable toilet, table, mirror and the sole of a boot. These customs officials were genuinely serious in their search for any concealed merchandise.

Surprisingly when the officials returned they processed our documents in double-quick time. We drove out of there sharpish, but steadily, not to attract undue attention, especially as we had had no search, not even a casual glance at our vehicle and its contents.

As always when we drove along I tried to note anything that was different to what we had previously seen. For starters, here we found that fuel sold at thirty-four pence a gallon – now that was a bargain; we could do with more of that. There were petrol stations everywhere along with an increase of vehicles and even double-decker buses. Although there were still many horse and carts used for transport. Not everyone drove with safety in mind, as we saw from the number of wrecked cars and lorries alongside the good tarmac roads.

Money was being invested in the towns and many new buildings were going up: orderly, neat surrounds, with pavements for pedestrians, manicured lawns, colourful flowerbeds and pools with fountains to delight the eye.

The countryside was varied with distant, dry, barren hills, then scrubby grasslands where herds of camels and flocks of sheep grazed. The shepherd boys did not badger us for anything; in fact they were totally disinterested in us, which was a welcome change. Where possible the land was farmed and crops flourished. Vivid yellow sunflowers stood tall with their heads tracking the sun in adoration.

On our third day of driving in Iran, we arrived at the capital Tehran and made a beeline to the post office. Sad to find not even one letter from home.

As we explored the city, we came across the Sepahsalar Mosque, an extravagantly embellished building with colourful floral and geometric tiles on the gateway, inner courtyard walls and adorning the summer mosque. The caretaker took us around the winter mosque, a fine marble room decorated with onyx and alabaster. Crystal chandeliers hung from the ceiling. We also visited several palaces, the Royal Mosque and the archeological museum – all ticked off on our 'must see' list of tourist attractions.

Out on the bustling streets we came across a stall selling freshly pressed drinks – apple, pear, orange, melon and carrot. Unfortunately non-filtered water was used in the process, so we resisted the temptation to buy.

Although when in a city we would search out the overlanders' campsite, we were unaware of one in Tehran at that time, so for our first night we parked behind the post office under the shade of trees. We had seen a lot of police around guarding various buildings, but nobody disturbed us.

On the second day in the city, after a morning of sightseeing, we had lunch in the Land-Rover, a thick tomato soup with pasta, followed by fruit loaf and a cup of tea. Afterwards I read and Alec slept.

Several policemen checked out our Land-Rover during the afternoon, and at six, one of them told us to move on. I think we had inadvertently parked opposite the police headquarters. We drove to the northern part of the city and parked in a back street, then went on a walkabout before returning to prepare supper in the Land-Rover. Later on a police motorcyclist stopped by and peered into our window, but he didn't say anything so we stayed there for the night. It proved to be a noisy location and we slept poorly.

The following day was a Saturday. I cleared away the breakfast things whilst Alec went to the bank for cash, before we drove to the Afghanistan Embassy. A strange place – full of hippies! There we discovered that we could obtain our visa at Mashhad, the last major town we would drive through in Iran en route to Afghanistan.

Our next call in Tehran was at the Iraqi Embassy. It was one crazy drive along the one-way streets with traffic galore and no one taking any notice of pedestrian crossings, traffic lights or signs. At the Iraqi Embassy we were informed that we'd have to wait two months for a visa to be granted. We left empty handed, as we were unable to remain in Iran for that length of time. I had read and seen photographs of the Marsh Arabs of southern Iraq, who lived in large, arched houses made from plaited reeds on manmade islands in the wetlands. I was keen to see that fascinating culture and Alec also would have liked to explore the ruins of Babylon, but it was not to be.

We returned to the main post office but there were still no letters for us. Popped to the tyre street – yes, a whole street of shops selling tyres – where we purchased a new one for thirty-four pounds. All errands done, we were grateful to leave the city of Tehran with its tangibly oppressive atmosphere.

But we were in for a treat: the best scenery since our arrival in Iran lay ahead, as we drove northeast through the Elburz Mountains. The lower brown hills were watched over by the snow-capped mountain of Damavand at 18,963 feet high. Down below the road was a deep, narrow valley with lush green trees growing by a fast-flowing river. We stopped in the hills at a lay-by and enjoyed a refreshing lunch: cold tomatoes with unleavened bread followed by delicious watermelon. A shepherd came by, dressed in a pinstriped suit and desert boots; his sheep and goats were clambering on the hillside far below.

In the afternoon, we continued our drive in the mountain range, through many tunnels, even a few that appeared carved out of snow. We made camp early by the river and I put my barber skills into action and cut Alec's hair. I wrote in the diary to record the day's antics, as was my daily habit. It was a romantic evening, sitting out eating our supper of rice and sauce, kept warm by the burning brushwood that Alec had gathered nearby. No visitors – yippee!

We overslept until seven in the morning, but we both felt well rested. We drove on to Amol, where the new tyre was fitted to the spare wheel. Notably smelly open drains ran alongside the town roads. Lads came by wanting to swap their coins for English ones, not that we had many of those at that point. We continued on to the Caspian Sea, thinking we might take a swim, but were put off by the murky water and rubbish on the beach. The air was very hot and clammy and we were only comfortable when driving along, feeling the rush of air cooling us through the open windows.

On the coastal road there were many villas being built. At Bâbolsar holiday resort we saw a couple of restaurants, a hotel and an attractive promenade with trees, flowers and palm-leafed plants. We checked out one jolly shop selling plastic woven mats, grass mats, blow-up plastic balls, swimming rings, flip-flops etc. – everything that one might need for fun by the sea.

We stopped to chat with five English guys, medical students travelling in their Volkswagen van in the opposite direction to us. They were returning to England following a two-month study in the Kashmir valley in northern India, tracking the blood pressure readings of the local people. We exchanged travel news and they forewarned us concerning the Afghan border, where the officials searched everything.

Our journey continued on eastwards where the landscape was very green with much farming. We saw cotton and tobacco crops growing. Water buffalo and packhorses became a common sight. I was pleased to see that the countrywomen's faces were uncovered, unlike the fully shrouded women of Tehran and the surrounding towns. These hard-working women of the land wore colourful dresses and had their babies strapped to their backs with cloth, just like the African mothers. A few women were doing laundry and washing their kitchen pans in a stream.

We drove through a green-forested gorge that was a national park. We hoped to find somewhere to stay for the night, but parking was only allowed in marked areas and for some reason these were gated off. Driving on through a tunnel, we passed a sign saying 'Bon Voyage', so we figured we had left the park. Unfortunately time had moved on to evening and darkness made our search for a campsite very tricky. Eventually we decided on a suitable place and settled in for the night. At nine, just as we were about to eat dinner, the police stopped by and informed us that we were in an unsafe location known for armed bandits. So after our meal, we journeyed on until we found a petrol station and parked in a clearing nearby. It was ten o'clock.

The following day we noticed that the terrain was back to dry and barren with stubbles of brown grass dried by the hot sun with temperatures in the nineties. We drove to Shahabad, where we refuelled, then continued on through the Kuh-i-Aldi hills and saw flocks of sheep and goats grazing. In the distance nomads rode their saddled camels along a trail. The odd village was here and there, with an occasional strip of green where a vineyard flourished on the hillside. The owners' children sold bunches of grapes and apples alongside the road.

At the town of Bojnurd it was time to stretch our legs and buy some supplies. Displayed for sale on the pavement were goat heads and lumps of white, greasy fat. One lady was walking along with skeins of natural wool in one hand and a pair of sheep lungs with a windpipe dangling from the other! We tasted the cheese on display at an open stall then bought a melon and some apples.

The route continued on good tarmac roads. It must have been a holiday season for the Iranians, as we passed many full cars with loaded roof racks and some folks were camping along the roadside. As we approached the major town of Mashhad, we decided to stop for the night near to the hospital and a military camp.

Unfortunately Alec was up for most of the night, suffering with diarrhoea. The smell was atrocious, not that he could help that at all. Whilst I'd been in and out of sleep, he'd moaned and groaned as he sat on the chemical toilet in the corner of the Land-Rover. So awkward to use at night when the bed was in position, as you couldn't lower your feet. The situation became so bad that I finally had to get up and fold the bottom half of the bed to make it easier for Alec to cope. I gave him plenty of water and added a dash of salt and a couple of spoonfuls of sugar to keep him hydrated, plus a dose of Lomotil tablets to stop the diarrhoea.

'What do you think caused your tummy bug, Alec?' I enquired at breakfast time.

'Maybe it was that cheese we tasted yesterday. There were a lot of flies buzzing around the stall.'

'How are you feeling now?'

'Not too bad. Eating this dry bread is helping, and having a sweet morning cuppa.'

'Will you be able to drive?'

'I think so,' replied Alec. 'I'll just have to take it steady.'

We had the windows and the back door wide open, to allow plenty of fresh air to blow through the inside and were thankful that the toilet chamber chemicals had neutralized the offensive stink.

Fortunately, with the worst of Alec's tummy bug over, we

were soon packed up and on our way into the centre of Mashhad. A clean, new city with many roundabouts displaying various statues and monuments in the middle, and neat flowerbeds enhanced the scene. First we had to locate the tourist office to pick up a local map and find the whereabouts of the Afghanistan Embassy. The receptionist at the Hyatt Hotel gave us some directions, but we were still at a loss.

Whilst waiting at the traffic lights, a local car drew alongside and the driver asked us where we were going and offered to lead the way to the tourist office. He was a clever chap, as he hoped we'd then go on with him to see the local carpets for sale. In fact we had a dozen or more guys stop us as we walked or drove along the streets in Mashhad, hoping we would be interested in viewing carpets. Alas, we disappointed them all.

The tourist office gave us the information we needed and we made our way to the Embassy of Afghanistan. There we filled in the visa application and handed over our passports, plus fourteen American dollars. They were very particular that the dollar bills were pristine, with no damage in any way. As we walked back to the Land-Rover, we bumped into an English truck driver who told us the whereabouts of the travellers' campsite. He and his mates worked for a British firm transporting steel from Mashhad to Kandahar in Afghanistan and regularly used the camp.

On arrival we found it to be surprisingly posh, with large brown tents in place and sixteen brick chalets. It boasted a swimming pool, clean showers, flush toilets and hot water! One pound each, per night, if we used our own accommodation.

That afternoon Alec went back into town to collect our passports from the Afghanistan Embassy, grateful for the quick service. He also bought bread, eggs and a can of engine oil for the Land-Rover. The bread was a large, broad sheet of wafer-thin, crispy dough with a puffy, uneven surface. I popped all the air bubbles to remove any tiny, trapped pebbles, for it had been cooked on a bed of hot stones.

As I washed our grubby clothes and the bed linen, I spoke to an Irish fella who'd just graduated university with a degree in architecture. He'd left Northern Ireland at the beginning of July and had cycled to Mashhad on his way to Australia. We met several other overlanders during the afternoon from Denmark, Sweden and Austria. Later Alec changed yet another broken leaf spring, and swapped the wheels around to balance the wear. Several truck drivers came by and exchanged travel adventures and news of the route.

The next day the chores continued: I finished the pile of washing, checked the contents of the roof box and polished our shoes. Alec cleaned and serviced the petrol cooker, washed the Land-Rover, replaced the dud bulb in the left rear break light and emptied the toilet. By noon, everything was fine and dandy so we left the campsite.

We went first to the city centre to see the Imam Reza Holy Shrine, a magnificent mosque with a circle of lawns all surrounded by a wall. There were hundreds of pilgrims in and around the building. As the mosque officials recognized us as infidels, we were only allowed so near.

Then we called in at the post office, popped to the bank, disappointed a few more carpet salesmen and drove way out of town to camp for the night on a gravel hill.

Fortunately our only late-night caller was a fox trotting by on a midnight hunt.

Total distance driven = 24,540 miles

Bureaucracy

15th to 18th September 1977
Afghanistan

The Iranian/Afghanistan frontier was ahead of us and there was no knowing what challenges we'd encounter in the coming days. Leaving Iran was straightforward: no search by the customs officials and our passports were stamped to say we had exited the country. As we drove across no-man's land, we saw the border post of Afghanistan ahead, a few simple mud huts. What a crazy border, full of hippies on the hash trail. An Afghani official in blue overalls checked over our vehicle and fortunately we didn't have to remove everything. Apparently we would have that to look forward to on departing the country. Not too much hassle, just slow formalities that included our vaccination records being checked.

It was late afternoon as we drove away through lovely countryside along a straight road for a while, then it twisted and turned between little brown hills, past domed mud hut villages. Nomads in their black tents were way off in the distance with their herds of one-humped camels already settled for the night.

Eventually we arrived at the olde worlde city of Herat and drove to the main hotel. There were a few guests, mainly overlanders camped around the back. We introduced ourselves to Simon and Rose from England, travelling in their short-wheel-base cream Land-Rover. We also met Jean-Luc and Martine, a Swiss couple with a six-cylinder, long-wheel-base, green-and-cream Land-Rover. Our conversation was brief as it was getting dark and we needed to prepare for bed.

We were so eager to be out and about that first morning, exploring Herat: a fascinating city of mud dwellings with a few modern buildings, including two-storey structures along the main street. The back streets had earthen roads. There were only a few cars around, as transport was predominantly horse-drawn gigs. Many of the horses were in fine condition, striding out, heads raised proudly with decorative red pom-poms bobbing up and down on their bridles. Black and white Toyota taxis ferried their customers to and fro. The merchandise trucks, with wooden, slatted rear cargo bays, were brightly painted. Tinsel, beads and trinkets hung inside the drivers' cabs and the dashboards were bedecked with luxurious ruby-red or royal-purple velvet.

The men about town were dressed in long-sleeved, loose, thigh-length shirts with baggy trousers that were cuffed at the ankles. Many wore dark waistcoats or jackets and embroidered pillbox hats or turbans. Most were wearing plastic shoes; just a few had leather footwear. The boys were dressed in a similar way.

The women had on wide, baggy trousers and were totally covered from head to toe with full burqas made from pleated, silky cloth in dull colours of dark blue, maroon, dark green or brown. A skullcap was incorporated within the design and a crocheted grill visor for the lady to peer out on the world. Little girls were clad in matching dresses and trousers with headscarves covering their hair.

It was Friday, the Muslim holy day, so very few shops were open. We couldn't even window-shop, as every shop had its merchandise behind padlocked, heavy wooden shutters. At one place that was open we stopped to buy biscuits to snack on and a fourteen-year-old lad bade us follow him. He took us to his father's shop, where ethnic silk, embroidered shirts and dresses were for sale.

Next we passed by a tearoom. Men sat on a high, large platform made of mud and covered with hand-woven wool carpets. Tea was brewed in two big copper urns with taps on and poured into small tea glasses. The tearoom was the local men's domain, where they put the world to rights.

We walked by the city castle, which was originally built for Alexander the Great in 330 BC. It has had a few different owners and facelifts over the centuries.

Apparently there used to be twelve minarets standing in Herat until the Russians knocked seven down, according to two teenagers we came across, as we went to view the remaining five. We walked through the street together with the lads who were keen to practise their English. The older boy pushed his bike along as he shared with us his aspirations to train to be a doctor one day.

We went back to the Land-Rover and then returned to the hotel, where Alec was soon engaged in resolving various mechanical issues of other owners' vehicles. I enjoyed a chance to relax and drink mint tea with a few travellers, before I fixed our supper of spaghetti and sauce. It was a pleasant evening as we sat outside together with the occupants of the two nearby Land-Rovers to discuss the route ahead.

'See here on the map, the main surfaced roads go in a diamond shape,' Jean-Luc pointed out. 'You can drive from Herat north to Mazar-i-Sharif to Kabul, or from Herat south to Kandahar and then up to Kabul.'

'So which direction are you going?' asked Alec.

'Neither.' Jean-Luc smiled, with a glint in his eye. 'We're going this way, straight across the Hindu Kush from Herat to Kabul.'

'Really… and what about you, Simon?'

'Too damn right, we're driving the Central Route too. After all, that's what Land-Rovers are built for. It's cross-country all the way.'

'But don't forget to mention the military orders,' chipped in Martine.

'Oh – and what are they?' I asked.

'No one is allowed to drive alone. You have to travel in convoy,' Jean-Luc replied.

'Does that mean with an army vehicle too?' asked Rose.

'No, that's not necessary. We can just team up with one another,' Simon clarified.

'Well, you all seem to have it all worked out. Can we drive along with you too?' asked Alec.

'*Oui, oui, bien sûr,*' Jean-Luc readily agreed, as they all did. 'Tomorrow we'll apply for the official papers to authorize our crossing.'

'Yes, we'd better get to bed, as we should be at the police station by eight in the morning,' Simon said, folding up his stool.

'Goodnight,' said Rose.

'*Bonne nuit.*'

Our replies faded into the night air as we dispersed to our own Land-Rovers.

'Well, I didn't realize that Afghanistan was going to be like this,' I said to Alec as we snuggled close together in bed.

'No, I haven't researched much on travelling in this part of the world. I guess we were focused on Africa, what with the Sahara crossing an' all.'

'Jean-Luc sounds well read on this country, so it's great that they're up for us to go along with them,' I said, quite unaware of what we were letting ourselves in for!

'Night, night, Darling.'

'Sweet dreams, my love.'

The six of us – Simon, Rose, Jean-Luc, Martine, Alec and I – were at the police station promptly at eight the next morning. We acquired the official travel documents and were told we needed two stamps. The police gave the first stamp of approval to go across the Central Route, but we then needed an official stamp from the tourist office.

'It's not possible to stamp these forms.' The tourist official handed them back.

'Why ever not?' Simon demanded. 'The police stamped them without a problem.'

'Well, there have been reports that the road is blocked.'

'Blocked by what?' an irritated Simon replied.

'That we do not know, but you can come back at two this afternoon.'

Disappointed, we all walked out of the clerk's office and split up to do our own thing. Alec and I went to the bank and found it closed, so no money until the following day. We managed to change a ten-dollar American bill in a shop, then explored more of the town, munching on sugared almonds, a local sweet treat that I bought from a roadside stall.

I noticed that milk, eggs and yogurt were available at the Herat dairy. Watermelons were on sale in abundance. You could buy a whole one or just a slice or two. The sweet coral-pink flesh in the open melons provided a welcome playground for the local flies. Having seen that Simon and Rose were growing bean sprouts in a small plastic box in their Land-Rover, we bought a kilo of mung beans to have a go at producing fresh veg.

It was a hot day and so, feeling thirsty, we searched for a tearoom. But our next stop was at a shop selling rice displayed in big sacks with rolled-down tops. The owner offered us a glass of tea. Smart salesman, as after being refreshed we readily bought a couple of pounds of rice.

Further along the street, we were invited into an industrial workshop and we stayed for over an hour. They were making scissors and small knives for carpet looms. The raw materials were old car springs. One of the men held a spring with long tongs in a bed of smoldering charcoal embers that heated and softened the iron. His clothes were peppered with tiny holes, burnt by the sparks that flew out of the hot fire. Another man and a young teenage lad sharpened scissors on a revolving stone wheel.

They gave us each a stool to sit on and were eager to know the English names for their tools and other things in the workshop. Alec drew pictures of the items on a piece of paper and wrote the English name alongside, saying out loud the word as he completed each drawing. The air was hot and smelt of sweaty men and smoke. Tea was brewed and shared around.

When it was time to take our leave we asked the price of a small carpet knife, but the men insisted we had it as a gift. I gave the lad the remaining sugared almonds as a gesture of thanks for their kindness.

At the bakers, the unleavened bread was baked in an earthen pit in the ground with a fire burning at the base. The thin, pliable length of dough was thrown into the pit and it clung to the side of the hot walls. Shortly afterwards, the crisp strip of baked bread was removed with a long-handled, wide-pronged metal fork and tossed onto the wooden ledge before us. I juggled the hot, thin bread from palm to palm until it had cooled down as we wandered back to our parked Land-Rover. We found Jean-Luc and Martine's vehicle close by. It was two o'clock and they'd just been back to the tourist office. They were told to return again at five!

So Alec and I went and explored the old city and were delighted to find it crammed with open shops selling saddles, harnesses, metal boxes, rifles, bullets, carpets, fruit, food, fabrics and clothes including ladies' burqas. After an afternoon soaking up the sights, sounds and aromas, we returned to the tourist office, only to be told to come back again in the morning. We were not amused!

Back at the hotel car park, Alec changed the gear oil in the overdrive. He found he was unable to change the rear differential as the head of the drain plug had smashed off, leaving the actual plug still in situ.

We were in bed by ten, both eager to see what the next day would bring.

Waking early we washed, dressed and ate breakfast, then prayed and did our daily Bible study. Everyone else on the campsite was still in the land of nod. By eight we were champing at the bit as we drove into town. First we went to the bank, where we waited for one hour and forty minutes for the bank to change our traveller's cheques. Alec then went into the tourist office and came out smiling, waving the stamped official travel permit. The other four had yet to collect theirs, so we ventured off to buy a few more supplies for the journey ahead.

We also called in to see the police to ask about the road situation and there was no mention of any roadblock, so we could leave any time. Returning to the hotel, I made a vegetable pizza for lunch. Simon and Rose came back also, having collected their completed permission paper.

Unfortunately, we four were left hanging around the campsite for the rest of the day waiting for Jean-Luc and Martine. They had misunderstood that we had planned to be on the road that afternoon and didn't arrive back from town until early evening. Oh well, rather a wasted day, but with our travel documents in hand we could all leave in convoy first thing the following day.

Total distance driven = 24,888 miles

Afghan Encounters

19th to 20th September 1977
Afghanistan

I woke up with that tingly, excited feeling in my tummy, knowing that we were off on a fresh adventure, rather like crossing the Sahara, full of uncertainties and possible danger. We would be driving an estimated 900 miles across the Central Route, through the Hindu Kush from Herat to Kabul.

'So – are we all set?' Alec asked the convoy team at eight-thirty.

'Sure, let's go,' called Simon.

'Bien sûr, allons-y,' affirmed Jean-Luc.

Our Land-Rover led the way out of town, followed by the Swiss and backed up by the other Brits: three Land-Rovers fitted to the hilt with cross-country equipment, winches, shovels and spare parts, and topped up with fuel and water. We looked pretty cool as our convoy drove out of Herat and headed south along the Russian-built concrete road. The trees lined the road in salute as we proudly went by. The miles were clocking up very nicely as we zipped along, enjoying the buzz of anticipation.

*

'Oh my goodness, look at that!' Alec exclaimed as he slowed down our vehicle. In the corner of his wing mirror he had seen a black object racing diagonally forward from behind.

He pulled onto the side of the road and we climbed out, just as Jean-Luc and Martine's vehicle tucked in behind us. We were aghast to see Simon and Rose's crippled Land-Rover bearing down on its left front brake drum, scoring a groove in the concrete as it skid along. It came to a sizzling halt, looking dejected and shameful. Its left front wheel had since rolled way into the scrubland, until it toppled over and lay flat and still.

'Are you alright?' I shouted as we all ran to Simon and Rose's aid. We found them shaken and bruised, but fortunately nothing more.

'Damn,' said Simon, 'I knew I should have checked and tightened those wheel nuts again this morning. I was so eager to be away that I forgot.'

'It's alright, Simon, we're not hurt. It's okay,' said Rose.

'Are you crazy?' shouted Simon. 'This is the last thing we need! What are we going to do now?'

Alec offered a practical solution: 'I'll go and retrieve the wheel, whilst you all look for the wheel nuts.'

Amazingly every one of the five nuts was found within a short distance of each other. The wheel was soon refitted firmly to the ailing Land-Rover and we continued on along the main road. We soon reached the dirt track on the left that we had been looking for, opposite a signpost on the right to Shindand.

It was an endless track going on and on and on, past several villages, until we stopped at one that had fuel: a hand pump attached to a forty-five-gallon drum of petrol. We all promptly topped up our tanks and jerry cans again. Simon enquired where it might be possible to buy a new brake drum to replace their damaged one. None of us were surprised with what he discovered: he and Rose needed to return to the main road and continue driving south to Kabul, via Kandahar.

Our convoy was down to two vehicles.

As we drove along the Central Route towards Farsi, the cross-country track was very visible. It was encouraging to see local traffic coming along too, reassuring us that we were on the right road as marked on the map. The terrain was dry and dusty with shades of beige to pink earth on the gravelly, rolling hills.

Two loaded lorries came towards us, packed to overflowing with merchandise and people. Sitting way up high, on top of the piled goods, were rugged, turbaned men hanging on to their baggage. Inside the cab, the long bench seat was bulging out with more men, even one between the driver and the cab door. The front mudguards provided a seat to a man either side of the bonnet. Not to miss the chance of a ride, there were outriders standing on the step up to the cab, holding on to the open windows of the doors. At the back of the trucks several men gripped tightly to whatever they could hold onto, as their feet perched on the back bumper.

One of the trucks waved us down and asked if we could sell them any fuel. We obliged and sold two gallons from one of our jerry cans. It was a hot day, with temperatures above 100°F; it was unbelievable that many of the men were wearing heavy overcoats or army jackets over their traditional dress.

Thirty miles west of Farsi we arrived at a village just as it was getting dark and we decided to stay for the night. There was a mud-hut hotel where the four of us had a glass of tea observed by the local men and lads. Our Land-Rovers were parked at the edge of the village. Later, after supper, a big truck loaded with men, women and children stopped nearby to camp for the night. They all slept outside on the ground under the stars, pulling their clothes and any blankets they might have tightly around them. The strength of the howling wind rocked the Land-Rover through the night.

At one point a pack of dogs turned up; some were tall and hairy with big feet and floppy ears, others, slender with short, curly hair and long ears. They eerily howled as they prowled around the camp. Someone sent a few stones flying their way and the dogs yelped and scarpered back to the village.

'Cock-a-doodle-doo,' crowed the village cockerel as the travellers clambered back on the lorry and were away at first light. We were not far behind, leaving at seven-thirty. En route we saw many nomadic camel trains. The camels were loaded with tent poles, carpets, coffee pots and the odd chicken or two. Children and old people rode aloft the camels and donkeys. Men, women and older children walked alongside as their dogs trailed behind.

The irrigation system used extensively in that area cut channels across the dirt road, making careful, concentrated driving essential to avoid being jarred. Any land that could be farmed was abundantly irrigated. The fields of golden corn were being harvested by hand, using a sickle and stick, then gathered into a pile on the ground. Five cows trampled around and around on the sheaves of corn, releasing the grains of wheat.

Every so often we passed by a graveyard. Each grave was denoted by a pile of stones covering the earth with a larger stone at each end. New graves had leafy branches from a tree stuck in the ground, top and bottom. Tied on to the branches were strips of material fluttering in the breeze. Cattle horns and china pots were displayed on some of the graves.

Our one-hundred-mile drive of the day went well and it was good to chat with Jean-Luc and Martine at natural stops along the way. We drove through stunning valleys, passes and gorges. We saw many nomadic encampments with black tents pitched and fires glowing brightly where the women were cooking. Children ran to the roadside, waving excitedly to welcome us. We waved back with joy.

Going through Tulak en route to Sabrak, the night was drawing in, so we stopped at the next village. Three men approached our parked vehicles and we asked through sign language if we could stay there for the night. They amicably agreed and there soon gathered an intrigued crowd of locals watching us. They were fascinated when we put up our extending roof. I was busy with taking the cooker, kettle and other stuff out of the cupboards ready to prepare the dinner. I pumped water to make it flow out of the tap on top of the worktop as I filled the kettle. Alec was doing an all-round check of the vehicle, including the air pressure in the tyres. Jean-Luc and Martine were doing the same in their vehicle. We were putting on quite the show, and our audience chatted excitedly as they commented to one another about our curious antics.

Then a man called my attention to come out to see his wife. She was a short lady, dressed in a burgundy, floral-patterned, heavy cotton, midi-length dress with long sleeves. The bodice and wide cuffs were intricately embroidered. Over her braided, long black hair she had a matching cloth that reached down to the hem of the dress. Below that I could see she had on loose black pantaloons that were cuffed at the ankles and her feet were clad in embroidered leather shoes with pointed, curved-up toes. She was adorned with rings on her fingers, wide solid-silver bracelets and an elaborate double chain of heavy silver jewellery that was draped from her shoulder across her body to her waist. It was made up of a solid-silver purse and other solid shapes that were inset with ruby gems.

She held her hand to the side of her swollen face. She was in great pain. I looked into her mouth and saw a broken, decayed tooth, so I applied drops of clove oil and gave her a paracetamol tablet.

Another lady came forward complaining of toothache and backache: paracetamol for her too and deep heat ointment to rub into her back.

With the crowd of inquisitive villagers I patiently waited before cooking supper. After some time a man told everyone to go home. He bade us goodnight with his raised hand and closed our door.

I cooked, we ate, and after a game of Scrabble we organized our bed and settled down to sleep.

That night, another howling dog pack was on patrol.

Total distance driven = 25,025 miles

Up Close and Personal

21st to 23rd September 1977
Afghanistan

'Looks like you might have some more patients this morning,' Alec said, as we finished our breakfast.

'Really!' I responded, leaning across him to raise the blind a little at the back door. I could see a group of locals quietly waiting for us to emerge from the Land-Rover.

'Oh, right, better get cracking and see what they want,' I declared, as I packed away the kitchen stuff to be ready for the ongoing journey.

They had mustered up someone who could speak a little English and he helped me to understand what ailed the people. Two old men complained of gastric trouble and one had a headache. I gave them basic medication. A toddler had mucky eyes: her eyelashes were stuck together with dried yellow crud. I took some cotton wool and soaked it in boiled water and bathed her eyes clean. She struggled in her mother's arms as I worked quickly and gently, but the sweet girl was unsure about this strange, tall white lady who was messing about with her face.

The lady, who had had a toothache the night before, came back all smiles and insisted that we took a photo of her. She hoped we could send a print back, but to where? A young man offered his address, which he wrote down in Arabic script. Hmmm… not sure that could be followed through, especially as it wouldn't happen until we returned to England. That was too difficult to explain, so we took her photo and afterwards her solemn face for the camera, beamed once again.

Nearby, the mobile butcher arrived and dismounted from his horse to set up shop. He sat cross-legged on the ground with a carcass of meat and lobs of fat before him, that he hacked into chunks for his waiting customers.

Just as we were about to leave, an elderly man brought his son to us and asked if we could help him. I looked at this twenty-something young man's face and saw his sallow complexion with sunken, yellowed eyes. He looked weak and tired as he stood there with his head bowed, shoulders slumped and his breath smelling of fresh vomit.

I walked back to Alec and conferred with him.

'He's very sick and needs medical help,' I whispered.

'Well, there's no knowing how far we'll have to go before we find a doctor,' Alec replied. 'But if you think it's necessary then we should take him along.'

As the young man climbed into the back of the Land-Rover, we could see the relief on his father's face. He had been at his wits' end to know what else he could do to relieve his son's suffering. Jean-Luc and Martine, who had been patiently waiting to leave, supported our decision.

Driving across the vast, open land, we reached a river that was right across the main dirt road. Alec led the way and found the water was wide but relatively shallow. He stopped on the other side of the river, jumped out with camera in hand to photograph Jean-Luc as he drove across.

Shahrak was the next main town we reached. It was throbbing with people. We tracked down a primary health-care worker at his primitive clinic and presented the patient to him. He agreed that the young man should continue on to Chagcharan Hospital to be treated there. No English was spoken at all, but our sign language to one another did the job. The patient was weak and nauseous and he agreed to go along with the plan.

As it happened we were in for a treat of a ride over a mountain pass where we drove way up to 9,800 feet, according to the aviation altimeter screwed to the dashboard. We saw breathtaking views of magnificent, rugged mountains, resplendent in tones of reds and browns.

At a fork in the road we unknowingly chose the wrong track. A group of children waved us down and pointed in the other direction. The correct track was a narrow, rough road that steeply climbed as it zigzagged up over the pass. We then drove deep down into a tight gorge to follow the path of the river. There the Land-Rovers were literally climbing one wheel after the other over huge rocks that lay on the dry riverbed. On several occasions Jean-Luc stopped his vehicle to jump out and watch to see that the metal guard protecting the engine oil sump of our Land-Rover would clear a boulder. Alec did the same for him.

Then – behold – we turned a corner, still in the shadow of the walls of the gorge, and saw ahead the Minaret of Jam towering high in all its glory, centre-stage in the spotlight. The steep walls of the gorge framed the spectacle in a V-formation, backlit by the bright sunlight beyond.

We had only driven fifty miles all told by the time we called a halt. Alec and Jean-Luc were exhausted from the strenuous driving, as they had ensured our vehicles kept upright and unscathed by the rugged landscape we traversed.

Our night's camp was in a prime location hidden in the heart of the gorge where the River Jam intersected with the Hari River that flowed fast and furious down below. We parked just a few yards away from the famous Minaret of Jam. It stood alone with no mosque by its side, but with its own backdrop of grand, natural rock walls. Built in the twelfth century using baked mud bricks, it was an elaborately decorated tower that soared over two hundred feet high into the sky. The diameter of its base was twenty-seven feet, but it gradually tapered in the higher it went. There was an inscription made from turquoise ceramic tiles set in the mud, halfway up the historic tower. Because of its cultural importance there was a local mud hotel nearby, where we took our patient to stay. No dogs to contend with in the night, so we all slept peacefully, lulled by the constant sound of the river cruising by below.

Alec and I woke before six and rose early to read our Bible. As we studied together we learnt more and more of the Christian faith. Knowing Jesus Christ in a personal way had magnified our appreciation of all that we saw around us. Our senses had been heightened and our desire to really relate to the people we met had strengthened, even though we were hampered by language limitations. But everyone understands a smile, and being able to interact more closely with the local people in recent days had been a genuine blessing. Oh, if only we could tell them of the eternal truth we had discovered.

While I cooked porridge, Alec went to invite our travelling companion to join us for breakfast. We had arranged with Jean-Luc and Martine that we would wait for the sun to rise above the gorge before driving on. That was in order to take photos of our Land-Rovers crossing over the precarious bridge high above the river. The bridge was made from planks of wood tied with rope horizontally to the massive logs that reached from the cliff edge, crossing high above and over the river to the ongoing track on the other side. Whilst cattle could be herded across the bridge, we saw horses walking through the river, both hazardous activities. Side-to-side the bridge was wide enough for the Land-Rover to be driven along, with its wheels within the edges of the outer logs.

Prepared for all eventualities, Alec instructed me to be the photographer. I crossed the bridge on foot, climbed down the embankment to the right and stepped out onto a huge boulder just above the level of the rushing water.

I looked across to Alec, who was all set to cross. Our patient sat in the back, wondering what all the fuss was about. I gave Alec the signal to go. Heart in my mouth, I watched as he skillfully edged across the bridge whilst I took care not to fall in the river. I snapped just one photo, wary of our limited stock of films.

'How was it?' I asked as I clambered back inside the vehicle.

'Great fun, but freaky! When I reached the middle, the weight of the Land-Rover tilted the bridge the other way.'

'Yikes.'

'Did you get a good picture?' Alec enquired.

'Well, I hope so. Time will tell.'

We thought the previous day's drive had been a challenge. Well, we had seen nothing yet! We soon found ourselves on a hairy drive through a narrow gorge, just twenty feet wide with the cliff face towering above us on either side. The actual track was even narrower in some sections, and as we drove over the boulders we were thrown from side to side within the vehicle. We met locals walking and others on horseback, herding their cattle along the uneven, slippery, rocky ground.

Eventually the track led out of the gorge into a wide-open valley of multi-coloured hills with soft golden grass. Tall green and golden trees swayed in the breeze. The river meandered through the hills in a horseshoe shape. The scene was stunning! We passed by several villages of mud huts and round grass-mat huts with white or black roofs and wooden or grass doors. The local people were dressed in brightly coloured clothing and greeted us with friendly waves as we drove along. It was a scene of pastoral contentment.

But not so in the Land-Rover when I turned to check on our patient sitting in the back.

'Oh, Alec, you'd better stop – our passenger is looking rather green,' I cried out. The young man was very anxious and about to throw up. Alec immediately stopped and I let our patient out just in time. After we rested for a while I gave the young man a glucose drink to restore his well-being.

We had parked by a village and soon our vehicles and ourselves became a point of interest when a group of men walked across to greet us. Their lads were not far off their heels and soon were badgering us for baksheesh: free gifts like a pen, a ruler, a notebook, Alec's watch and my wedding ring. My, my, their list was more extravagant than usual, but Alec was not about to hand over his watch, nor me my ring. We knew that even handing over the cheapest item like a pen would only encourage the habit of pestering foreign travellers, so we ignored their requests.

Alec and Jean-Luc decided to go and check out the nearby water-powered flourmill. We discovered that it was a public holiday in the area, so Martine and I walked along to greet the ladies, who were wearing their finest dresses and jewellery. These country women were not veiled. What a joy to see their faces and respond to their shy smiles. But an old lady amongst them was wary of us. She waved her clenched fist and shooed us away.

As we took to the dirt road again we passed by two horses, each carrying a man and a woman. The women were regally dressed, one in a cloak and veil of rainbow colours. Their horses had hand-embroidered felt blankets under the saddles.

The track climbed again, high out of the valley over the crests of the hills, up and down, up and down, until we came to another valley where the river flowed through. The town of Chaghcaran was before us. Now was our chance to find medical help for the patient.

We located the hospital and fortunately found a French-speaking doctor, so Jean-Luc explained the situation and introduced our travelling companion of the previous thirty-six hours. It was agreed the young man could stay at the hospital and we handed over enough money to pay for his stay, thankful that he would then receive appropriate treatment. We said cheerio, and he gave us a weary smile, nodding his appreciation.

It had been some time since we'd seen any fresh bread, fruit and vegetables for sale. Much to our delight, we discovered such foods available in the little town, so we bought plenty of extra goodies.

'Jan, look, over there.' Martine nudged me to look across the street.

'Why, there's just a group of men standing around?' I responded.

'Yes, but look who's with them.'

'Oh no, I don't believe it! What's he doing there?' I exclaimed.

'Alec, Jean-Luc, do you see our young man from the village is over there?'

'Really… what's going on?' Alec replied as we all walked across the street. 'Shouldn't he still be in the hospital? He can't be cured yet.'

And so it was through the help of a local man we discovered that after we walked away, the patient was promptly asked to leave the hospital and go home. The doctor had told him that on the following day the Minister of Health would open their new hospital and they didn't need any patients around.

Ours was not to reason why – different culture, different ways. Our thinking we were being helpful was not necessarily so. We threw up our hands in exasperation and left the young man to find his own way back to his village.

Going about our own business, we looked for the petrol pump in town and refuelled the vehicles. It was mid-afternoon as we drove away and onwards a few miles, before stopping by the river to eat a late lunch. Munching on fresh bread with sliced tomatoes, we quietly regrouped and relaxed for a while, just the four of us.

Afterwards we took the dirt road eastwards and drove on for another thirty-five miles through rolling, gravelly hills. We went down into a small valley where we came to a mud village nestled close to the foothills. By then it was early evening and time to make camp for the night. We pulled onto a flat, grassy area with room enough for two Land-Rovers to park at a comfortable distance from one another, to allow for intimate privacy. We always sought out the flattest land, to ensure the kettle or saucepan and its hot contents wouldn't slide off the paraffin cooker. It was unusual for us to choose to park so near to a village again, but a wise choice in this wild country, where you felt anything could happen.

A local man came by, so we checked if we were okay to stay. We were becoming quite adept at using hand signals and body language to communicate our requests. Being reassured that it was fine for us to remain where we were, we asked where the village tearoom was. He shook his head, as there was no such thing there, but thrillingly he invited us to follow him to his home instead.

Entering through the low doorway, I noticed how thick the mud walls were. We removed our shoes in a small room and then went through a hole in an inner wall into a large, dark interior. Here we were directed to sit upon the felt-cloth-covered mud bench, formed out from the wall. Dried plants were set alight to initiate the fire in the sunken earthen dish that sat in the centre of the room. Tiny golden sparks floated up towards the chimney, which poked out of the blackened, sooty roof of the house. Dried dung patties and wood were added to the fire and they began to burn steadily, radiating heat and a rural fragrance around the room. My eyes smarted with the haze of grey smoke. A blackened, heavy kettle hung on a metal tripod, which was positioned over the fire.

The soft glow of the firelight enabled me to see the extended family gathered inside the room, fascinated by their unexpected visitors. Delightful faces peered at us, young and old. Two elderly women with weathered faces admired the cardigans Martine and I were wearing. They felt the wool with their rough, wrinkled hands. Several of the young girls aged about twelve years old were pregnant and well adorned with jewellery – a peer group all sharing the same life experience, which comes very early compared to what we know in the west. The couple whose home it was had two young children, about eighteen months and three years old. The older one, a bonny bairn, was cheeky, laughing, singing and clapping to everyone's amusement.

The water boiled and tea was made. The man's young wife kindly gave us each a glassful of sweet black tea. She then took down a bundle from a shelf hollowed in the mud wall and knelt down, placing it on her lap. I was intrigued. From out of the small, rolled-up, woven rug she took a wonderful loaf of bread. Tearing off a hunk, she handed it to one of the pregnant girls to pass on to me. She repeated the same for Alec, Jean-Luc and Martine too. As we took our time to sip the tea and eat the delicious bread, I felt privileged and humbled by the generosity of these villagers. With limited conversation, after a while the silence felt awkward, so we bade them farewell and returned to our Land-Rovers.

The next morning we noticed the condensation inside the vehicle on the windows and metal trims had frozen overnight. Alec checked the temperature and saw it was only 34°F. We were up by quarter-to-six but kept the door closed whilst we accomplished our morning routine. We might have been trying to be private, but the local lads thought our Land-Rover needed exploring. They climbed up onto the bonnet to pull on the chains that secured the jerry cans on the roof rack. They scattered as soon as Alec jumped out of the back door. Scallywags!

Just as we were about to drive off, a mother walked across to show me her toddler's right leg, which had been badly burnt. I got out of the Land-Rover to examine the child. Fortunately the burn was healing well and scar tissue had formed. There was no sign of infection. She must have been scalded with boiling water or tottered into the hot embers of an open fire. I wondered how often that occurred within their poorly lit homes. I smiled to reassure the mother that all was fine.

'It's alright, Alec, we can continue, thank goodness.'

Alec gave the thumbs-up to Jean-Luc and our mini-convoy departed.

Total distance driven = 25,165 miles

Such a Beautiful Land

23rd to 25th September 1977
Afghanistan

During the day we drove 110 miles, up in the mountains, down to the valleys, everywhere having a magnificent panorama. Shepherd boys watched out for their families' flocks of sheep and goats. The nimble animals searched the mountainsides for tufts of coarse grass poking out from the clefts in the rocks. Farmers in the valleys harvested their crops by hand, whilst their women wove cloth on looms outside their homes. Turbaned horsemen rode by on their sprightly steeds. Camouflaged mud and stone villages were tucked away in the dips of the land. The naked hills of rough browns, beiges and coral pink shades of earth gave way to dark-green-leafed trees and golden-yellow corn that grew in the orderly and well-managed farmland below.

We took a break at a café in the town of La'lōsarjangal where we had a glass of hot black tea and ate bread. As we sat relaxing, there drove by many jeeps belonging to United Nations and Save the Children. Perhaps they were on their way to the official opening ceremony of Chaghcaran Hospital?

The Land-Rover was only doing nine miles to the gallon as we drove along the soft, silky, sandy tracks that produced a cloud of dust behind us. We took it in turns with Jean-Luc and Martine to lead the way. When following we kept a good distance behind, to ensure we could actually see the terrain that we were travelling through.

That evening we parked in a fallow field and were glad that only a few villagers came by, as we were all exhausted from the rigorous drive of the day.

'Happy Birthday, Darling,' said Alec with an early morning kiss when he handed me five birthday cards as we lay snug in bed. Imagine – my twenty-sixth birthday and there I was in Afghanistan on a fascinating and challenging adventure. With delight I opened my cards and read loving greetings from our families back home in England. I didn't feel homesick at all, but was very happy that they had remembered me.

We planned to visit a very special location during the day, but our intended early departure at seven-thirty was thwarted when Jean-Luc's Land-Rover failed to start. The longer we travelled with this couple, the more grateful I was that Alec was an experienced mechanic and understood the workings of a vehicle. Fortunately, up until then our Land-Rover had not had any serious engine problems. This was undoubtedly due to Alec's daily checks on oil, water and so on, plus regular maintenance, changing the air and oil filters etc. On the other hand Jean-Luc, who probably was an excellent schoolteacher, only knew how to drive his Land-Rover and where to put the fuel in. Consequently their vehicle was liable to cough, splutter and die from time to time, so Jean-Luc and Martine appreciated that we were driving in convoy. Alec hoped Jean-Luc was picking up some useful maintenance tips for daily and future care of their means of transport.

The two men leaned over, peering into the engine of the ailing Land-Rover. Alec guided Jean-Luc on how to troubleshoot and repair the problem.

'Shall I put the kettle back on and we'll have another cup of tea, Martine?'

'*Oui, oui, bien sûr.*'

I unpacked our folding chairs. Martine and I sat down, drank tea and enjoyed the quiet interlude by writing letters home. In the field opposite, the men were busy harvesting the wheat. Another two came by leading their donkeys, which were dragging along heavy logs tied by ropes to each side of their girth straps. The pleasant aroma of the cut corn was accentuated by the fresh, fermented, grassy whiff of donkey dung. I breathed in the rural smells and was reminded of days in the English countryside as a teenager, riding my horse, Amber.

After two hours the repair was done, so we set off and continued to enjoy the drive through the farmed valleys. Mud-brick-built villages and tall, green and golden trees were surrounded by the rugged Hindu Kush mountain range.

At the town of Yakawlang we stopped and I bought seven mini loaves of bread, six eggs, two pounds of tomatoes and a dozen apples.

'*Vite, vite.*' Jean-Luc called us all to get a move on.

'Well, I hope Band-e Amir lives up to Jean Luc's expectations,' Alec said as he and I climbed back into our Land-Rover.

'Yes, he has these landmarks etched on his mind and he's dying to see them,' I responded. 'We've certainly benefited from all his research. First there was the imposing Minaret of Jam, so tall with fabulous, creative artistry all over the tower. How they built that in the twelfth century, I can't imagine.'

As we recalled that wonder created by man, we drove another thirty miles and the altimeter needle indicated the track had climbed to an elevation of almost 10,000 feet. We came to the brink of the road and there, displayed before us, was the majestic Band-e Amir panorama created by God: a series of six lakes of descending height, with water cascading down from one lake to the next and the next;

crystal-clear sapphire-blue water against a background of soft creams and brown rocky hills and pillars; natural dams of travertine, a form of limestone, separating the terraced lakes.

Jean-Luc was grinning from ear to ear when we saw him, after we parked the Land-Rovers on a jutting-out promontory of rock that overlooked the lakes.

'*C'est magnifique, n'est-ce pas?*' he said.

'*Oui, oui, mon cheri, c'est formidable,*' agreed Martine as they stood arm in arm, gazing in wonderment at the glorious vista.

'Come on, let's go for a walk,' Alec called to them, as he and I set off along a windy footpath that cut down through the soft, rocky pillars surrounding the lakes. The rock surface of the natural dam shimmered in the sun as the water flowed over, highlighting its beauty. Trees grew between the lakes, and reeds and tall grasses swayed in the breeze. The snowy white sandy beach leading to the water, invited its visitors to come a little closer.

This was a tourist attraction for sure, and some distance beyond were a couple of basic hotels and restaurants. As a birthday treat for me, we all hired horses to ride around the lower lake. It was a tangible way to connect with the breathtaking landscape. I was thrilled to go for a ride, and it must have been the first time that I had seen Alec on horseback. He did okay. His horse was very slow but he did manage to jolly him on and canter a short distance. Mine was a high-spirited mare, which suited me well. The saddle was a wooden frame that straddled the horse's back on top of a thick, folded blanket. A tired, padded cushion separated one's rear end from the wood frame. The ride was only an hour long, so the discomfort was bearable and well worth it to bask in the spectacular location.

Still up for exploring more and always wanting to see what was around the next corner, Alec decided to go further. He wanted to drive up the rough track that climbed beyond the highest lake. We headed up the hill alone, as Jean-Luc and Martine chose to relax by the lake, near to their parked vehicle.

The track took a direct route following the curve of the hill and the lake was immediately down on our right. Very soon we realized we were on a perilous route when the track was no longer flat, but sloped away to the right. Gradually the vehicle began to slip down the steep bank towards the water.

'ALEC! We're gonna tip. I'm getting out.'

'Don't you dare! If you abandon ship, she's definitely going over.'

He gritted his teeth as he quickly put the gear into four-wheel drive and accelerated sufficiently to carry the Land-Rover forward. He turned the steering wheel steadily leftwards as the wheels turned and climbed tentatively towards the top of the hill. I hung on for dear life, holding my breath as I prayed to God that we would make it.

The Land-Rover ground on up to the crest of the hill, where fortunately there was a handkerchief-size piece of level land on which to safely stop and park.

I jumped out. 'What on earth did you think you were doing?'

'Me! What about you? Ready to abandon me, that's really encouraging!'

'Why do you always have to go that bit further? Look at Jean-Luc and Martine; they're content with the view down there. Alec, it's never enough for you!'

'Well, if we've come all this way, I wanna see all I can.'

'So how do you propose we get back down? I don't see any other tracks.'

'Well, it'll have to be the way we came up.'

I gulped. Should I walk back down? That definitely was not my forte, walking down slopes. Would I get back into the Land-Rover and risk the danger again of falling into the deep lake?

'Are you getting in?' asked Alec, already in the driver's seat.

I chose to join him for the risky ride.

'Pray hard,' Alec said as he looked directly into my eyes, switched on the engine, put it into gear and released the handbrake. He manoeuvred the awkward machine backwards and forwards, shunting it around to face the way we came. Like turning on a saucer.

'Ready?'

I nodded and gripped the edge of my seat.

'Let's go,' Alec said.

He skillfully negotiated the sloping dirt track as quickly and carefully as he could. I held my breath and intensified my grip, which as we all know keeps everything from falling, like when you're flying in a plane.

Alec safely and thankfully reached the point at which the track levelled out, and within a few minutes we were parked alongside the other Land-Rover.

'So how was the view?' asked Martine.

'Amazing!' replied Alec, giving me the eye. We both realized that our escapade had totally stolen the limelight and we'd only given 'the view to die for' a fleeting glance.

For supper I prepared chicken curry and rice, decorated with sultanas, diced onions, tomatoes and apples, followed by peach mousse and walnuts with a mug of coffee. As we were washing and drying the dishes, a minibus drew up containing four men, one of whom was a policeman.

'No good camp 'ere. You must come to 'otel,' said a man with a gruff voice.

'Really? But it's such a peaceful place to be,' Jean-Luc responded.

'Yes, but crazy man's 'ere and Frenchmen missing. Already this month, three people dead!'

'Sounds like a good idea to me to go to the hotel,' I offered, looking towards Martine, who nodded a 'yes please'.

'Sure, why not? They might have some cold drinks there too,' Alec said and Jean Luc unanimously agreed.

We duly followed the minibus in the dark along the dirt track for the short distance to the hotel area, parked nearby and settled for the night.

Band-e Amir – what a great place to spend the day. In the morning, after a treasured lie-in until seven, we had breakfast, then began the chores. Alec and Jean-Luc fitted a new cylinder head gasket to Jean-Luc's vehicle, whilst Martine and I did laundry. I took our dirty clothes, a bar of soap and a plastic bowl across to the falaj: where the water flowed along a manmade, open, narrow channel from the nearby lake, to provide running water for the locals. It beat pulling water from a well I thought, as I scooped the fresh clean water into my bowl. Martine and I were joined by a couple of other travellers washing their smalls and discovered that the word was out: the two French tourists had turned up alive and well.

'That's a relief,' I sighed.

'C'est vrai,' Martine agreed.

'Well, look who's over there,' I exclaimed as I looked up from scrubbing the dirty collar on Alec's shirt.

A cream short-wheel-base Land-Rover had driven into the camping area.

'Why, it's Simon and Rose,' Martine observed and smiled.

Kettle on, we all took a break to chat over a cuppa as we caught up on all that had happened since Simon and Rose left us. They had driven on the southern route all the way to Kandahar, then northeastwards to Kabul, where the fractured brake drum of their vehicle was replaced. Afterwards they drove west along the Central Route to arrive at Band-e Amir.

It was an enjoyable day out in the warm fresh air, having the occasional interaction with the other travellers. Alec's face lit up when I handed him a mug of tea, plus a mini apple pie that I had discovered and bought from the grass-hut shop over yonder.

That evening Jean-Luc and Martine invited us out to dinner to show their appreciation for Alec's help with their Land-Rover, plus to celebrate my birthday in style! We removed our shoes before entering the local mud-hut restaurant, then sat cross-legged on the firm cushions placed on the floor. The walls and ceiling were clad in a deep-aubergine cotton fabric, which was softly lit up by the light of the paraffin lamps. Green-leafed plants set in large terracotta pots stood in the corners of the room.

We enjoyed eating the delicious palaw, which was fried rice, with sultanas, carrots and chunks of very tasty meat. This was followed by chai, a spicy, milky tea flavoured with crushed cardamoms.

What a pleasant way to end the day.

Total distance driven = 25,464 miles

To Kabul and the Khyber Pass

26th September to 4th October 1977
Afghanistan – Pakistan

'Any more tea in the pot?' Alec asked as he ate the fresh bread he'd bought from the baker that morning. The baker's business was booming with the custom from the thriving hotels and visiting overlanders.

'Yes, sure.' I carefully poured us both another mugful, avoiding splashing our Bible, which lay open on my lap. 'Alec, listen to what it says here in Colossians[2]: "This is what I have asked of God for you: that you will be encouraged and knit together by strong ties of love, and that you will have the rich experience of knowing Christ with real certainty and clear understanding. For God's secret plan, now at last made known, is Christ himself. In him lie hidden all the mighty, untapped treasures of wisdom and knowledge."'

'Gosh, that says it in a nutshell,' said Alec. 'When I think back to when the Osbornes gave us that Bible, its meaning seemed totally locked up when we tried to read it.'

'Yes, now we can take on board so many nuggets from God's truth.'

---

[2] Colossians 2, verses 2 and 3, TLB.

'I reckon it's knitting us together more,' responded Alec. 'I feel much more willing to forgive you when you're a pain in the neck.'

'Me? Now when would that be?' I said with a mischievous giggle as I tickled him, running my fingers around his waist.

'Oh you know, when you fall asleep sometimes as we're driving along. I bring you all the way out to see these marvellous places and there you are, nodding away, while I'm trying to keep the Land-Rover straight on the rough roads.' He laughed as he tickled me back and I giggled even more.

'What's going on in there?' called Simon as he knocked on the back door. 'Sounds like too much fun to me.'

Alec opened the door and climbed out. I followed.

'Morning, Simon, what's up?' Alec said with a smile.

'Well, I was just chatting with Jean-Luc and we're thinking of driving onto Bamiyan after lunch. Will that suit you too?'

Alec looked at me and I nodded in agreement.

Early that afternoon our three Land-Rovers left in convoy to drive the forty miles over a mountain pass at 12,000 feet, down through another narrow gorge and out onto the broad, sweeping Bamiyan Valley. We all parked at the overlanders' camp by the Karavan Hotel at the foot of a long stretch of magnificent rocky cliffs. The six of us went to the hotel restaurant for tea and doughnuts, which we enjoyed whilst sitting in comfy wicker chairs around a smart table.

Bamiyan Valley was famous for containing the world's tallest-standing Buddha, at one hundred and seventy-three feet, equivalent to the height of an eighteen-storey block of flats. A second Buddha stood at one hundred and twenty-one feet. They were hewn out of the sandstone cliffs in the sixth century BC and were protected inside their own arch within the cliff. There were also caves in the cliff face that had been Buddhist monasteries at one time, but now the local people dwelt in many of them.

'So, Jan, are you coming?' asked Alec.

'No, you go on up. I'll wait down here,' I said, knowing that I might freeze halfway up and not be able to move up or down.

Alec followed the others to the stairway entrance. He paid the soldier for his entrance ticket and began to climb the stairs cut into the sandstone. Within fifteen minutes he had climbed all the way up to the top of the tallest Buddha and I could see him as he walked around the Buddha's head. The face was unfortunately no longer intact above the mouth. From that vantage point Alec had an extraordinary view across Bamiyan Valley.

The following day we all set off in convoy out of the valley to enter a deep gorge between the mountains following the course of the river. In some areas the gorge widened and grass-thatched houses stood on the verge. Camels followed a track up a hill in the distance. At Doabi Mekh-i-Zarin we traversed the river via a bridge and the track led us to the most beautiful valley of all, Ajer. The green, fertile valley was bordered by imposing mountains of many shapes and colours: brown, grey, green, pink and white, like bottled layers of sand. In one area the mountains were like dominos of fallen grey rock lying against each other. A fast-running river flowed through the valley, churning up the riverbed. The valley was terraced-farmed with each plot of land watered by an irrigation system of open water channels. Cattle, sheep, goats, donkeys and horses grazed contentedly on lush pastures.

At one village a boy threw a stone at the Land-Rover and Alec stopped to tell him off but he quickly scarpered. Alec then heard air hissing and found the right rear wheel was punctured, so he set about changing the wheel right there on the narrow track. The other two Land-Rovers were blocked in behind us. We'd not seen any other traffic for at least an hour, but – typical – a local truck suddenly turned up, all in a rush to pass us by. The driver and several of the passengers decided to help, and one man managed to wedge the jack in the wrong place under the Land-Rover. For Alec, being a man who prefers to work quietly on his own, this was extremely irritating and only lengthened the whole process.

Eventually we were all on our way again and we drove to the end of the valley, where the mountains curved around in a dead end. We came across a modern bungalow, the former Shah Mohammed Zahir's retreat. He was ousted in a coup d'état in 1973. The building was being used for tourists and we could stay for $20 in the modern bungalow or pay $10 to sleep in our own vehicle parked alongside. The high costs and the manager's villainous looks had us continue on along the dirt track, where we discovered there was indeed a way through the wall of mountains.

Afghanistan's landscape outdid itself at every turn. You thought you couldn't be more impressed or surprised by any other formation of rocks, cliffs, rivers and so on. Now we entered a hidden, narrow, formidable gorge that was awe-inspiring. We drove as far as we could until we came to a lake, where the track virtually disappeared, and we left our vehicles to walk and explore the area. Mighty cliffs towered above us. A waterfall gushed forth from a natural spring, flowing down the rugged, rocky wall and splashed luxuriantly into the lake that we walked alongside. What a privilege to be standing there in the midst of a secret treasure of natural, raw beauty.

Suddenly two men from the Shah's retreat four miles away mysteriously turned up on foot. One of the men, the 'villain', was holding back a jet-black guard dog that growled and snarled its teeth at us. They warned us that we couldn't stay there for the night, as we had planned to do. Falling rocks apparently – but who knows what story they made up to force us to leave that mystical location. We obliged and actually responded to the men's request to give them and the dog, which by then was wagging its tail, a ride back to the Shah's retreat. We declined again to stay there but instead chose to head back to the nearest village to park for the night. By then it was dark and we were only too glad to call it a day.

Having explored the fascinating route across the Hindu Kush, we were eager to reach the capital city of Kabul. It took two days to drive the final hundred or so miles, across spectacular terrain following the dirt track. At one point we stopped to give a ride to a policeman, his wife and their sick child who needed to go to the hospital. Finally we reached the main tarmac road heading into the city and paid the required toll fee. As always we were glad to travel on a firm surface again, for a while at least, just to catch our breath. We delivered the family to the hospital and then searched the city to find the Green Hotel, the overlanders' campsite.

'So what did they say?' I asked Alec when he returned with Jean-Luc and Martine after their early-morning mission on the next day, a Saturday. They had been to check in at the Pakistan and Indian Embassies in the city.

'No problem, we don't need visas after all,' Alec replied. 'Are you going to be finished with the washing any time soon?'

'Why, what's the rush?'

'Well, you're going to love exploring this city, with all its busy streets and lots of interesting stuff for sale. We don't want to waste time hanging around here.'

'Okay, so if you string the washing line up between those two trees over there then I can quickly peg out the clothes.'

Alec obliged and I soon had everything sorted out and was ready to go. Just a short walk from the Green Hotel we found fresh fruit and vegetable stalls. A colourful display of apples, pomegranates, pears, melons, strawberries, broccoli, beetroot, cauliflowers, red and white cabbages teased our appetites. Then we saw the stalls that sold traditional, local crafts, a temptation to any souvenir hunter. Carpets, wall hangings, woodcrafts, clothes and jewellery were all on display. We checked in at a fabulous bakery that sold bread, croissants, buns, cookies and cakes, and came away with a selection of goodies.

Venturing along to the main bazaar that was located near to the river, we found streets of countless stores stashed high with goods: many fabric shops run by Indian merchants, shops selling nothing but teapots, and then a whole street of shops stocking new car spare parts. In a back alley we found traders dealing in second-hand spare parts taken from old or crashed vehicles. Our guys were all smiles.

That evening for supper I fixed tomato soup with herbs, followed by tuna fish, bean shoot salad, tomatoes, apples, radishes and a sprinkling of sultanas. Then fresh strawberries with milk and sugar, enjoyed with a coffee. Scrumptious!

We spent three days in Kabul, doing maintenance and chores. Plus I pressure-cooked fresh beetroot, then sliced and bottled it in vinegar. I made a few particular purchases as well: a supply of toilet rolls, as we'd heard they were expensive in India and of poor quality; a batch of razor blades to use as future bartering currency; plus twelve tins of powdered milk for an excellent price. I bought a comfy pair of baggy cotton trousers, plus a nomadic tent trim of woven burgundy wool with a geometric design, about a foot wide and ten feet long. This would normally be wrapped around the exterior middle of a Bedouin tent as decoration. It would be interesting to see how I could use it in the future, when we were no longer nomads.

Alec and Jean-Luc spent time together at the back-street second-hand spare car parts dealers' and mechanics' workshops. Our vehicle had a whacking thick leaf added to the rear spring since it had broken a few days previously. Alec hoped it would fix the blighter for good. The punctured wheel was repaired and Jean-Luc's exhaust pipe welded. Alec's nifty, ingenious repair using a clipped-on, empty tomato can had initially solved the problem by muffling the raucous din of the blown exhaust.

*

On the Tuesday we were up at six. We did our morning ablutions, had breakfast and were packed ready to leave the Green Hotel an hour later. We would exit Afghanistan and enter the northern frontier of Pakistan via the infamous Khyber Pass. Jean-Luc and Martine had a different itinerary planned, but we would rendezvous with them in Amritsar, India, on the 15th October. Simon and Rose also had their own schedule.

After refuelling the tanks and six jerry cans, we took the highway through the Pal Par Pass and into the Kabul Gorge. The good surfaced road took us through several tunnels in the mountains. Camel trains, cattle, donkeys, sheep and goats were also using the road, being herded along by their owners. The mountains rose steeply as we drove through a gorge that opened out onto a plateau. A river fed into a lake, which in turn was used to irrigate the farmed land. It was very hot at 90°F. At the town of Jalalabad, where the main street was lined with an avenue of trees, Alec stopped and bought us each a glass bottle of Fanta Orange to quench our thirst.

Further on, nomads were camped out in white tents on the grassy, rolling plains and their cattle and donkeys grazed nearby. We were delighted when we reached the Afghan border and had no problem leaving the country. We had expected the Land-Rover to be thoroughly searched for contraband.

The border post into Pakistan was buzzing with life: teahouses, shops and many moneychangers. The passport office was straightforward, but the customs officials were so slow processing all the vehicles and people. In the end they just checked our documentation and we were cleared to go, having paid the toll to drive through the Khyber Pass. Dusk was creeping up on us as we continued onwards through the ominous, rugged, mountainous terrain. It was not the best time to venture there.

Following in the trail of Darius the First, Alexander the Great,

Genghis Khan and many other warriors, we could see how the local tribespeople had the advantage in this strategic military location. Mindful of the western movies of cowboys and Indians setting up an ambush for their enemy, it was easy to picture how the landscape leant itself to such tactics. We passed fort-like villages, but there were few people about.

Once across the pass without any untoward incident, we stopped at the toll gate and handed in our ticket. Then a man asked us for a ride to Peshawar. We directed him to climb into the back of the Land-Rover. By the time we reached the main city it was pitch black. As we drove near to the centre, the man asked to get out. He offered to buy us a cup of tea, but we declined, knowing we needed to find somewhere suitable to park for the night.

The local police were helpful, but we had difficulty understanding one another even though they were speaking English. Eventually we arrived at the Dak tourist bungalow, which was sadly in a state of disrepair with broken windows. Inside there was a tap four feet above the floor that served as a shower and the toilet was smelly, due to the water being available only two hours in every twenty-four.

It had been a tense, stressful day as we had expected the worst scenario at any moment along the journey. Feeling shattered, we were glad to be able to unwind in our own private living space in the Land-Rover. I prepared an easy supper and soon afterwards we settled in bed for a well-earned sleep.

Total distance driven = 25,869 miles

Vignettes from Pakistan

5th to 13th October 1977
Pakistan

We were all set to explore our first city in Pakistan – Peshawar. I dressed up for the occasion and wore my brand-spanking-new, dark-green, cotton, baggy trousers along with a suitable loose, long blouse. Didn't I feel snazzy. The weather was showery, so I took an umbrella as we went for a ramble around town. The uneven edge of the road was slippery as the rain saturated the accumulated dirt and grime into a slimy gunge.

'Yow!' I shrieked as my feet slid out from under me and I floundered – splosh – in a murky, oil-slicked puddle at the side of the bustling road.

'What are you doing down there?' Alec laughed, as he gave me a hand to pull myself up.

My bottom was sopping wet and filthy water trickled down my legs. I looked a proper charlie.

'Oh, great! I guess we'll have to go back now,' I grumbled.

Fortunately we had not walked far, so I soon washed and changed, leaving my latest fashion piece soaking in a bucket.

We returned to the streets of Peshawar, which throbbed with passing traffic. The buses were amazing – converted Bedford trucks, colourfully painted and decorated. Their cabs were festooned with tinsel and novelties hung from the rearview mirrors. There were red, yellow and blue perspex windows for the passengers to look through as they sat in the back on wooden benches.

We walked over the bridge that crossed the railway track and on to the town centre. There we saw a sign for an insurance agent and entered the office to buy the required third-party vehicle insurance for Pakistan. A complimentary cup of tea was part of the deal.

Next we needed to find the pharmacy to buy tablets to treat a persistent dose of dysentery. Ever since we'd eaten that birthday meal in Band-e Amir, we'd been out of sorts. Maybe we'd picked up a few intestinal worms. The chemist assured us that his recommended medication would kill and cure everything, so we gave it a go.

As the rain was pelting down we took refuge in a shoe shop stocked with handmade leather shoes, sandals and slippers. We had fun trying on the local styles. Some felt comfortable and some not so. After visiting several shoe shops along the street we made our purchase. Alec bought brown leather sandals that would be very practical, whereas I was drawn to a pair of glitzy, gold-thread-decorated leather slippers like a genie would wear. Typical – as I love glittery things!

Our next stop was at a workshop where mechanics rebuilt engines. The men welcomed Alec's obvious interest and on the kettle went for another cup of tea. So the day continued as we explored the fascinating town, street-by-street and shop-by-shop.

The next day we drove twenty-five miles south to Dara, an infamous town where craftsmen made weapons copied from Kalashnikovs, rifles and pistols down to pen guns. We wandered along the street, stopping to peer in the multiple workshops. Men were fashioning bullets by the hundreds. At one workshop there was a right ingenious

Heath Robinson creation. It had a big electric motor mounted on a bracket that was fixed high on a wall. It drove a set of machines, belts, pulleys and fans, all connected to one another and doing all sorts of engineering activities, including polishing the interior of rifle barrels.

Every so often a gun was fired outside towards the sky – a prospective buyer, testing the goods. BANG! BANG! The sudden sound made me jump every time.

We asked a craftsman the cost of his weapons and he showed us two rifles, which looked similar but varied considerably in price. Apparently the cheaper one was more dangerous to the user than what he would be shooting at. If you had the money, you could buy whatever you wanted.

We left Dara and drove ten miles to the north, where we were stopped at a police checkpoint. On our journey down a policeman had insisted we pay him money, but we refused and drove on. This time a policeman put his hand into the open window of our Land-Rover and grabbed our radio. Alec swiftly snatched it back. The policeman was ranting and raving – 'Hashish!' – so we made a quick getaway.

There was no telling how officials would present themselves to you because later that evening the police at a timber checkpoint stopped us. Were we carrying any wood? We assured them we were not and they offered us a cup of tea and granted our request to camp nearby for the night.

After a good sleep, we left the police checkpoint by seven-thirty to venture through Swat Valley. It was a bright sunny morning, and it felt good to be alive and well. Every day we had a new opportunity for discovery and appreciation of different cultures.

As we drove northwards we passed nomadic families migrating southwards for the winter months. Young children and chickens were carried along on pack donkeys. The men and older children were shepherding tall sheep and goats. Mothers carried great baskets filled with kitchen utensils on their heads. Small mongrel dogs scampered alongside, stopping every so often to sniff in the grass.

The windy road ran parallel to the rushing river of clear blue water that washed over the rocks lodged in the riverbed. Mud and stone flat-roofed houses were perched on the hillside. An old man dressed in striped pyjamas had a bright-orange, henna-dyed beard. He sat on the edge of his wooden-framed bed, strung with plaited string, enjoying the warmth of the morning sun as he watched the world go by.

Black water buffaloes grazed on grass or wallowed in muddy water. Crops of maize and rice grew on the terraced land. As we drove deep into the hills, the pine forests looked resplendent with their rich green adornment.

At Kalam we crossed the river over a bridge and found ourselves on a rough track for six miles, winding onwards and upwards to a village built close to the source of the Ushu River. We were surprised to see camels up there, arriving with sacks of potatoes from the lower valley farms and returning loaded with firewood. In the distance the magnificent Mount Falakser at 19,415 feet, stood proudly. We enjoyed the spectacular view as we stopped for lunch, before making our way back down to Kalam. We were waved down a couple of times to exchange travel news with overlanders in their vehicles. It was refreshing to have this western contact along the way, to encourage each other in unfamiliar territory.

That evening we chose a campsite well away from any village, but were soon discovered by a group of twenty local boys and girls, who persistently hung around and even climbed up onto our Land-Rover. It annoyed us to have this intrusion into our personal space at the end of the day. Even after travelling for so long, we remained disquieted by this cultural clash.

*

On Saturday 8th October, it was 8 months since leaving England and we had driven 26,352 miles. During that day we drove almost two hundred miles over mountain passes and along farmed valleys. Most of the main roads were tarred and we actually saw one being made. Humbling to see the job was all done by hand, using shovels, buckets and wheelbarrows – there was no mechanization at all.

Alongside the road under construction, several women sat cross-legged on the grass verge with a heap of football-size rocks on one side and a growing pile of gravel on the other. They painstakingly broke up the rocks with hammers and chisels. Their small toddlers played close by, scooping up the gravel in their pudgy hands to let it go from a height and watched the dust fly away in the breeze. A mother, with her crying baby wriggling in a cloth tied to her back, paused from her work for a moment to reposition her baby to suckle at her breast.

The men were swarthy and muscular, blackened by the smoke that rose from the stinky, molten tar that they carried in buckets to pour onto the prepared road. A labour-intensive operation: there were even two men operating one shovel – one man dug the earth, whilst the other pulled the shovel by the tied-on rope, to move the soil in a synchronized motion.

Lahore was the city we reached after a further two days of travelling. A key location for us, as it was the next Poste Restante collection point. At the post office we were rewarded with eight letters from family and friends. Such a treat to be reconnected with loved ones and read their good news.

We stayed in Lahore for three hot, humid nights. We strung up our net to keep out the clouds of whining mosquitoes. They were out on the battlefield, eager to suck fresh, British blood. They were restless nights of tossing and turning, only to be woken at the crack of dawn by the mullahs' call to prayer from the minarets that towered above the rooftops.

Washday at a farmhouse. Romania 11/8/1977

Lenin stood over Sofia. Bulgaria 20/8/1977

Ferry terminal at Galata Bridge, Istanbul.
Turkey 25/8/1977

Lakeside lunch break. Turkey 29/8/1977

A Kodak moment for Jan in Esfahan. Iran 31/1/1978

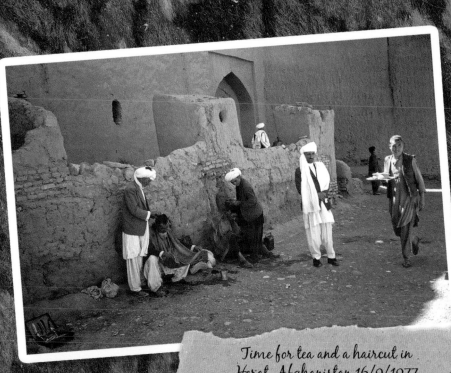

Time for tea and a haircut in
Herat. Afghanistan 16/9/1977

Fabulous fruit stall in Herat. Afghanistan 17/9/1977

Nomadic family and their home on the move.
Afghanistan 20/9/1977

The village lady who had a toothache.
Afghanistan 20/9/1977

Jan, the patient, Jean-Luc & Martine. Afghanistan 22/9/1977

Steady as you go! Afghanistan 22/9/1977

Driving across a wobbly bridge by Minaret of Jam.
Afghanistan 22/9/1977

A memorable birthday at Band-e Amir. Afghanistan 24/9/1977

The standing Buddha overlooks the overlanders' campsite, Bamiyan. Afghanistan 27/9/1977

The standing Buddha's eye view of the Bamiyan valley. Afghanistan 27/9/1977

How hot do you like your curry? Pakistan 8/10/1977

En route to Leh, Ladakh in north-east, India 19/10/1977

Captured moment in Leh, Ladakh. India 20/10/1977

Highest Point Of The World's Highest Road,
18,380 feet, Ladakh. India 21/10/1977

Jan, Jean-Luc & Martine on 'magic' bikes
touring Srinagar, Kashmir. India 2/11/1977

Pushkar Fair, Rajasthan. India 25/11/1977

The ghats of Varanasi leading down to
the River Ganges. India 2/12/1977

Making our way to Kathmandu. Nepal 11/12/1977

*'Where do you want to go to, mister?'
wondered two little girls in Patan.
Nepal 14/12/1977*

The Nyatapola Temple, Bhadgaon. Nepal 18/12/1977

The Taj Mahal, Agra. India 7/1/1978

The Golden Temple, Amritsar. India 16/1/1978

A spot of lunch on the beach. Greece 28/2/1978

Sunset view of Mount Olympus.
Greece 27/2/1978

The overlanders' campsite in Lahore was in the grounds of the Salvation Army centre. We were thrilled to make use of their showers. It felt good to be in fresh clothes and to have clean hair, especially when a local Christian who worked at the centre invited us to his home for dinner.

Early evening the man came to meet us and we drove together in our Land-Rover to his home, just fifteen minutes away. We were introduced to his wife and eight children, who all lived in a small, simply built house with an inner courtyard. For dinner we enjoyed a delicious lamb curry and rice with bread, apples, bananas, sweets and a choice of water, tea or Coca-Cola to drink. Such generosity!

We heard from the host about life as a Christian in that Muslim country. Apparently if the opposing party came to power then no new churches would be allowed and all Christians would be required to wear a uniform. We were disturbed by this revelation, as we had never really thought about the life of Christians in other countries. Our own faith and understanding of the Church was in its infancy. We exchanged addresses and photographs and hoped to keep in contact with the family.

Back at the campsite we found that Jean-Luc and Martine had arrived a day earlier than expected, and before we had all reached Amritsar. We exchanged news of one another's adventures during our time apart and planned for the journey to come.

Before retiring to bed, Alec and I poured over the map of India and were full of wonder and anticipation of what we might see and experience there. We checked that all the official documents were in order, and then reckoned up our foreign cash and traveller's cheques for declaration at the customs post the next day.

Total distance driven = 26,866 miles

Tibetan Treasures

14th to 20th October 1977
India

Back in convoy with our Swiss companions, we left Lahore at seven-thirty and went along the Grand Trunk road that led to the border crossing. The road was already in full swing with a mixture of traffic and animals moving along. It was unfortunate that early on the journey we had a puncture, so we all waited for Alec as he switched the damaged wheel with a spare one.

In Pakistan, we were impressed by the smart, military police and customs officials and we were equally taken by the striking, turban-wearing soldiers at the Indian border. There the efficient customs clerk had an eye for detail, when for the first time in all our travels he noticed a discrepancy on our car documents. He observed there was no registration number on the vehicle carnet and the chassis number was incorrect. Suspicion aroused, he informed the officer in charge. Then the Captain himself carried out a thorough inspection of the contents of the roof box and all the storage space within the vehicle, including underneath the bed. Fortunately he found nothing untoward and gave us the go-ahead, despite the inconsistencies on our documents. Thankfully Jean-Luc and Martine had no problems.

We drove a distance away out of the vision of the border guards and pulled onto a clearing beside the road, shaded by the trees and overlooking rice fields. The adrenalin surge from the uncertainty of the outcome at the border had given us all an appetite for lunch. A small herd of water buffalo ambled by with their young herdsman, who walked along with his stick held behind his neck, his hands holding each end. He stood for a while and watched us, before hustling his animals along the road, from where they had stopped to graze on the grassy verge.

In the following days we headed north, firstly to Kashmir in Srinagar, where we stayed one night, and then northeast towards Ladakh, little Tibet, a region we hadn't anticipated visiting. Five days after arriving in India we were high in the mountains. At six in the morning it was only 32°F, rather fresh to say the least. The water in the vehicle had iced over and the engine was slow to start as we prepared to set off.

A beautiful, clear morning as the sun highlighted the stunning view below, where the river meandered along the valley floor. Rugged mountains were all around, with Namikala, at 12,198 feet, regally adorned with its glistening white snow cape.

At the village of Mulbekh we noticed the striking architecture of the houses in the region: very attractive, sturdy white houses, two- to three-storeys high; some had balconies and all had smart glass-paned wooden framed windows. On a few houses, the windows were creatively installed together on two walls, at the corner, affording spectacular views.

The road took us up and through the Namikala pass, a rocky brown mountain landscape. A military convoy overtook us, as we enjoyed driving along the excellent tarmac road. Men and women were busy with road maintenance. It was an incredible climb to reach the highest point of the Srinagar-Leh road at 13,479 feet.

The descending, winding road was an amazing feat of engineering. The attractive scene of Lamayuru region was laid out before us, with the stunning, coloured rockfaces being explored by a small flock of mountain goats and sheep. Their nimble shepherd boy, boldly jumped from rock to rock.

At the bottom of the pass the road followed the course of the striking turquoise-blue river for several miles. Then it left the riverside and followed a dry, barren valley, climbing out onto a plateau where the road was unusually straight and flat. We could see for some fifty miles ahead with snow-capped mountain ranges all around. Leaving the high plateau, the road wended its way down to a forested valley in all its autumnal glory.

We were thrilled to arrive safely in the town of Leh and we parked in the grounds of the New Leh Motel, prepared and ate supper, then went early to bed.

After a delicious pancake breakfast we were ready explore. The town was a buzz with the locals, who welcomed us and were quite happy for us to take their photos too. There was little traffic on the streets.

An old man held the wooden handle of his personal prayer wheel. The cylindrical, carved wooden barrel turned around and around as he mumbled prayers under his breath.

A younger man was wearing a wide-brimmed hat and his long hair was in two plaits tied together. Dressed in earthy-coloured clothes, he looked like a tracking scout from a wild west movie.

The Tibetans' clothing fascinated me: very warm ethnic outfits with a dramatic addition of distinctive hats. The women and teenage girls wore straight and loose trousers, either brightly coloured or in a sombre, dark tone. Over the trousers they wore heavy, wraparound, long-sleeved, midi-length coats which were made of either woollen cloth, corduroy or velvet in black or brown, lined with a brightly coloured fabric. Over the coats they each had a brocade waistcoat with a mandarin collar and draped from their shoulders was an embroidered, tasselled shawl. Their thick, black, plaited hair reached far down to their lower backs. It was interwoven with wool, and the two plaits were tied together with ribbons at the end. On their heads they wore fascinating, tall hats with deep wings on each side, made from either quilted brocade or velveteen in black, brown or purple, lined with red. A couple of women each wore a black fur hat of a slightly different shape with an extra flap of stiff fabric, which curled back from the forehead and went down over to the nape of their neck. This panel was decorated with flat chips of turquoise stone sewn in place. High, cosy boots made of knitted wool with leather soles completed their outfit.

The men wore similar coats, some made of sheepskin, others a maroon woollen fabric. Their hats were lined with sheepskin and they had boots like mukluks. Babies and some of the children wore knitted woollen hats. The women carried their babies on their backs held by lengths of fabric tied around their middles. Some of the ladies were busy knitting gloves, socks and hats using four steel knitting needles each, creating intricate, colourful designs with seemingly no printed pattern.

The intimate social interaction between the people was very noticeable, especially after weeks of travelling through Muslim countries where men and women had separate daily activities and were clearly not free to show any warmth to each other in public. Here, amongst the Tibetan people, we saw men and women holding hands as they walked along the street. I saw teasing, laughing and much smiling amongst the people of all ages. It was warm and appealing and made for a comfortable atmosphere for us foreigners.

The teashops served hot, milky tea in glasses, savoury snacks and fudge-like sweets to tempt us. The general shops sold everything from tea leaves to bras. The butchers had very primitive facilities. There were also cloth merchants, tailors, hat makers and boot craftsman. The embroidered felt boots were fashioned with thick soles.

Vegetable traders, mostly women, sat on the ground with a cloth spread out displaying their limited produce: carrots, cauliflowers, cabbages and potatoes.

A pack pony down from the mountains, with his rugged, wild-looking owner, had come to Leh to collect supplies.

Tourist shops were open to cater for the few intrepid visitors who ventured so far in the northeast of India, hundreds of miles away from the typical Indian tourist sites that we had yet to explore. Buddhist prayer wheels, metal bells, jewellery, embroidered shawls, traditional clothing and very attractive, small, dragon-patterned carpets were on sale.

We stopped to examine the precious and semi-precious stones on display. I was attracted to the rich, deep purple Alexandrite stones that were ready cut. I thought one would make a pretty ring, being in one of my favourite colours and bearing the name of my man. There was one weighing four carats that caught my eye. At twenty-five rupees a carat that would be one hundred rupees, which was roughly seven pounds and fifty pence, an expensive souvenir for us at that time, so we didn't make a purchase.

The town well explored, we wandered along the back alleys and through low, dark tunnels connecting the houses. The warm, rural smell of the cows in their sleeping quarters wafted our way. Walking close to the houses, we could see the attractive, carved woodwork of the doors and windows that showed another example of creative and detailed craftsmanship. A full and satisfying day drew to a close.

Back at the Land-Rover, I cooked the fresh white cauliflower I had bought from one of the veggie ladies and poured over a tasty, hot cheese sauce made from cheese powder. This was followed by sweet, warm pink blancmange and tea.

We enjoyed a peaceful, contented sleep that night in a remote and fascinating part of the world.

Total distance driven = 27,480 miles

Exploring Ladakh

21st to 24th October 1977
India

We were up at five-thirty, dressed and packed, and away by six, as were Jean-Luc and Martine, to go on a daredevil adventure together, when an early morning start was to our advantage. It was still dark as we drove in convoy, taking the road north out of Leh. We passed by big signs written in English – 'Tourists to Report to the Police' – 'Do Not Drive One Mile North of Leh'!

But there was also another sign along the road: 'To the Highest Point of the Highest Road in the World'. For Alec, who had stood at the South Pole in Antarctica, this was a priceless opportunity not to be missed. The road climbed steadily up and up and the scenery became more spectacular the higher we went. Giant snow-capped, mountains surrounded us.

I felt the jitters as we went past a public works camp as quickly as we could in our Land-Rovers. The loud engines were full on, steadily ascending the mountain road. Wisps of grey smoke puffed out of the tent chimneys, but no one stirred and my jitters fluttered away.

Fifteen miles from Leh stood another sign: 'No Visitors Beyond This Point'. The barrier bar was raised high in the air and the guard

251

was sound asleep in a small khaki tent beside the road. Nothing ventured, nothing gained, so we pushed on, aiming to be as far away from the military post as fast as we could, before anyone was alerted. The switch-back road with its hairpin bends enabled us to gain height rapidly, until after another ten miles we reached our destination. Our Land-Rover had exerted itself to the full, burning a gallon of petrol every seven miles of the steady ascent.

We proudly took photos of the Land-Rovers and ourselves at the formidable mountain site. Behind us was a giant sign declaring that we were at the 'Highest Point of the World's Highest Road – 18,380 feet'. The panoramic vista of majestic mountain peaks, ridges and steep descents took our breath away in more ways than one. Being six thousand feet higher in such a short time since leaving the town, our oxygen levels were severely depleted and we all felt quite heady, thus we moved about slowly. To celebrate the significant moment, we ate our breakfast with a highly elevated cup of tea.

Four public works department lorries came by and continued onwards along the road that led to the border with China. It was tempting to drive on to see what else there was to discover, but wisdom prevailed: we knew it was indeed forbidden territory. Reluctantly we began the descent to Leh. On reaching the military post, the barrier was down and the armed soldier was now fully alert and on duty.

'Where are you going?' he demanded.

'To Leh,' Alec replied.

'Didn't you see the sign? This is a military zone.'

Better to act dumb, Alec thought, as he shrugged his shoulders.

The guard raised the barrier and waved us on: a shrewd decision not to call his officer, knowing it was he who had slumbered when we'd passed by at dawn.

Back in Leh we made straight for the teahouse and sampled the samosas – triangular, deep-fried pastries filled with yummy potatoes and curried bean sauce.

Later on that day we all four went to explore further in the Ladakh region, heading south along a wide valley. There were many attractive villages and herds of ponies grazed on sodden grass. Built at strategic points along the valley were a great number of stupas: Buddhist shrines shaped like solid mounds or domes.

Twenty-five miles from Leh we came to another barrier across the road. The military policeman had us write down the details of our Land-Rovers and passports in the official records book. We were surprised to see a young European woman walk out of a teahouse near to the military checkpoint.

'Hello. Any chance of a ride to Hemis Gompa?' she asked. It turned out that she'd been living in that village for the past year.

Jean-Luc and Martine welcomed her into their Land-Rover whilst we carried her groceries and fresh vegetables in ours. Not a bad idea to give a ride to someone going to where you want to go, when you are a stranger and the signs are few and far between.

We branched off the main road and crossed a bridge. Then we followed the route into a small valley, climbing steadily as we passed more stupas, which were connected by stonewalls. We reached the village by Hemis Gompa, which was built on the side of the hill. Men and women were laying a cobble-stone road and the women sang as they worked. We drove as far as we could and then parked on a level clearing. The young woman disappeared with her shopping into the labyrinth of village pathways between the substantially built houses.

On our visit to Hemis Gompa, the biggest Buddhist monastery in Ladakh, we found it to be an impressive building, both in structure and detail. There were many colourful wall paintings depicting Buddha. A huge golden Buddha statue was on show and prayer wheels small and large were set into alcoves in the walls. We climbed right up to the flat roof of the building and saw men, women and children carrying grey soil in baskets on their backs to other men who were renovating the monastery.

In next to no time dusk had fallen, so we returned to our vehicles and drove away from the village to find a suitable private place to camp for the night.

The following day we had the opportunity to venture beyond Hemis Gompa when we walked for an hour along a rocky dirt track. It led us deeper into the valley and higher up the mountainside to a small, hidden monastery built into the rock face. The climb was tiring due to the altitude, but well worth the effort for the welcome that we received from the middle-aged lama, the Buddhist monk who lived there. He invited us to sit on his balcony beside a pile of onions. In the corner, dried dung was stashed away, waiting to be used for his fire. Golden marigolds, blue cornflowers and pink stocks grew strongly in tin boxes alongside the wall of his home, adding vibrant colour to the otherwise grey backdrop.

In his generous spirit the lama served us rancid, salted butter tea, a drink favoured locally and so suited to the cold and tough environment. The tea tasted strange to our western palates, but the butter moistened our lips. Our tummies warmed, we were then invited into the monastery. After removing our shoes we entered a cold room with a wooden floor. Colourful fabric was fitted from floor to ceiling, covering the mud walls. It was fixed in place with a painted wooden trim. Buddha statues and photos of lamas were displayed around the room. Several glass cabinets were set against the walls, providing storage for the many 'books' piled deep on every shelf. The books were in fact made up of four to five-inch wide strips of handmade paper, which were inscribed with printed religious script. A collection of these paper strips were bound in leather and kept between two flat pieces of wood.

The lama beckoned us to follow him outside, down a few steps and around several corners until we reached a second room with a similar layout to the first. In a central glass case was a four-foot-high, sitting golden Buddha statue. We were in the printing room. I noticed a cupboard that stored many wooden blocks with the script carved out in reverse.

The lama proceeded to give us a demonstration of how a print was made. He sat on a rug with a wooden block in front of him on which he placed a carved wooden slab. Taking a metal dish containing soot, he mixed in a little water and poured some onto a flat rock. He rubbed it with a shoe brush and stroked the sooty water onto the carved wood, then pressed a piece of rice paper onto the blackened, carved wood slab and the print was made. We bought a copy each – an authentic souvenir.

From there the lama directed us to the nearby house where he banged a stone on a rock to gain attention. An elderly, barefooted man with a wispy beard invited us in to see his shrine. First we walked through his dwelling, where the walls were adorned with several tankas, cloth scrolls painted with Buddhist themes. This led into a cave with rock paintings and five statues. Money and coins were stuck to the rock face.

After a fascinating morning we took the easy climb down the mountain to reach the Land-Rovers by noon, and returned to Leh in time to explore the handicrafts again. I really wanted to buy an Alexandrite stone for a ring and managed to find a beauty for just twenty rupees.

The drive from Leh to Srinagar took three days. There had been significant snowfall on the higher passes, making the task a greater challenge.

We stopped en route at the Lamayuru Monastery, located in a village that clung to the side of a mountain. It was a real spectacle to see the monastery in full action. We were invited in by the cheerful lamas to see the bright paintings on the walls in the entrance hall of the monastery. Incredible images of their gods were depicted. Inside the building, the pillars and the wood-beamed ceiling were all colourfully painted with geometric designs. Statues of gods stood at the far end of the room. Long, narrow carpets partly covered the floor. We were welcomed further into the heart of the monastery to a prayer shrine. Four men from young to old, clothed in flowing, orange fabric, sat cross-legged on carpets, each with a traditional loose-leaf book open before him. They read and chanted prayers to the beating of a drum and the sound of ringing bells, creating an eerie atmosphere.

Total distance driven = 27,747 miles

Fine Work

25th October to 2nd November 1977
India

It poured with rain all the next morning as we drove the last 70 miles back to the region of Kashmir. We arrived at Srinagar, a country city nestled in a valley, surrounded by the foothills of the mountain range we had just explored. We made a beeline to a teahouse, as we were parched, chilled and hungry.

As we tucked into sweet tea, buns and peanut cookies, a pleasant, young man approached us. 'Good morning,' he said with his palms together and with a slight bow. 'Welcome to my city. Please may I take you to the shops to see all the beautiful things?'

It must have been the effect of the wet, miserable grey day, for surprisingly we agreed to have a guide.

The high street was lined with great wooden buildings and well-stocked shops, each entered by a door, rather than the whole shop being open with goods displayed directly on the streets. The town was indeed a treasure trove of alluring mementoes. There were useful boxes and small tables made from papier mâché, decorated with delicate hand-painted patterns, edged with gold. Carved wooden objects were displayed in another shop. I bought a steel carving knife and fork with carved wooden handles. The blade and the fork slid into a slot in the handle of each other, forming a wooden fish that rested in a swimming pose on tiny brass feet.

Mohammed & Sons was a store with a selection of quality leather and fur clothing. I was drawn to a fabulous, navy, suede jacket, the two front panels elaborately embroidered with pastel-coloured flowers. I couldn't resist trying it on and was thrilled that it fit. Even the sleeves were long enough. It would look great with a plain, navy, suede skirt, which I ordered there and then. Alec decided on a made-to-measure, dark-brown leather jacket.

Next the young man ushered us into a linen shop with wooden shelving along the walls, stacked high with white cotton tablecloths. The owner was exceedingly enthusiastic about the goods he had for sale. He showed us a vast selection of tablecloths of different sizes – round, square, rectangular – all with matching napkins. 'Fine work!' he exclaimed in a rich, deep-toned voice. He said this every time he shook out a cloth and laid it on top of the previous one. 'Fine work!' By the time he'd finished, the display table was piled high. Such a choice, so many varied designs and coloured threads. Some just right for English afternoon tea, with spring flowers embroidered on. Other cloths would go well with an oriental tea set, to complement the artistically sewn, fiery dragons. Between the four of us we bought several tablecloth sets as ideal gifts for folk back home, especially our parents. The fact that the traders could accept personal cheques made the purchases possible.

We asked our guide, Ali, if he knew of a good jeweller and he led the way to a silversmith whose jewellery was on display. His was such excellent craftsmanship with intricate filigree details that I was happy to leave my Alexandrite gem with him to set into a ring.

The day was drawing to a close and it was time for supper. Ali suggested we dine at a houseboat on the lake for just ten rupees each. We parked close to the lakeside and boarded a shikara, which was a local taxi, something like a gondola. It wasn't far across the lake before we reached one of the many wooden houseboats moored along the edge of an island, only accessible by water.

We entered the salon and were invited to sit at the table. A pot of tea was served first, by the young cook who'd been standing by in the hope of someone coming on that wet, chilly day. A few Soviet Union magazines were available for our perusal while we waited for dinner. Rice, chicken, curried cauliflower and dhal were well received and we even had seconds. The shikara taxi man waited for our return custom as we planned to spend the night in our vehicles at the tourist camp, which was a right quagmire with the constant rain.

Fortunately the rain did ease off during that night and the sun peeped through the morning mist. After breakfast, Alec took the opportunity to climb up onto the bonnet and check our wooden storage box on the roof rack.

'Oh no, Jan, you're not going to like this,' he exclaimed as he opened the lid and pulled out some items. I left the dishes to go and investigate. He handed me my midwifery textbook, which was sodden from the rain seeping into the box on the one side. I'd brought it along on the trip in case I found work along the way.

'Not worth keeping, Alec. How are the other books?'

'Oh, they feel damp, but still readable. We should find a dry space inside the Land-Rover to store them now.'

He handed me all the books, plus the engine gasket set, which was soaking wet. I placed the latter on the flat surface of the mudguard, hoping the fragile gaskets would dry out.

Jean-Luc and Martine needed to replace their roof box with two metal boxes they had bought in town the previous day. Jean-Luc had unfortunately wrecked their box when he had reversed into low cables at a mountain village in Ladakh. He used some of the wood to create two small cupboards in their Land-Rover and Alec took the two large panels and made a shelf above our heads in the cab of both vehicles. It was fantastic to have more storage space. Along with that task, Alec replaced the broken leaf springs he had discovered on both vehicles. We were all busy throughout the day with routine maintenance, cleaning and sorting.

Our first taster of the houseboat experience enticed us to give it another go, but with an overnight stay. We booked two one-bedroomed houseboats side by side. Jean-Luc and Martine joined us in our salon to have supper. A young boy had the challenge of keeping the wood burner fired up all evening. The fire began well with some dry tinder, but the damp logs struggled to catch alight. Everyone had a go at blowing into the open metal door, trying to encourage a lasting flame. The activity caused the smoke to waft out into the room, forming a woody-smelling haze that counteracted the musty, damp odour of the humble boat.

Tea was served once again. The Indian style of serving tea was so delightfully British too: a little milk poured into a dainty china cup, followed by scalding black tea and a spoonful or two of sugar.

We were entertained during the evening by visitors, who seemingly invited themselves in. One Indian fella constantly interrupted our conversation with many questions, all spoken with that wonderful accent and accompanied by the nodding of his head from side to side.

'Vhat 'ave you been doing today?'

'Vhat did you buy?'

'Vhat vill you do tomorrow?'

A tailor turned up, smartly dressed in his pinstriped suit. He tried to persuade Alec and Jean-Luc to order made-to-measure suits: a two-piece for only thirty pounds and a three-piece of the finest quality cloth for fifty pounds. Sadly for him they declined his offer.

We waited and waited for our evening meal. Eventually our impromptu visitors left and we wondered if we were ever going to be fed. Unfortunately when it arrived it was lukewarm from the cold plates; but never mind, it was still delicious: roast duck, carrots and potatoes. Between the four of us the portions were rather slim, so we had extra rice and dhal, followed by stewed apples and more tea.

Alec and I slept well in our houseboat that night. Unfortunately Jean-Luc and Martine had a rough night, sleeping in a damp bed and with a draught of cold air breezing in through a broken window.

In the morning we ventured onto Jean-Luc and Martine's boat to use their rather smarter, clean shower, thankful that there was hot water available. Omelettes, toast, butter and orange marmalade were served outside on the deck with plenty of hot tea. Our overnight stay with meals included cost just ten rupees plus ten packets of razor blades.

Back at the Land-Rovers we stashed away our overnight belongings, before returning to our shikara driver. He had two crafts – *Son of Kashmir* and *Light of Asia*. We booked the latter for a four-hour tour around Dal Lake. The boat had fully sprung seats, a canopy and tied-back curtains. There was a small bench seat and a large bedlike seat for the passengers, so we took turns with two hours for each couple per seat.

It was an enchanting activity on a warm, sunny day with a gentle breeze blowing. The foothills and mountains began to emerge as the morning mist evaporated. The shikara was skillfully guided between floating carpets of deep-green, waxy, flat leaves crowned with exotic, magenta lotus blooms. A vibrant-blue kingfisher clung to a tall reed, swaying from side to side, as he keenly watched for a tempting morsel to swim by. He would not go hungry for the lake was well stocked with fish.

The boats used by the local tradesmen and women were slim wooden canoes, pointed at one end and square at the other, with a bench seat across for the oarsman. The lake was a busy market place in itself with canoes laden with fruit, bottles of drink, biscuits, sweets, toilet rolls, washing powder, jewellery, saffron etc. Young girls sang a lilting song as they enticed customers to buy their stunning lotus flowers. Women provided a laundry service for the occupants of the houseboats, collecting and delivering clothes, towels and sheets. Other women were on the lake harvesting edible plants out of the water, that could be cooked and eaten as a vegetable.

Our ride on the shikara went along the waterways between two-storey houses built on the banks. The locals made good use of the easy access to water and had flourishing gardens growing root crops and squash. Children played in the branches of trees that overhung the canal.

Our boat floated by many waterside shops, pipe sellers, grocery stores, butchers, tailors and handicraft workshops. Craftsmen were cutting willow branches to weave into baskets.

The tour included a visit to Nagin Lake, a quieter location where houseboats could be rented for a peaceful retreat. The four hours drifted by all too soon as we relaxed with not a care in the world.

On our way back to the tourist camp we stopped at the leather and silversmith shops to collect our consignment. The leather goods and my stunning ring were well received.

The following morning we all went to Smith's bicycle store and hired four bikes to go on a grand tour of the city. We rode through the busy streets, darting in and out between buses, trucks, bullock carts, local cyclists, pedestrians, goats, cattle and water buffalo. I felt vulnerable and unprotected and was glad when we headed off along the narrow side streets that were mostly used by pedestrians.

Cycling along at a gentle pace, it was easy to stop at any time. We happily responded when a carpet salesman beckoned us over. He invited us into his workshop where a beautiful silk carpet was being woven on a grand, old, motorized machine. He then directed us to climb the exterior stairway up to a balcony that stretched the full length of the house. The first open door we passed led into the kitchen, where his wife was attending to her morning chores. Pots, pans, ladles and spoons hung on a wooden frame that was attached to the wall. Our host spoke to his wife as we went by.

We were directed to go into the next room along the balcony, a simple room with mud-plastered walls. There was rush matting on the floor with a cotton sheet spread over one half. In one corner was a pile of bedding and a few items of clothing hung on wooden hooks on the wall. We removed our shoes and sat on the mat as instructed by the friendly man. We were each given a blanket and a kangri to keep warm, even though it was a mild day. A kangri is every Kashmiri's companion during cold weather: red-hot, glowing charcoal, smoulders inside an earthen clay pot that is encased within a willow basket. This is placed under the holder's wool coat or blanket. Cosy!

Soon afterwards, our host's wife entered the room and set a tray before us. It was laden with a white china tea set, slices of bread and crunchy Ritz crackers to nibble on. Their generous hospitality was humbling and it was not even a ploy for us to buy a carpet; in fact there was no sales talk at all.

From there we cycled on and took a grassy, tree-lined track out of town. Water canals that simplified irrigation, intersected fields of vegetables. Wooden bridges led across a mini canal and other tracks to individual houses. It was a tranquil ride to the other side of the lake and up onto a tarmac road. Being out of the bustle of the city, there was only an occasional vehicle as we pedalled on and on through pleasant countryside, passing by a village now and again. The fresh, invigorating air blew onto my face and through my hair as I blissfully ventured along the road to our destination.

Shalimar Gardens – what an entrancing terraced landscape of formal flowerbeds, lawns, waterways, fountains and pavilions in the romantic style of the Moghul dynasty. It was commissioned by Emperor Jahangir to be built for his wife, Nur Jahan, in 1619. It was such a delight to visit the imperial summer residence of the royal court from centuries ago.

On our return to the city we rode along the busy main street, which had fascinating architecture and a variety of shops. Some lads were standing at the roadside, making a few rupees for the family by selling sheep's eyes and hooves. A group of men crowded around a medicine man. He was selling medication for urinary and stomach problems in hand-labelled, slender-necked, brown bottles with glass stoppers. He was doing a roaring trade with his slick, convincing banter.

We saw a solemn-faced bridegroom dressed in a pink, long-sleeved brocade tunic over matching trousers. Around his neck hung a gold-and-silver paper medallion. His groomsmen walked by his side as they made their way to meet the bride.

Whenever we stopped, people surrounded us and insisted on touching our bikes and ringing the bells, almost as if their local bikes became magical when foreigners rode them.

What a wonderful day we had had. After returning the bikes we walked back to the tourist camp. For supper I made pizza topped with cheese sauce, chopped peppers, onions and tomatoes, followed by a dessert of natural yogurt with slices of banana and apple, drizzled with honey.

Total distance driven = 27,886 miles

Delhi Dealings

3rd to 21st November 1977
India

Air Mail

Tourist Campsite,
Delhi, India
19th November 1977

Dear Mum, Dad, David and Paul,

Hope you're all well. Writing to you from hot, hot Delhi. Alec and I are both wearing our t-shirts and shorts today at the campsite, whilst we're busy doing maintenance and chores. I don't ever wear my shorts out and about in public on this trip, as it would be inappropriate in many of the countries we've been visiting.

The first thing we did when we arrived here a week ago was to check out the Poste Restante. Found two letters from you, one from Alec's folks and one from our new friends Nigel and Helen in Vienna. Plus the replacement rubber diaphragm for the water pump arrived too, which is a great help – thanks, Dad, for organising that.

Mum, did you win a prize for 'The Changing of the Guard' floral exhibit you created? Do Auntie Barbara and Auntie Peg still go to Floral Art?

We called by the British Embassy yesterday and read in the Daily Telegraph that Princess Anne has had a baby boy.

Hope the bread strike is finished. For the past few weeks we've been eating unleavened bread. A novelty at first, but I've eaten enough for a lifetime and it's now a pleasant change to have sweet bread rolls here in India.

Oh, my birthday – yes, I had a lovely time. Thanks for the cards from the Aunts, Brenda, Jane and yourselves, of course. Also mention to Auntie Barbara that the little battery Kenwood mixer she gave us before we left is marvellous. I use it every day to mix powdered milk in water.

To answer David's question, up until today we have used 2,070 gallons of petrol travelling 28,876 miles, which works out to almost 14 miles to the gallon.

Amazing to think we've been travelling for over 9 months. It's become another way of life and it'll be strange to be in one place for a long time once again.

So we left Srinagar a week ago to drive over 900 miles south to Delhi via Kishtwar, Kyelang, Batoke, McCleod Ganj and Dharamsala. There we had a bit of an accident. The road was busy as we left the town and there was a traffic jam as we drove down the hill towards Manuli Khad Bridge. The bridge was only wide enough for one vehicle and the traffic was waiting for a bus to cross over. Directly in front of us was an Army truck full of troops and close behind us was our traveling companions Land-Rover and close behind him a taxi and so on. Suddenly the Army truck began to reverse towards us. I yelled and waved as Alec honked the horn. We were hoping the soldiers in the open back would alert the driver too, but no, the truck kept coming and coming until it rammed hard into our right wing.

So the rest of the day was spent at the military checkpoint, filling in forms in triplicate. They gave us 200 rupees as compensation, enough for a repair, but not for new parts. At the end of the day we were just thankful the accident wasn't any worse.

We drove in the next couple of days through Mandi, Aut and south towards Simla. Both Land-Rovers found it tough work to climb the Jalori Mountain Pass at 10,280 feet along the steep tracks. As the engines needed to cool down at the top we took a wonderful hour's walk along the ridge and saw the magnificent, panoramic view of a deep valley with its pine-forested slopes. The snow-capped mountains in the distance heralded the beginning of the Himalayas.

Celebrations for Divali, the Hindu festival of light, were in full swing as we passed through towns and villages. Families were out in great numbers, strolling happily along in their best outfits. Stalls were decorated with festive paper-chains and piled high with displays of colourful sweets and sticky cakes. Music, singing and firecrackers resounded in the evenings.

The closer we got to Delhi, the crazier the driving. We had several near-misses with buses overtaking and vehicles pulling out of side roads without even a glance to see if there was any oncoming traffic. No indicators are used; you just honk your horn the loudest and make a move.

Being here in this vast city is quite an eye opener. One evening we were wandering along the back streets, dodging between hundreds of people, bikes and trishaws. (Trishaws are a form of local taxi, a tricycle with a canopied seat fixed across the back two wheels, for passengers or goods.) Beggars crouched near a chapatti café, hopeful of a bite to eat. Many other people including whole families were bedding down for the night along the dirty, uneven pavement near the open gutters.

As for us, we were fortunate to be going back to our own mobile home and tucking into a good square meal at the camp restaurant. Chop suey, pork chow mein, naan bread, a mango lolly and a lovely coffee, all for sixty-five pence. A world apart from the locals, just down the street!

This campsite is a melting pot of nationalities. An Australian couple with a baby and young son are en route home, driving in their Land-Rover campervan. There's a French guy with his pregnant girlfriend. The usual Encounter Overland and Exodus tour companies are here with their big groups all travelling in trucks. A Swiss nurse, who lived in Tanzania as a child, is journeying alone on public transport. This mix creates a hubbub of lively interaction in the evenings.

Shopping for food in Delhi is quite a challenge, probably because it's a vast city and we don't know our way around. Fortunately on a street near to the campsite there's a good fruit and veg market, plus bread and eggs are available too. I was delighted to find India's equivalent of shredded wheat in the form of eighteen-inch-long, straight strands of processed wheat. Broken up into a bowl and soaked in hot milk, they make a delicious breakfast.

Our travelling companion Jean-Luc needed a number of spares for his Land-Rover and we were directed to Nehru Marg International Market where the car spare parts traders are. When the brakes failed recently on Jean-Luc's vehicle, Alec investigated the problem and discovered that the seals in the brake hydraulic system had become soft and squidgy. This caused the fluid to leak around the seals, making the brakes useless. Alec realized the wrong fluid had been used and it all tracked back to an unfortunate mistake made by a mechanic, months before in Switzerland.

Jean-Luc handed the plastic bag of ruined seals of various diaphragms to a store owner, Mr Singh. He was very obliging and looked high and low in his store for all the seals required, taking down this box and that and sizing up the individual seals to find a perfect match. The Land-Rover in question – a six-cylinder Series 3, Safari model – is not imported into India right now, and consequently seals with the exact catalogue number aren't available. Whilst the search was conducted, we sat on stools drinking tea prepared by the gofer lad. When all the seals were assembled in a pile on the counter top, Jean-Luc asked how much he owed. The storekeeper replied, 'You are a visitor in our country. For this reason I wish to give you these seals as a gift. There is no need to pay me anything.' We were flabbergasted by such generosity to us foreigners and sincerely thanked the kind and honourable man.

Alec and Jean-Luc worked for four solid days on Jean-Luc's Land-Rover. As soon as they finished one thing, something else cropped up. They went back and forth to buy spare parts at Mr Singh's shop and encouraged other overland vehicle owners to go there too.

As we were staying in Delhi for a few days, Alec arranged for a garage to have our vehicle in each day to repair the dented wing. The mechanics worked steadily and produced an excellent result for seventy-five rupees less than the compensation the Army gave us.

Leaving the Land-Rover parked at the garage, Alec and I took a rickshaw for a helter-skelter ride to the bus station. (A rickshaw is a three-wheeled, motorized, open-sided mini-cab that you can hail for a perilous ride amongst the crazy, noisy traffic.)

We decided to treat ourselves to a city coach tour, which took us first south of the city, where we visited the Qutab Minar, the tallest minaret in India. Built in the early thirteenth century out of red sandstone and marble and is adorned with intricate carvings and inscriptions of verses from the Koran.

Birla Temple in New Delhi is located just off Connaught Place and was commissioned in 1933 by the Birla family of industrialists. It took six years to build and was inaugurated by Mahatma Gandhi in 1939. It's a magnificent pink and white temple guarded by great stone elephants. On the interior of the temple, paintings and statues of Hindu gods are displayed.

Jantar Mantar Observatory, designed by Maharaja Jai Singh of Jaipur in 1724, was another interesting architectural construction we saw that incorporated a sundial within its structure.

We stopped for lunch at a large Punjabi restaurant frequented by many Indian tourists. There we ate a delicious hot meal of chicken curry, rice and chapattis with mango juice. As we dined, a military parade of smartly dressed soldiers with bright-red turbans marched along the street.

Nearby in a public garden two workmen were taking a nap in the shade of a tree. They had been hard at work, one leading a cow that pulled a large lawnmower that was being guided across the lawn by the second man. While the men napped, the cow helped herself to the cuttings in the grass box, the fruit of her labour.

The coach continued to take us to other historical sites, including the tomb of Mahatma Ghandi and the great Red Fort. Delhi is a fascinating city with old and modern buildings side-by-side, just like the rich and poor living in sight of each other. It's a cultural explosion of humanity in all its exotic charm, elegance and raw degradation.

Well, on that highfalutin note I'd better finish as Alec says he's hungry! We're going to the camp restaurant for one of their tasty burgers.

Lots of love from
Alec and Janice

xxxxx

Total distance driven = 28,876 miles

To Pushkar Fair

22nd to 26th November 1977
India

We had heard that it was worth taking a trip west, to the region of Rajasthan, for a rich cultural experience. Happily we were not disappointed as we explored the region along with Jean-Luc and Martine. Our initial drive out of Delhi took us through pleasant countryside with its rolling plains of sandy soil, supporting small-leafed shrubs, cacti and trees. Old forts stood at strategic locations on outlying hills. The men worked on the land with their ploughs pulled by sturdy camels, as the women cut and gathered tufts of dry grass. This they carried in baskets on their heads to their palm-thatched, rectangular houses.

Amber was our first, enchanting port of call. Love the name. As we arrived, there was a golden glow upon the historic city as the sun shone warmly on the soft-yellow-toned buildings. Long-tailed monkeys ran along the lofty ledges. The palace, positioned high on a hill, overlooked the lake. We parked the vehicles and walked the steady climb along the sloped road to the palace, passing alongside powerful elephants robed in exotic, colourful, gold-tasseled cloth, which accentuated their painted, patterned ears, faces and trunks. Paying tourists rode up high, experiencing the bygone age of the Raj.

Amber Palace was very grand. The hall of public audience, built of pink stone with white trim, had many supporting pillars decorated with Hindu symbols of elephants and lotus flowers. The doorway into the harem was adorned with natural, vegetable-dyed frescoes of floral design. Only the king, his wives, concubines, children and eunuch guards were allowed in the harem. What a stud the king must have been! In the royal living quarters the ceilings and walls were elaborately embellished with mirror work, miniature stained-glass windows and floral-decorated marble.

Jaipur was our next destination that day, a coral-pink city with white-painted accents, designed by Maharaja Jai Singh. It was the 250th anniversary of the architect's accomplishment and the city was in a flurry of festivity. There were few cars on the streets, but many trishaws, rickshaws, holy cows and people. The conglomeration of road users required the presence of a traffic policeman at the crossroads, a smart chap dressed in a pristine white uniform topped with a white British-Bobby-style helmet.

Initially we went to the tourist office, to gather information about the celebrations, and enjoyed a complimentary cup of tea. Jaipur Inn was the place for overlanders to go and park, which we did before finding food. I was famished! We all bundled into Jean-Luc's Land-Rover and went back into town to eat chapattis, potato puffs, vegetables and sauce, washed down with hot, sweet tea. Our meal was delicious and very cheap.

Next to savour the richness of the city bazaar. Ambling along, our eyes feasted on all the fabulous goods for sale. There were gorgeous, vibrant-coloured fabrics with tiny mirrors sewn on, silver jewellery, brass and copperware and small wooden elephants decorated all over with mirrors.

Two women sat on the ground with tired, broken-spoke umbrellas set open behind them, offering little shade against the sun's hot rays. In front of the ladies were large enamel bowls piled high with vivid orange marigold flowers, which they strung into garlands. The strong aroma of the flowers made me sneeze.

In amongst all the razzmatazz, I spied a local dentist with a selection of dentures and dental tools displayed on a cloth on the ground. I was glad I didn't require his services. No doubt he was a dab hand at extractions and probably put on quite the show for all to see.

Exploring further in the city, we heard an amateur band playing tuneless tunes as hundreds of pigeons took flight off the rooftops. A group of women walked along wearing their finest clothes and jewellery. One wore a gold-threaded cloak – a bride on her way to matrimony.

The day drew to a close as we returned to the campsite, relaxed and satisfied.

The following day we set off to further explore Jaipur. First we walked to the palace, avoiding the rats scampering along the open drains. The exterior of the building was a romantic coral hue with white painted flowers. Marble elephant statues stood on guard at the main palace gateway. Chandeliers hung in one courtyard, whilst in another were two giant silver urns once used to store holy water from the River Ganges. (The urns of holy drinking water accompanied Maharaja Sawai Madho Singh ll when he traveled to England for the coronation of King Edward Vll in 1902.) The ornate doors were inset with colourful peacock designs. A fine collection of miniature paintings was a delight to see in the art gallery. There was also a costume exhibition, plus arms and weaponry on display, including some gruesome knives. Only one interior room was open to the public, exhibiting red-velvet-cushioned, gold-painted chairs standing beside a silver-inlaid table presenting an ornate hubble-bubble pipe.

At lunchtime we ate vegetable samosas with curry sauce and

drank tea, served at the café in one of the palace courtyards, where musicians and jugglers used to entertain the maharaja and courtesans. A holy guru stood there with an unusual cow. She had two extra legs growing from her withers and was highly revered, wearing a pink, decorative cloak draped across her back.

After lunch we went along the lively streets of Jaipur, taking photos of the dramatic, colourful scenes around us. We stood for a while to admire the famous Hawa Mahal, the Palace of the Winds, an imaginative coral-pink structure with an unusual façade of decorative screens built in, behind which the royal ladies would view the street goings-on without being seen by the commoners.

There was much to see in this region, so we took a short drive along a country lane to Galta. It led us into a pretty gorge where a group of sacred buildings were situated along the road. We parked and walked on the pathway going up the hill towards the Sun Temple. Shrieking peacocks strutted along, showing off their plush plumage.

We were wary of a gang of monkeys that made sudden, darting movements and were often too close for comfort. They were renowned for grabbing tourists' cameras, as for some reason they objected to having their photo taken, which was quite bizarre. But they too were regarded as holy and they definitely ruled the roost in their own temple territory.

Wizened old gurus with long, white, matted hair and beards, each wearing a simple white muslin sarong, carried their only possession, a brass bowl, as they roamed about the edifice.

On our return to Jaipur we stopped for a cup of tea at a roadside stall. We were served the original chai latte made with tea leaves, root ginger, crushed cardamoms, sugar, milk and water all boiled together in a saucepan. There we sat on wooden benches at a simple rustic table with a well-worn, faded, blue-and-white-checked, plastic tablecloth. Flies flitted to and fro, supping at drops of sticky-sweet tea spilt on the cloth.

Our day was topped off in flamboyant fashion. For just sixpence each, we attended the 250th anniversary celebration of the city of Jaipur, held in the magnificent Moghul Gardens complete with gushing waterfalls. Dancers in gorgeous, colourful, sequined costumes told the story of the city in an hour-long theatrical performance with dramatic light and sound effects.

In the morning we awoke an hour later than planned, but still took time to enjoy breakfast and to read our Bible. Verse by verse, chapter by chapter we were gaining further understanding of God's truth through his extraordinary love letter, written to mankind to draw people back to himself, through Jesus Christ. We were surrounded by Hindus, sincere in their beliefs which includes Jesus as one of their hundreds of gods. But we discovered that they were haunted by their karma. They needed to perform many acts to placate their gods and rise to the next level towards nirvana, through reincarnation. People whose lives were downtrodden – forced to live in the street gutters, begging and scavenging to survive – were considered to be receiving their just deserts from their former, misspent lives. We had much to process in our minds as we travelled amongst the variety of cultures and beliefs, briefly seeing through the 'windows' of people's daily lives.

Contemplation set aside, we got back to the nitty-gritty of travel. We called at the petrol pump for a fill-up and bought the most expensive fuel so far on our journey. The road from Jaipur to Ajmer was initially through flat countryside with occasional hills. Then it ran alongside treeless marshlands with long, lush green grass that swayed in the breeze. We stopped at Dudu for tea and delicious cream horn pastries, and were delighted to sit on comfortable bamboo-woven armchairs with strung webbed seats. A bicycle tyre was slotted over the string-bound, circular base rim of each chair to give it durability as the chair stood on the rough earth floor of the outdoor café.

Driving on through the bustling town of Ajmer, around the

outskirts of the lake beyond, we knew for sure we were travelling in the right direction. Thousands of pilgrims were making their way to Pushkar for the annual religious festival and camel fair. Many walked, others rode their camels, whilst still more travelled by public transport and in private cars. The pilgrims carried very little, some with just a blanket balanced on their heads.

The road climbed up over a steep rise and then a smaller one until we reached Pushkar, a town built beside a holy lake. Soldiers were directing the traffic and we asked the location of the tourist bungalow. We were to drive towards the lake, but the streets were throbbing with hundreds of pilgrims, shoulder to shoulder, men, women and children all heading that way. If our Land-Rover had been made of cardboard, it would have been unwittingly carried along by the crush of humanity. A sea of people before us, yet no other vehicles. Alec gingerly drove along at a snail's pace whilst I sounded the Swiss cow horn we carried in the Land-Rover. But to no avail: this was their town, their festival and their right of way. We were the outsiders. We were no longer the centre of attention.

'STOP, ALEC, STOP!' I shouted.

A woman carrying a baby had fallen forward in front of the left wing of the Land-Rover as her flowing robes had caught under the wheel and pulled her down. At that same moment Alec slammed on the brakes and stopped the vehicle.

I jumped out and went to the woman's aid, but she had already been assisted to her feet. She and the baby were unharmed, just a little shocked at the sudden tumble. They did not stand around to lodge a complaint, but were swept forward in the surge of the crowd.

Back in the Land-Rover, I breathed a sigh of relief, knowing how fortunate we were. Had a death or serious injury occurred, we might have seen a different side to the jubilant crowd. People in intense mobs can become volatile when there has been a negative action against one of their members, even if they do not personally know the individual.

Alec reminded me of when he served in Hong Kong with the army. They were warned that if involved in an accident whilst out driving, they should keep going and head for the nearest police station to report the accident. To get out of your car at the accident scene could end in a lynching if a local person had been run over and killed.

Alec drove even more slowly as I persistently blew the horn, trying to alert the noisy crowd to allow us through. Eventually we arrived at the attractive tourist bungalow and parked on the grass bank between the wall of the bungalow and the holy lake. We backed up against the wall, but soon realized the area was being used as a public toilet, so Alec turned the Land-Rover around. Our opening back door then faced the lake, a much more agreeable view.

We then ate a curious lunch. With no bread available I decided we'd have a second breakfast of shredded wheat with sliced bananas and milk. As an added extra we dipped into our survival ration packs. When Alec was in the Antarctic, the cook told the men at Adelaide Island to go through the box of vacuum-sealed, high calorific foods that were leftovers from the scientific expeditions. A great acquisition to use in camping trips back home, so Alec took his share with our trip in mind. Now here we were in the midst of an Indian festival, surrounded by a hubbub of pilgrims, savouring ten-year-old Antarctic treats – processed cheese, toffees and chocolate!

Lunch over, we were eager to venture out into the mass of people. Being on foot was far less stressful, as we observed the fascinating gathering of Rajasthani people whom we walked alongside. Women admired and bought fabrics, necklaces and bracelets. Men looked at various leather goods on sale: sandals, cows' collars with bells on and camel saddles. They stopped for a drink, or a dish of food prepared by the wayside tradesmen and women. Sugar cane or a drink made from the same was particularly popular.

There were many lepers crouched on the floor with deformed hands and feet. They wistfully stared up at the passers-by, holding their old, rusty tin cans between their fingerless, scarred hands, which had weeping sores.

Holy gurus were at the festival in great numbers, with their long Rastafarian hairstyles, white-painted faces and minimal clothing, one just in a g-string. Not always elderly, there were men of varying ages who had been called to that religious way of life, dependent on the generosity of others to meet their daily needs.

The sea of people naturally moved out of the town to the surrounding sand dunes and the crowds dispersed to their chosen camp location, which could be a particularly comfortable dune or a welcome isolated tree that gave shade and a little coolness in the heat of the day. The children ran freely here and there, enjoying the holiday mood. Campfires burned, heating large cauldrons to boil water for cooking rice. Hundreds of fine camels and holy cows were ambling or hobbled on the dunes. Men were in lively discussion, trading and making a profit as their animals exchanged ownership.

The Rajasthani people were dashingly dressed. The men wore plain turbans in vivid red, yellow or orange. Their clothing consisted of a white shirt or a white vest and jacket. The majority wore 'skirts' fashioned from a fine white cloth folded to be a skirt-cum-trousers. Some of the men wore jewellery: earrings and chokers.

The women were robed with variations of style and colour according to their ethnic group. All wore full cotton skirts from waist to ankles with differently designed blouses, often revealing a bare midriff. Every lady had a cloth veil, from head to ankle, with one corner tucked into her skirt. The vibrant red, yellow and orange outfits were embroidered with silks and embellished with tiny mirrors and shimmering, gold, decorative trims. The ladies wore silver jewellery on their heads and their long, black hair was braided into thick plaits. Some had a solid-silver choker around their necks. Many were wearing earrings and bracelets and one particular group had multiple bracelets reaching from their wrists to the top of their arms.

We walked towards the marquees of the county fair and the agricultural exhibition, where competition winners of the finest cattle, sheep and chickens were on show with their proud owners. We went past the refreshment tents to the funfair. There were target-shooting stalls, pick a lucky number, *the Well of Death:* a display of daredevil motorcyclists riding around a vertical circular wooden wall, plus chairaplanes and even a small, hand-operated wooden ferris wheel. This had four large boxes with slatted seats upon which sat laughing ladies, enjoying the novelty of rising high into the air as the wheel was turned.

Back at the Land-Rover, we found it bedecked in clothing from the pilgrims, who were using it as a clothes horse to dry their wet garments. Each pilgrim had immersed himself or herself in the murky, sacred waters. Even city gentlemen arrived in their suits and leather shoes. They undressed to their underwear then walked along the slippery, muddy beach to take their turn amongst the hundreds of pilgrims and dipped themselves into the holy waters.

It was an auspicious night, with a full moon that lit the spectacle of men and women participating in the religious, sacred ritual. The women's voices rang out in song as they celebrated together.

We had a sleepless night surrounded by the constant movement and voices of the pilgrims.

It was not surprising the next day to hear that Martine was feeling unwell after such a restless night, so she and Jean-Luc drove off back to Ajmer Lake. Whilst Alec and I looked forward to seeing the arena events scheduled for later that day. The streets were even more congested with gregarious, festive people. Some of the men carried swords and axes, and we were particularly wary of them, especially at crossroads when there was a lot of shoving and barging, much to the men's pleasure. A few women and children were toppled over into the gutter by the gung-ho movement of the men.

We reached the main grandstand of the arena where other

foreigners and the press were welcomed. After a long, two-hour wait the events began, with camel races, a police horse display, tent pegging, a donkey race and a fun women's tug of war between the Indians and expatriates.

Mid-afternoon we left Pushkar, carefully driving against the flow of pilgrims as we negotiated our way out of town. We drove back to Ajmer to reunite with our friends and were glad to see that Martine was feeling much better.

Total distance driven = 29,206 miles

Indian Pot-Pourri

27th November to 4th December 1977
India

Ajmer – Deoli – Bundi – Kota – Baran – Shivpuri – Jhansi – Khajuraho took three full days, driving 467 miles through varied countryside, from farmland to lakes and marshlands, fording rivers and alongside uncultivated terrain with distant hills. We stopped at wayside cafés for chai and tasty savoury snacks: curried chicken, curried potato and cauliflower, rice and chapattis were a welcome break. It was then that the four of us took the chance to chat and check our maps for the route ahead.

There were so many people in the towns and villages and whenever we stopped we soon became the focus of attention. We were guests in their country and we tried to be patient, even though we were often hassled by groups of noisy, rambunctious lads, encircling us as we walked along the streets. At times this proved so overwhelming that we retreated to our Land-Rovers and drove on.

Along the roads we wove between the assortment of road users from big trucks to bullock carts that transported people and goods. Whole families were on the move, migrating with their animals.

Their water buffaloes carried wood-framed, rope-strung beds across their backs with baby goats, chickens and brass pots perched on top. As we drove through the villages we regularly saw toddlers tottering along, completely alone on the road, such little ones who were quite unaware and unprotected from the dangers of the traffic trundling by. We had to be prepared for anything and everything.

'Watch out for snakes!' someone called as we climbed out of our Land-Rover at the Khajuraho tourist bungalow campsite. I turned, having heard a familiar voice.

'Simon – Rose – how are you?' I responded, delighted to see our fellow travel companions from the Afghan route.

'Lost any good wheels lately?' Alec asked, tongue in cheek.

'No, fortunately not,' Simon chuckled. 'It's great to see you. How's it going?'

We were thrilled to catch up on news all together, along with Jean-Luc and Martine. The kettle went on and the chatter flowed for a good hour.

Before turning in for the night, I cautiously pulled Rose to the side and asked, 'What did you say before – about snakes?'

'Oh, apparently this area is known for its snakes, although we haven't seen any yet and we've been here since yesterday.'

'Well, I shan't be roaming about in the dark, that's for sure,' I replied.

When Alec checked around the Land-Rover in the morning he discovered the front right tyre was flat. He thought the Schrader valve was leaking, so he changed the wheel first thing before we headed off to visit the famous Khajuraho temples. Twenty-two of the original eighty-five temples remained. Built out of sandstone, a few were remarkably well preserved considering they were over a thousand years old. Set in pleasant, well-kept gardens, the temples were astonishing for their grandeur and hundreds of artistic sculptures: figures of animals and gods plus erotically posed nudes in sexual embracement that would take an Olympic gymnast to perform. Statues of men engaged with one or two women boldly showed the enlarged detail of their amorous body parts. It was staggering to see the skill of the craftsman who created these extravagant works of art in such abundance centuries before.

Early in the afternoon we left the campsite to continue on towards Varanasi, driving alongside farmland with a few trees here and there. There was not much to note for the remainder of the day, and we parked up for the night on a fallow field. I fixed supper: cheese and onion omelette, new potatoes, sweet macaroni and stewed apples. Gawpers were kept away when rain fell during the evening. Its pitter-patter on the elevated roof lulled us to sleep.

We awoke to a radiant sunrise; the air smelt of damp earth, and a new day had begun. After waiting patiently for Jean-Luc's Land-Rover to cough into life, we set off, initially heading towards the small town of Rewa. There we refuelled the vehicles and had potato fritters and tea, to top up our energy levels. As we continued en route to Chachai, the road passed through prosperous farming communities. The farmhouses were built of mud with clay-tiled roofs. At Chachai we saw the cascading waterfalls that dropped over 300 feet into a gorge in the otherwise gently rolling land. It was very hot and humid.

There was always something new to notice every day. The curiosity of that day was several sedan chairs carried by sedan bearers walking one behind the other along the road. The occupants were completely hidden within the fabric-covered box. There was a long pole slotted through a bracket on either side of each box, with a person to the fore and aft holding the end of a pole in each hand, like one does with a stretcher.

We stopped at a pleasant location for lunch, but soon became the locals' curiosity with thirty children, a few men and women, plus a family of monkeys, all intent on watching our every move and every mouthful.

Leaving the agricultural plain, we drove up over a rise to where the land had slabs of brown and orange rock formations – like a giant's chocolate bar with orange filling. The roadside was bedecked with green and beige wild grasses sprouting from the rich red earth. The Land-Rovers climbed up to an escarpment, which became forested the higher we went. Over the other side, the rolling farmed plateau was spread out before us as we continued to Mirzapur, a bustling, topsy-turvy town with traders' goods overflowing onto the road. Many potters were creating clay pots on their wheels as they sat in front of their mud houses. Finished pots dried in the sun. Countless children and adults were about, and rickshaws, bullock carts, cyclists and all manner of vehicles caused chaos and confusion along the streets. Fortunately the railway crossing was manned, as we waited for two electric trains to pass by.

We heard the strange zonking sound of flour mills operating as we went through some of the villages. Dusk was falling as we drove along a main street lined with pottery stalls next to one another. Each was illuminated by its own hurricane lamp, showing off clay pots of all shapes and sizes. Thirty miles short of Varanasi, we drew to a halt a good distance from the closest village and parked for the night.

Another glorious morning and off we went again, passing through many more villages on the way to the city. We saw shopkeepers trading merchandise, barbers cutting hair and women collecting animal manure from the road. They made dung cakes and carried this freely available fuel in baskets on their heads. Camels with their riders and heavily laden donkeys were being led along. Children clad in smart uniforms were walking to school. We passed several trishaws loaded with cauliflowers.

Arriving in Varanasi, we drove over the great bridge and crossed the sacred Ganges River. It was a nightmare driving through the narrow, congested streets with so many slow-moving vehicles. I misread the map and we found ourselves heading for the university. I asked a pedestrian or two and we were redirected to take the right road to the tourist bungalow, a large building in the midst of the frantic city. There we enjoyed refreshments within its quiet courtyard and again met Simon and Rose.

Alec and I spent the afternoon on vehicle maintenance, washing and grocery shopping. We learnt that the best time to view the city was early morning, so we went to bed soon after supper, in anticipation of experiencing the mysteries of the Ganges at dawn.

We arose at five, washed, dressed, ate a quick breakfast of locally produced puffed rice with milk and sugar, downed a mug of tea and were soon ready to climb onto a trishaw. Jean-Luc and Martine came along in another one too. Dawn was breaking as the young men cycled along the slowly awakening city streets. People slept on their rope wooden beds outside their shops, whilst some had already awoken and were packing their bedding away. A man toasted bread over the red-hot coals of a glowing fire, which had kept the night chills away. Teahouse owners were making their first brew for the early risers. As the trishaw-cyclists pedalled down the narrow streets that led to the river, we passed many small temples and heard priests chanting to the rhythm of a drum. As we passed along the dimly lit streets we noticed brightly painted statues of gods set in candlelit inglenooks within the temple walls.

We alighted at the riverside and paid the trishaw lad his due before we walked down the steps, known as a ghat, to hire a boat: one rowing boat between the four of us, plus two rowers, who took turns at rowing. One of the men was also our English-speaking guide. He shared with us the rituals of the people by the river at that time in the seventies.

As we floated quietly along the sacred Ganges River, the grey morning mist hovered above the water. The city came right to the water's edge. Many of the buildings once belonged to maharajas from all over India and their architectural design certainly portrayed their origins. The oars dipped in and out of the brown waters in a gentle fashion, as the oarsman drew close to the riverside. There we could observe many Hindu worshippers who had come to take to the waters – men wearing just a loincloth, and the women a cotton cloth that modestly covered their body. Down the ghats they walked, right into the river's shallow waters at the edge. Each carried a brass pot to partake in the religious rituals of scooping up water, turning around so many times, and dipping in and out.

Priests sat on mats at intervals along the steps in the shade of their grass umbrellas, ready to mark the foreheads of the pilgrims with red powder, after their sacred ablutions. Meditating gurus sat cross-legged on the steps in yoga fashion. One man in a loincloth did his exercises, which included a lengthy headstand in the high alcove of a building.

Further on we came to the funeral pyres, where understandably we were forbidden to take photographs. The bodies of the dead arrived on bamboo stretchers, the dead men covered with white cloth and the women with red cloth. The families carried their loved ones to the holy river within a few hours of their death. With high temperatures, especially during the day, this made sense. On arrival the body was immersed in the Ganges before being placed on the pyre, a pile of burnable sticks and grasses. It would take four or more hours for the body to completely burn, then the ashes would be scattered into the river, leaving the pyre available for the next body. Holy cows and stray dogs roamed between the funeral pyres and the grieving relatives. Our guide informed us that children under ten, holy men and anyone who had died of smallpox were not burned, but placed in the river with a large rock tied to them, so that they would sink. That seemed incredible to us – but that's what the man said!

After the solemnity of the funeral pyres and the stench of the smoke wafting across the waters, we were taken further upriver to see the cottage industry in the Muslim sector of the city. There we were invited into the home of a craftsman, who had a small showroom. Tea was served. We marvelled at the intricate work of the handmade cotton and wool lampshades, shirts and finely woven brocade. Unfortunately for our guide no sale was made, so we returned to the river to be rowed back to the same ghat where we had hired the boat.

It was still only eight o'clock when we arrived and the two trishaw riders had remained, hoping they could pick up another ride on our return, and they were not disappointed. We requested that they take us to the Durga Monkey Temple. There we saw many small brown monkeys roaming high on the temple's ridges. A garland of fresh flowers was placed around our necks as the priest welcomed us, but as non-Hindus we were forbidden to enter the temple.

We walked across a pontoon bridge to Ramnagar Fort, which had an excellent museum with interesting exhibits: armoury, sedan chairs, elephant seats, ivory carvings, pieces of china and a very old clock embellished with zodiac emblems. The fort also boasted the grand entertaining room of the maharaja.

By then we were hungry and glad to stop at a street stall for potato puffs with yogurt, chutney and curry sauce, with the standard cup of chai – naturally. Our exploration of Varanasi was not yet over, as we headed back across the bridge to take the trishaws to a university museum with its exhibit of sculptures and miniature paintings. Then through the maze of narrow streets of Chowk bazaar, a bargain hunter's treasure trove, to discover the Golden Temple tucked away down a side street, interestingly positioned close to the local mosque, whose white minaret could be seen beyond the temple roof. In an alcove of its own, within the temple wall, was a statue of Ganesh, the elephant god. Gifts of rice, flowers and holy Ganges water liberally adorned its base.

A call was made at another craftsman's home to observe a musical instrument, a sitar, being made from teak wood and a gourd. The friendly musician charmed us with a short rendition.

Our last call of the day was an hour's ride to Sarnath where Buddha was enlightened. There we saw several stupas and temples to Buddha; their construction was very plain compared to those in Ladakh.

What a full and interesting day. For dinner that night I made a tasty pizza and was thankful that the last purchase of flour was fresh and tasted good, not like the previous stale, weevil-infested supply.

The following afternoon we left Varanasi with Jean-Luc and Martine to drive towards Nepal. We shared the road with bicycles piled high with clay pots and baskets, leaving very little room for the cyclists. We overtook a line of elephants plodding along the highway, each with its trunk clasping the tail of the elephant in front. Their riders sat astride the thick necks of the obedient creatures, steering the giants with their feet from behind the huge, flapping ears. After sixty miles we found a clearing by the road to park for the night.

When we awoke the next morning it was a glorious, sunny day so Alec took the opportunity to change the engine oil, watched by a group of fascinated local spectators. The men observed closely, discussing amongst themselves the nuts and bolts of the task – men's talk. They were as pleased as punch when Alec gave them the old oil, plus the used filter and the shiny, empty oil can. One man offered us fresh milk and another gave us two sugar canes.

At Gorakhpur we mailed postcards to friends and family back home, then had lunch at a roadside café: rice, curried vegetables, dhal, fried chapattis and tea, all for ten pence each. We refuelled to full capacity, including six jerry cans in readiness for entering Nepal, where the fuel was reputed to be more expensive. Our journey continued along the road as we passed alongside banana and sugar cane plantations.

On arrival at the Indian border control we had no problems – in fact, no search at all. They didn't even check our declared items or money. The border post was right in the middle of the village where there was little room to park, as there are so many trucks and buses waiting too.

Into Nepal where the passport officials were quick, but customs were laboriously slow. They searched everywhere, including under our bed. They were looking for firearms and vehicle spare parts. It took so long for both Land-Rovers to be searched that it was dark by the time we left the border.

Several miles on we eventually found a big enough area of land beside the road that was not farmed or terraced and was suitable to park on for the night.

Total distance driven = 30,204 miles

In the Shadow of Annapurna

5th to 11th December 1977
Nepal

I opened the heavy back door and climbed down out of the Land-Rover. Away in the distance the soft amber glow of the rising sun, lit up the field of bright, yellow-flowered mustard plants nestled at the foot of the Himalayan Range. Standing with outstretched arms, palms raised to the sky, I breathed in the fresh mountain air.

'Good morning, Nepal. It's so good to be here!'

'Who's there?' enquired Alec, as he dressed inside the Land-Rover.

'Oh, no one yet. I'm just thinking out loud.'

After breakfast, observed by a group of young children, a few teenage boys and several girls each carrying a baby, we stashed away our overnight stuff and then began the day's journey. Interestingly we observed that the Nepalese drivers were particularly courteous and this we really appreciated.

At Butwal we stopped to pay a road tax and bought some fresh, juicy tangerines from a young girl at the roadside. Leaving the flat plains behind, we soon reached the foothills of the mountains. It was wonderful to be back in hilly countryside once again. There were charming one- and two-storey, thatched mud houses, painted white at the top and orange at the bottom. Thatched, open-fronted barns made of wood provided shelter for their animals, with a closed fodder storage level above.

The warm and friendly, round-faced Nepalese people welcomed us. The women were dressed in short-sleeved blouses that left a bare midriff, a straight, wraparound skirt and a long cloth bound several times around their middle, like a cummerbund. They enjoyed wearing jewellery, including nose rings. The men wore shirts with shorts or trousers or wraparound skirts and on their heads they had a traditional hat known as a Dhaka topi.

We gained height as the Land-Rovers climbed steadily along the winding tarmac road into the mountains. It was rough in places and partly missing in others where landslides had washed away much of the road. Spectacular scenery: green-forested mountainsides, deep valleys, snaking rivers and wherever possible the land was terraced to grow crops. There were red-leafed trees, like giant poinsettias, that gladdened the heart.

On sighting our first snowy peak in the distance, we four stopped at a village teahouse. The tea was made in a saucepan on a mud cooker with a wood fire burning underneath. It was spiced with ginger and served in spotlessly clean glasses. A pregnant lady, along with her elderly mother-in-law, ran the orderly teahouse. The latter reprimanded Alec who sat leaning back, balanced on just one leg of the stool. A tut-tut-tutting with a pointed, wagging finger put him in his place, like a naughty little schoolboy. With tea being a penny a glass, who were we to be offended?

Another road tax was paid before we entered Pokhara, the big town set deep in the Himalayas, overlooked by the imposing peaks of Annapurna and Machapuchare. We ventured first to Hotel Snowland, where Jean-Luc collected a written message from his brother Jean-Marc, who also happened to be travelling in Nepal at the same time. We enjoyed yummy apple custard pie and banana custard pie with tea at the hotel. There was a small kiosk across the road where wonderful loaves of brown bread and rounds of hard cheese were on sale. An immediate purchase was made. The Nepalese farmers had been taught well by the Swiss and had established a successful cheese production industry. The good milking cows had originated in the Alps and thrived in their new mountain home.

By early afternoon we had made camp at the peaceful, idyllic lakeside in Pokhara, on an expanse of flat grassland underneath the boughs of several tall, mature trees.

We awoke before six the next morning to watch the sun rise behind the clearly defined mountains. We were not the only ones to be up so early. An English couple travelling in a blue transit van came over to see us.

'Good morning. I'm Robert and this is Genevieve. Would you by any chance be going to Kathmandu today? Our van's big end's gone and I need to go and collect the spare part being sent from England.'

'No, sorry, we only arrived here yesterday and want to explore the area,' Alec replied. 'Have you checked out if there's a local bus?'

'Yes, that may be my best option,' Robert said, and they walked away in their quandary.

'So, Alec, how does brown bread, boiled eggs, a chunk of hard cheese, my homemade mango jam and a coffee sound for this morning's breakfast?'

'Scrumptious. I can't wait.'

At ten, Jean-Luc, Martine, Alec and I set off to walk through the town, calling first at the tourist office, where we found brochures on trekking but, strangely, no maps. The main street was very long with two- and three-storey brick-built houses and shops either side. It took us five hours to walk from the lake all the way to the end of the street and back again. One shop sold frozen chicken, pork and mutton, plus fresh cheese and butter. We checked in at a few of the cafés for snacks and tea throughout the day.

The road also took us near the perimeter of the runway at the airport. We watched a Twin Otter aircraft take off and soar steeply over the mountain peaks, in its striking fashion. The sound of the familiar PT6 engine stirred distant memories of Alec's first love of Twin Otters from his Antarctic days.

On the way back to the lake we called in at Hotel Snowland for Jean-Luc to meet his brother. They had a joyous reunion after being apart for nine months. A celebration meal in the restaurant was enjoyed as we all discussed plans to trek in the mountains.

The next morning we moved the two Land-Rovers close to the blue transit van for security, as Genevieve was waiting for Robert to return from his mission to Kathmandu. I packed our rucksacks with some basic supplies: food, sleeping bag, loo roll, torch, extra warm clothes etc. We slung these onto our backs and set out at noon, the five of us, including Jean-Marc. The first part of the walk was along a path between fields, on the flat land surrounding the lake. As the path took an upward incline I found the rucksack uncomfortable, as it hung heavily on my shoulders. They were cheap, khaki canvas rucksacks that we'd bought for such a day, but we soon realized in no way were we equipped for any serious trekking.

Part of the climb was steep and winding, while another section had steps cut out of the natural rock and then further on easier, gentle slopes. Eventually we reached Sarangkot to see the picturesque view of Pokhara Valley and the surrounding mountains enhanced by the warm colours of the setting sun. There was a hotel with a restaurant open, but we chose to stay with a local who had a stone hut we could rent for the night. The cost of one night's lodging included supper.

'Go, girl, go!' cheered on one of the other travellers who had joined us, as the Nepalese family's teenage daughter chased the chicken deemed for the pot. I wasn't sure if it was the teenager or the chicken he was rooting for. Jim, an Australian, and his Devonshire girlfriend Hilary were travelling from Australia to England by public transport.

We enjoyed the meal of rice, chicken and vegetables served in huge tin dishes and eaten with our hands. Second and third helpings were offered too. Surely not all from that scrawny, flighty bird? Jim, Hilary and Jean-Marc smoked cannabis after the meal.

The wooden plank bed for Alec and me was even narrower than the one in our Land-Rover. It was supported on four short legs and had a straw-filled sack for a mattress. Being wary of any bounding, biting bugs, we cast the itchy mattress aside. Jean-Luc, Martine and Jean-Marc pushed the other two beds together and shared the hut with us. Our sleeping bags gave little respite from the cold December night, thus sleep was sporadic.

It was a relief to rise early the next morning after such an uncomfortable night. We packed our rucksacks and hiked the final leg to the highest point at 5,223 feet. Unfortunately we saw little of any view, as the mountains were shrouded in clouds as dawn broke. Alec and I enjoyed our tasty breakfast picnic of brown bread, cheese, tomatoes, boiled egg plus rum fudge and chocolate from the Antarctic rations.

After eating, the seven of us left together to walk back to Pokhara, going down a trail of natural rock steps, which led to the flooded rice paddy fields below. We reached our vehicles by lunchtime and enjoyed a restful, lazy afternoon.

The following day we spent at base, catching up on chores that are essential whether you live in a house or in a Land-Rover. Whilst I washed clothes, having collected the necessary water from the lake, Alec cleaned and adjusted the petrol cooker. He needed to stop the flame burning yellow and leaving a nasty black soot residue on the outside of pans and our whistling kettle – a right messy botheration all around, hence I'd called the attention of my handyman to sort the trouble out.

Robert returned from Kathmandu and was busy repairing their van with the necessary spare parts. Jean-Luc was working on replacing a broken spring leaf on his Land-Rover.

It was a peaceful, pleasant day at the campsite. Welcome traders selling bread, tangerines and papaya came on by, walking on the soft green grass. The tranquil waters of the lake reflected the foothills and the majestic mountain giants.

'*VITE, VITE – JEAN-LUC!*' screamed Martine. We all turned and ran to their Land-Rover. The heavy beast had fallen off the jack and Jean-Luc was underneath.

'*Ça va, ça va, je ne suis pas blessé,*' Jean-Luc reassured everyone he was unhurt as he pulled himself out from underneath the vehicle, escaping its deadly weight. It was a valuable lesson to us all to make sure one's vehicle was securely raised before working beneath it. We sighed with relief as we returned to our chores.

In the evening we were all back at Hotel Snowland to enjoy the menu of the day: spring rolls and sweet-and-sour pork with fried rice. Why cook in the Land-Rover when the meals at the hotel restaurant were really inexpensive, yet so tasty and with extra big helpings?

I set the alarm to wake real early the next morning, as Alec was keen to see if we could catch a good, clear sunrise, and we were in luck. We drove through the town to a viewpoint that enabled us to capture the soft-pink blush on the snow peaks of Annapurna and Machapuchare as the sun rose. We parked overlooking a gorge; way down below, the turquoise waters of the meandering river flowed between the rocky cliff walls. Our early-morning venture gave us a good appetite for breakfast, which we ate as we read to the end of the book of Genesis in our Bible. Jacob's son Joseph was quite a man. Even though he became an important and rich leader in Egypt, he always looked to God to lead him.

Back at the campsite we prepared to drive on to Kathmandu later that day and Alec washed the Land-Rover at the lakeside. We arranged with Jean-Luc and Martine where we would next meet in the capital. While we enjoyed having travel companions, we loved the sense of freedom when it was just the two of us.

The day's drive of 136 miles along the excellent tarmac road, built and funded with Chinese assistance, was a breeze. The enchanting countryside was captivating all the way. Lush green foothills with terraced fields. The river flowed along the valley floor and banana trees flourished here and there. Villagers harvested their crops and their cows trampled on the heads of corn to release the grain. Others ploughed the land in readiness for the next season. The thatched terracotta farmhouses looked neat and well cared for.

An occasional truck and overcrowded bus were the only other road users. As the road began to climb, twisting and turning with a few tight hairpin bends, we travelled through the hilly countryside. Nearing our destination, we ascended to an escarpment and saw stretched out before us the valley of the city of Kathmandu.

Filled with excitement, we drove through the outskirts and ventured into the centre to find the general post office. 23 letters and Christmas cards were given to us. We eagerly located the tourist camp, parked up, put the kettle on and sat enthralled with news from home. To be sure, it was a day to celebrate, especially when we discovered that my brother Paul had become engaged to his girlfriend Joanne on the 5th November, Guy Fawkes Night.

Total distance driven = 30,458 miles

Kathmandu

12th to 17th December 1977
Nepal

We enjoyed a lie-in until eight, had breakfast, and then used the camp's showers, only to find the water was freezing cold. Oh well, at least we stripped off and washed all over for a change.

'Well, don't you look smart,' I remarked to Alec. 'Anyone would think you're going for a job interview or something.'

'Yes, well, I hope that will be the case,' Alec replied cheerfully. He was dressed in his cream trousers, brown check shirt with a tie, plus the patterned, azure-blue wool jumper from his Antarctic days, fresh socks and cleaned leather shoes.

We drove to the city airport, where Alec enquired at the maintenance department whether he could speak with the Chief Engineer.

'I'm sorry but he's away at a conference,' replied the young Nepalese technician.

'Can I speak to whoever is in charge in his absence?'

After a few minutes a smart, middle-aged senior engineer arrived.

'Hello, my name is Alec Forman. I'm from England. I've come by to see if there are any job openings right now. I'm an experienced Twin Otter engineer and would welcome an opportunity to work here.'

'The boss is away, but as far as I know there are no vacancies,' the man replied. 'You should check with Royal Nepal Airlines and see what they can offer. You'll find them in the grey hanger over there.'

Unfortunately their director of engineering was away in the USA and the personnel manager would not be in until four that afternoon.

Later in the day we returned, but there was still no personnel manager around.

'Come tomorrow and see the acting director,' the receptionist suggested.

Following repeated visits to the airport over the next few days, trying to connect with someone in authority, Alec discovered that there were no jobs. That was a real shame as I fancied living in one of those cute, two-storey, thatched terracotta houses. I could have fixed up my kitchen with those shiny copper pots and pans they sold in the market.

Well, it was worth a try. Alec had to do some serious thinking and research by letters to find a job in Britain by the next summer. We calculated that our funds would hold out until then, including the cost of the return journey.

During our stay in Kathmandu, Alec also tried to track down Ambrose, a retired Gurkha. Alec had served with the Duke of Edinburgh's own 2/7 Gurkha Rifles during his two-year posting to Hong Kong from 1969 to 1971. He was very impressed with the Nepalese soldiers' warrior spirit, work ethics and impressive, smart turnout. How was it that at the end of a hot, humid, sweaty day, every Gurkha looked as if he had just walked out of a bandbox? Alec enquired with Captain Dhandhoj Tamang at the British Embassy about tracing his friend Ambrose. Disappointingly after a few days this search drew a blank too.

*

On our first full day exploring the city of Kathmandu, we walked to the old Royal Palace. There outside the gates, atop a six-foot stone pillar, stood the shrouded statue of Hanuman, the monkey god. It was wrapped in a red veil and garlanded with fresh flowers. A red-fringed, white parasol was fixed in place, high above the statue. The local worshippers gathered close to it, bowing, touching and walking around it many times, muttering their mantras. The entrance to the palace was guarded by lavishly decorated statues of exotic, four-legged white creatures with red eyes and mouths, ridden by oriental figures of eastern gods. Entering through the palace's giant golden doors, we saw the statue of Narasimha, half-man and half-lion, killing the demon Hiranyakashipu with its long nails. Portraits of the past and present Nepalese kings were displayed inside on the palace walls.

We climbed a nine-storey pagoda to enjoy an excellent view over the city and Kathmandu Valley. The rooftops spread far and wide before us as the pagoda towered high above the white-painted walls of the buildings and distant houses.

From there we visited several other temples located in Durbar Square. In its own mini alcove was a very small statue of Ganesh, the elephant god. It attracted many locals bringing sacrifices of food, ringing bells and dabbing their fingers in the red powder by the base of the statue, to mark their foreheads.

We visited the well-known location of Jhochhen Tol, popularly known by travellers at that time as 'Freak Street'. As we ambled along we passed a number of tourist shops selling clothes, trinkets and Japanese and Chinese prints on silk and rice paper. Also on sale were crocheted cream or white yarn lampshades, formed with metal rings creating long, cylindrical shapes and decorated with natural spice pods strung like beads.

Kathmandu was the final destination for many overlanders who hoped to sell their vehicles there and use the money to fly back to Europe, or go on to Thailand and eventually Australia. Many of the western travellers were hippies seeking enlightenment, who came by public transport, braving the uncertainty of where they would lay their heads each night. They put up with the unpredictability of what food would be available, plus the frequent chance of drinking contaminated water. We saw a number who were the worst for wear, bedraggled and unkempt, with a thin, gaunt appearance and glazed, sad eyes. Unfortunately the route east provided a ready source of drugs, which trapped them further in their vulnerability. Walking along Freak Street, drug traffickers offered us dope, but we declined. We were fortunate not to have trodden that path and had no interest in doing so.

Interestingly there were other young westerners offering an alternative way.

'Hello, my name is Jeremiah. Welcome to Kathmandu.' A bearded, lanky Swiss guy approached Alec and handed him a pamphlet on 'Health and Christianity'.

'Thank you,' said Alec, never one to pass up a leaflet. 'What are you doing here in Nepal?'

'Oh, I'm with the Children of God team.'

'And who might they be?' Alec enquired with curiosity.

'Why don't you come and find out? We meet every evening at Joe's. Sing some, eat a bit, have a laugh – it's pretty cool.'

'Where's Joe's place?' I asked.

He vaguely explained how to find Joe's. We bade him farewell and went our separate ways as we continued along to Durbar Square.

'Bonjour, mes amis.'

We turned to see Jean-Luc and Martine running to catch us up.

'Well, hello, you're here already. How was the journey?' asked Alec.

'Great. No problem with the Land-Rover at all.' Jean-Luc grinned with satisfaction.

'Are you hungry?' I asked.

'*Mais oui.*'

'We're just on our way to a café we've heard about down Pie Alley,' I added.

'*Allons-y.*' Martine set off enthusiastically and we ran to follow.

Arriving at the New Style Pie Café, renowned amongst travellers, we entered a simple, cosy establishment arranged with tables and chairs. Apart from delicious pies and chai to enjoy, the management encouraged the clientele to stay and play board games and cards, to while away their time. Between us we tested the apple pie, banana cream pie, walnut cream pie and banana cake. We reckoned the owners were onto a winner there, for we knew we'd go back again for sure.

The following day Alec and I decided to explore Patan, a town not too far away, worthy of a bike ride. Bikes cost next to nothing to hire and we were soon on our way after a brief call at the bakery to buy doughnuts. Such a splendid sugar boost before we tackled the uphill cycle ride to Patan.

The town had narrow streets with two- and three-storey redbrick houses. Each had carved wooden shutters, but no panes of glass in the windows. At Patan's Durbar Square, we saw more temples with intricate carvings of gods and creatures. A royal bath was sunken in a courtyard, guarded by two carved, stone serpents and a statue of the monkey god. We had to remove our leather shoes before entering one temple courtyard. Suddenly a fat rat ran across our path, well satisfied from stealing and eating the food offerings to the gods.

Just off Durbar Square, on a side street, we came across a bookshop and went inside to search for a local guidebook. Scanning the shelves, my eyes were drawn above to the top shelf where a Bible was displayed. I pointed it out to the shopkeeper, who then beckoned us behind the freestanding bookshelf, where we discovered dozens of Christian books written in English on sale. Quite remarkable! We were delighted to purchase three for a pound. Useful books to inspire and lead us on in understanding God's truth.

We later found out why he had hidden the books. At that time there were seven hundred Christians across the country. If a Nepali Christian encouraged another Nepali to become a Christian, the first could be sent to prison. This shopkeeper, who worked for a Christian organization, was imprisoned a year after our visit. We were so new to being committed Christians that we were completely unaware of how some believers have to choose to make a stand for their faith, knowing that they could be persecuted for what they believe and for telling others.

Another cycling trip took us on a road out of Kathmandu going past Pashupatinath Temple, which was situated near to the river. Locals bathed in the water or washed their clothes. Nearby a dead body burned on a pyre.

We cycled onto Bouddhanath Stupa, one of the biggest Buddhist shrines in the world. It had four pairs of painted eyes, a pair on each side of its golden tower built in the centre, rising out of a huge white dome. The eyes faced north, south, east and west and were protected above by a blue, yellow and red band all around the tower, with a rippling dark-green fringe. Above, the squared tower tapered off to narrower dimensions and was decorated with a golden band trimmed with red tassels. All around the base of the stupa, in alcoves cut out of the wall, were placed vertical, carved wooden prayer wheels. These could be spun on their spindles offering prayers to their gods. Surrounding the stupa was a circle of shops selling clothing, handicrafts etc. The place buzzed with activity as pilgrims and shoppers mingled together.

We retreated from the hustle and bustle to a quiet place beyond the village and sat in the shade of a tree to enjoy our picnic lunch. Later we cycled along a dirt track that wound back through the village along by terraced farmland where the locals lived and worked. The weather was glorious: bright, crisp and clear.

Later, on our return to Kathmandu, we delivered our bikes to the man who'd hired them out and then we went in search of the Children of God team. We tried to remember the Swiss guy's directions within the labyrinth of alleyways and thought we had found the right doorway. Walking through and along a low-ceilinged tunnel out into a courtyard, it didn't look right, as there were only Nepalese families tending to their domestic duties. We turned to walk away when a lad came towards us and we asked him if there were any Europeans about. He directed us up a poorly lit stairway to the top floor. A babble of voices and laughter drew us to an open door. Removing our shoes, we left them on the balcony with many other pairs, and then entered a crowded room where some twenty or so westerners sat cross-legged on the floor.

'Hello – it's Alec and Jan, I believe,' welcomed Jeremiah. 'Come, sit over here.'

'Hungry?' he asked as we squeezed between the other folk to sit down. We agreed and Jeremy arranged for us each to have a bowl of rice and dhal with a mug of hot chai.

A guy was strumming a few cords on his guitar and soon everyone was enthusiastically singing Jesus songs. They all seemed to know the words, but there was a lot of repetition so we tried to join in with the choruses. They were a lively lot, especially the team who handed all the visitors a copy of a *Mo Letter*. Alec slipped one into his shirt pocket to read later on.

'Can you clear a space over here, as we're going to do a couple of skits,' Jeremiah requested, and the folk who were in the way shuffled on their bottoms to join the rest of us on our side of the room.

The first skit gave a sarcastic view of a Roman Catholic priest and the second was of a doctor doing an operation on a patient from whom he removed books, money, cigarettes and a bra. We were rather taken aback by the presentation and wondered what exactly the group was all about.

A Danish girl called Hosanna befriended us, but her overflowing, exuberant expression of her love of, and faith in God unsettled both Alec and me. We were glad when it was time to leave and returned to the campsite to bed.

After a relaxed start on the next day we took the Land-Rover out for a drive to Dakshinkali, a pilgrimage location for Hindus. On arrival we parked a distance away from the temple located down by the river's edge. The temple honoured the female goddess Kali, for whom young male goats and cockerels were sacrificed. The steps down to the river were lined with beggars and holy gurus. Traders sold fruit and floral offerings for the pilgrims to buy and pay homage to their goddess. Inside the temple many people paddled in blood in their bare feet, as they pushed their way to the statue to present their offerings. They carried brass trays on which lay flowers, rice, eggs, fruit and a goat's or chicken's bloody head. Bells rang out mesmerizingly. The slaughtered animals' bodies were taken to the shallow, slow-flowing river to be de-feathered or de-haired and thoroughly washed inside and out. After the families presented their offerings, they sat outside on the grass to enjoy their ritually laid-out picnic, served on banana leaves.

It was hard to watch the goings-on, especially the pressure amongst the pilgrims to reach the statue of the goddess, each pressing in through the crowds. How we longed to tell them that Jesus Christ, the Son of God, had made the ultimate sacrifice for sin, for all mankind throughout the world. It cut to the core of our being as we watched sincere pilgrims trying to appease their gods.

On our way back to Kathmandu we stopped in a quiet location by the roadside. We were heartened as we gazed at the majestic Himalayan snow peaks shown off in all their glory, against the cloudless blue sky. A few children came and sat nearby and we shared our tangerines with them. We were not in any hurry and nor were they, so I gave them each a piece of paper with crayons and they drew pictures. One lad showed us the pot of flowers he'd drawn. We were all too aware of our language barrier in most of the places we visited, but to take the time to try to relate in a positive, caring way was an enriching experience.

Driving on to the city, we took a turning along a road, past Tribhuwan University, to the old village of Kirtipur set high on a hill. We parked the Land-Rover at the beginning of the village and walked along the lovely, quaint, cobbled streets, noticing the intricately carved wooden window frames of the houses. Women carried brass pots to fetch water. At the top of the hill stood a temple, guarded by two stone elephant statues. Men were playing cards whilst the women removed lice from their children's hair and rubbed oil into their scalps. Everyone was very friendly.

Two young lads decided they would be our guides and showed us the various temples. One of the lads looked about nine years old and spoke a little English. They asked us to take a photo of them sitting on one of the stone elephants. We obliged and the older boy wrote his address in English for us, hoping that we might send the photo from England.

It had been a full and interesting day, with much to record in the diary that evening.

Total distance driven = 30,494 miles

Christmas

18th to 27th December 1977
Nepal

On the Sunday a week before Christmas we went in search of a little church we'd been told about. We attended the service there, led by a Nepalese minister, for a small congregation of mainly westerners. Afterwards we chatted with a few folk and they let us know about the seasonal events being organized for expatriates.

From there we went to the post office to send our letters and cards to Europe. We stood by the counter and watched the clerk postmark every stamp, to avoid pilfering.

Driving out of town towards Bhadgoan, we were unexpectedly directed by the police to pull over, along with all the traffic. We waited and watched to see what would happen next. The President of Bangladesh was visiting the country and he went by in a flashy car with outriders and a cavalcade of diplomats' vehicles.

Later on, when we stopped to take a photo of women working in the fields, Jean-Luc and Martine pulled up beside us and we continued the day together.

We visited the quaint village of Thimi and wandered on foot

along the streets. Potters were making vessels of all shapes and sizes and a mud kiln smoked nearby. Children ran and giggled as they played with two frolicking puppies. Alec was attracted to a stall selling colourful, simply made masks and bought two for his dad. They reminded him of the childhood stories his dad had told of mugwumps and pooh-bahs.

On to Bhadgoan, to its own Durbar Square, which boasted a big hanging bell and drums and was surrounded by temples. A great five-storey pagoda had large, carved figures positioned on the stairs that led up to its entrance. A lone, massive white bull wandered nonchalantly along the streets lined with open shops, as the people went about their daily routine.

Later in the afternoon Jean-Luc, Martine, Alec and I drove in our two Land-Rovers fifteen miles to Nagarkot to see the sun setting over the Himalayas, as the deep-orange sky outlined the black mountain peaks. The silhouettes included the forbidding Mount Everest at 29,035 feet, the highest mountain in the world. It was indeed a pinnacle moment of our entire journey.

We awoke early the next morning to find the hill on which we were parked was shrouded in thick cloud, just as the sun was rising behind the giant peaks to herald a new day. We were all disappointed, but thankful that we had captured on camera the splendour of the night before.

The next five days were spent in and around Kathmandu, doing chores and having a good sort-out to see if we could sell anything. It was an ideal place to sell goods, as the Nepalese were eager to have items from the west. We sold our sleeping bags, rucksacks, hiking boots and a few music cassettes that we were tired of listening to. The new owners were happy and we were glad to have a few more rupees in our pockets.

They were relaxing days when we also called by the pie café a couple of times to try the other delicious pies. Either there or when we were out and about around Freak Street, we would bump into the young men and women of the Children of God team. Members had been given a biblical name that was not their original one. It seemed that was all part of belonging to their group. Despite our disquiet from our initial visit to their gathering, they wooed us back. It was an opportunity to do something different on a cold, dark winter's evening than just sit in our Land-Rover.

We were gathering quite a collection of *Mo Letters* written by their overall leader Moses David, who was based in the USA. The leaflets were written in a comic book style and told Bible stories, intermingled with Moses David's teachings. There were always newcomers at Joe's place as other young travellers were encouraged to go along. It was a warm and welcoming place to be and there was usually a free dish of savoury rice for supper.

The pies at the café inspired us to try to bake pies ourselves. We tested several ways to cook an apple pie in a metal pie dish on top of the petrol cooker. On Christmas Eve we had success using a shallow, wide clay pot that we had bought from the dairy. It had been full of two pints of delicious, thick natural yogurt.

First Alec put three pebbles in the base of the clay pot and placed the circular metal lid from an oil can on the pebbles. The pie was all ready prepared, with the aluminium pie dish lined and topped with pastry, sealing sliced apples and sugar within. I placed the pie on top of the oil can lid in the clay dish and lifted it all onto the cooker. Then I covered the clay pot with a large metal pizza tray. Alec struck a match and lit the petrol, creating a ring of flames beneath. Left to cook for thirty minutes, the result was an excellent pie. We were chuffed to have mastered a new cooking skill in our humble kitchen.

After lunch we had a wonderful Christmas gift of hot water in the campsite showers. It was a refreshing and invigorating experience to properly wash my grimy skin. We dressed in our best clothes, walked along to Kathmandu's Durbar Square and took a rickshaw to church for the Christmas Eve service. There were Nepalese and expatriates, plus a few travellers present. Christmas carols were sung by different groups of the mission community, and a sermon spoken in Nepali then interpreted into English. Tea and festive cakes were served afterwards, a welcome treat. We walked back to Freak Street and called in at the tailor's to collect a waistcoat, a gift for Alec's dad. Then we returned to camp for supper in our Land-Rover and a relaxing game of Scrabble.

Ever since we had accepted Jesus Christ as our Lord and Saviour in the home of Nigel and Helen back in Vienna, they had been encouraging us to pass on that good news. In fact, in their last letter they enquired how we were doing in that respect, and we realized the answer was 'not so well'. Sure, we could make language an excuse, but we had not mentioned our belief in so many words, even to Jean-Luc and Martine, who could speak English. Oh, they knew that Bible study and prayer were included in our daily activities, but we hadn't told them why and they hadn't asked either. The enthusiasm of the Children of God team gave us a little more courage to speak out, so we asked Jean-Luc and Martine if they would like to come to a Christmas party being held in Joe's flat. Not surprisingly they declined, as they avoided those people like the plague whenever they saw them about town.

Christmas Day, 1977 was just an ordinary day for the Nepalese, except of course for those who were Christians, albeit for many a hidden faith. For Alec and me it was now an extra-special day and we wanted to celebrate it from the rooftops.

There were some lads who appeared to hang out all the time by the local temples; some even slept inside the buildings – real cheeky lads, who were always trying to sell little red books printed with the thoughts of Mao Tse Tung. Alec already had one back home from when he lived in Hong Kong.

So we came up with a plan. Alec went out and bought six warm, woolly balaclavas and I packed them into Christmas parcels along with marbles, a small ball, a pencil and a notebook in each. If the boys were at the square, we'd invite them to the pie café to eat, tell them about Jesus and give them each a parcel. The whole activity made me feel very festive and excited.

At four that afternoon we wandered along to Durbar Square in great anticipation, carrying the presents hidden in a plastic bag. Unusually, we did not come across even one boy, so sadly it was just pie and tea for two.

Later we attended the Children of God's gathering. Not as many people came as they had invited. The team acted out hilarious skits, after which we had a meal of potato salad, a spinach-and-egg-bake and beer. We walked back to camp at midnight and had to call out the guard to unlock the gates.

I felt deeply homesick that Christmas night.

Boxing Day was quiet and restful. We called over to see Jean-Luc and Martine and wished them well on their planned trekking venture. I hoped they had enough warm clothes as I'd heard a few tourists had died out in the mountains that season, due to the extreme cold.

We had our own Christmas celebration in the Land-Rover that evening with Nigel and Margaret, a couple of travellers on their way to Australia, whom we'd met two days before. Remarkably Margaret recognised me from Shenfield Technical High School; she had been in a year lower than me. They lived in Hutton, Essex, close to Brentwood where my family was. It was great to chat with them. We all enjoyed the feast I prepared of pasta, meat and vegetables, cheese, tomatoes, fried egg, yogurt, tangerines, apples, chocolate, biscuits and coffee.

The following day it was pouring with rain. I first washed all the pots, pans and dishes from the feast, whilst Alec went to change rupees into dollars from the money we'd gained from our sales. It was time to leave Kathmandu, which was quite a wrench after staying there for two weeks.

The conversations we'd had with the Children of God team made me feel as if we should sell the Land-Rover, give all the money to them and stay in the city to join their endeavour. Jeremiah said that it might not be what God required of us and that it was okay to journey on. He gave us the addresses of other teams in the major cities that we planned to visit en route back to England.

Goodbyes said, we drove to the dairy and bought four pounds of loose milk powder sold in plastic bags – much cheaper than in a tin. We also purchased eight pounds of the delicious Nepalese mountain cheese. The chilling rain was still falling when we came out of the dairy, so we made a dash to the Land-Rover and climbed in quickly with our shopping.

A rat-a-tat-tat on the door drew our attention to a soaked, bedraggled temple boy. He was barefoot, wearing ragged cotton khaki shorts and a threadbare shirt, with a thin grey blanket around his shoulders. He asked if he could sit in the front of the Land-Rover for a while and we gladly welcomed the shivering lad in, to feel the warmth from the fan heater.

Interesting that when we went looking for the lads on Christmas Day not one was to be seen. Now it seemed as if God had brought one to us. We took the chance and told him about Jesus being born, and that was why we celebrated Christmas. We gave him a parcel and watched with delight as he opened it up and examined the contents. I put the maroon balaclava on his head and it fitted well. How much he had understood about Jesus we didn't know, but as he climbed down from the cab clutching his goodies, he waved us off with a happy smile.

Our drive away from Kathmandu in the miserable weather hid the beauty of the foothills of the Himalayas. The road took us higher and higher on the Tribhuvan Highway into the mountains and the rain turned to heavy snow. We had to stop at a road-tax checkpoint and noticed a great number of trucks and buses parked. A European traveller walked across to let us know that the road was blocked further along. As we could still see traffic moving ahead, Alec continued on to see how far he could go.

After a few miles, the road became less distinguishable as the blizzard blew more heavily the higher we went. Suddenly we turned a corner and discovered traffic mayhem: vehicles were shunting this way and that. Several trucks, Land-Rovers and Volkswagen vans were in the traffic jam. The driver of one VW van managed to turn around and stopped beside us.

'No good going on, mate. There's been an avalanche ahead and the snow has totally blocked the road. No one is going anywhere any time soon.'

'Thanks for the warning!' Alec shouted, as the guy carried on towards Kathmandu.

Alec drove a short way on to where the road broadened out and we parked on the wide verge. To the left, the snow-covered hillside swept away down into the valley. To the right, we hoped that any vehicles moving along the icy road, only a few yards away, would maintain control, keep on the actual road and not swerve into us.

Alec found a couple of rocks to use as chocks behind the wheels. Up went the roof and I put the kettle on as we settled into waiting out the snow blockade.

Total distance driven = 30,594 miles

West

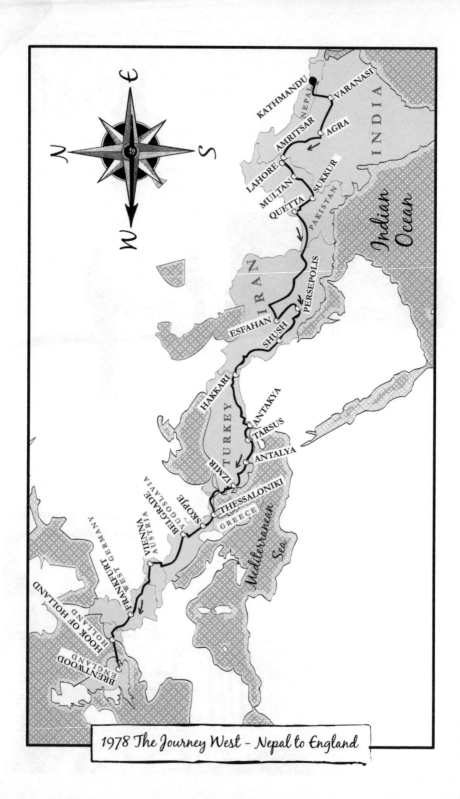

1978 The Journey West - Nepal to England

Avalanche to Crocodiles

28th December 1977 to 2nd January 1978
Nepal

Following an uneventful night, we were up and about when Alec saw a group of six hippies walking down the road from the direction of the avalanche.

'Hello, how's the road looking back there?' Alec called.

'Oh, it's not good, man. The route is blocked with at least sixty trucks stuck in deep snow, and that's beyond the avalanche, there's more over here,' replied the lead chap, putting his cold, bare hands under the armpits of his parka jacket, trying to warm them up.

'Really! Do you know how much snow there is further on?'

'Yeah, we were on a bus coming up from the other side yesterday and the snow's real bad for more than ten miles.'

'What did you do last night?' I chipped in.

'Slept in the bus. Jeepers, I was chilled numb,' said a young woman as she pulled her woollen hat snug around her ears, tucking in her long blond locks.

'Fancy a cuppa?'

'No, that's okay. The Red Cross have been giving out bread and tea to the stranded, so we're good.'

'And where are you off to now?' asked Alec.

'Well, it's gonna be a long time before the driver will have room to shift our bus and drive on,' explained a fella with ginger dreadlocks.

'Yeah, and added to the snow, the wind is so flipping freezing up there that the truck drivers have fires burning under their fuel tanks. Geez, that's crazy,' said another guy, his voice muffled through his long, hand-knitted, striped, psychedelic scarf, which was wound around his neck a couple of times and still hung down to his knees.

'Yes, I've seen that cunning trick too,' commented Alec. 'The diesel thickens up in the cold and won't flow through the engine.'

'What about your luggage?' I enquired.

'Oh, we've left our backpacks on the bus and we're walking to the next village this side of the avalanche,' replied the first guy again. 'See if we can catch another bus to Kathmandu.'

'Well, I hope you reconnect with your bags again,' Alec said, wondering at their wisdom.

'If you need a free meal when you get into the city, ask for Joe's place near Freak Street,' I informed them. 'The friendly guys there will give you a welcome. Just say Alec and Jan sent you.'

'Thanks,' said a slim girl. She walked away down the hill, her Doc Martin boots peeping out below her long, ruby-red, Indian cotton skirt.

'Well, that's that then, we're staying put today,' Alec concluded as we climbed back into our home.

The day was spent reading and writing postcards and entries in the diary.

You'd never believe it, but even at that risky camp location we had local visitors. A couple of boys came walking by, barefoot on the icy snow. Their clothes were totally inadequate for the climate. It was incomprehensible, but they didn't appear to be particularly bothered; they were really hardened to the harsh conditions of their poverty.

It was great that we could give them each a balaclava mystery parcel to take away and enjoy.

'Jan, what about using the meat from the Antarctic packs to bake a pie for supper?' said Alec feeling hungry in the late afternoon.

'That's a great idea,' I replied.

I reconstituted an eight-ounce dehydrated meat block with a measure of water. The dried onions, carrots and peas were softened in hot water, drained and added to the meat. I made the pastry and put the pie all together. Our ingenious oven cooked the pie exceptionally well and we had a scrumptious, hot, tasty meal.

The Land-Rover had warmed up nicely with the cooker on, so we decided to go to bed straight away after eating. I quickly undressed, then put on a vest, long johns, socks and a long winceyette nightdress – what a sight! We read our books for a while before nestling down to sleep.

'Can you see anything moving?' I asked Alec the next morning, as he lifted up the front blind at the bulkhead to check the road conditions.

'No, it's all quiet out there,' Alec replied.

'Oh good, we can have a lie-in – no need to rush about,' I responded as I pulled the duvet closely under my chin, keeping my hands tucked in. The exposed metal edges inside the Land-Rover glistened with frozen crystals of condensation.

By eight we were ready to be up and about, so we manoeuvred ourselves this way and that in order to pack the bedding and bed away without opening the door. Next we had to dress, which was a tad difficult as the carpet was sodden with water from the snow we'd brought in on our boots the day before.

Our faithful kettle was back on the stove, ready for the next pot of tea to enjoy with breakfast – porridge, boiled egg, bread and dried apricots that I'd soaked in water overnight.

A young Nepalese boy and teenage lad came along and watched

us for ages. We gave them coffee to drink. Then an English guy stopped by and enjoyed a mugful too. He was travelling by motorbike on his way to Australia via Kathmandu.

We read our books, played Scrabble and wrote several more postcards and letters as we waited and waited for the road to reopen.

I baked another pie for dinner, filled with egg and grated cheese, which was delicious with lentils and kidney beans, followed by sweet milk pasta for dessert. We'd had a long and pleasant day, and as darkness fell passing traffic increased, indicating the road had probably cleared and we could leave the following day. As we settled early in bed again, a vehicle pulled in front of us and its lights shone right into our window.

'It's only the bread and tea wagon,' Alec determined and lay back down. We were soon asleep, unperturbed that the Red Cross van had parked close by.

It was an early start the next day as we continued along the Tribhuvan Highway. Initially the road was navigable, until we met the bulldozer working to clear the snow. Multiple buses, trucks and a few private cars on the road hindered the driver's progress. They moved in both directions along the mountain road that was only wide enough for one vehicle. Passing points were few and far between. It took us five hours to travel five miles. We patiently sat and read, played Scrabble for the umpteenth time, drank coffee and munched on sweets and biscuits, as Alec slowly edged the Land-Rover forward.

Along the route we stopped at Daman, a small village in a strategic location, sixty miles southwest of Kathmandu. At over 7,611 feet, it commanded a majestic, panoramic view across the Himalayas, from Dhaulagiri in the west across to Mount Everest in the east. The clear-blue, cloudless sky afforded us a stunning scene to photograph as we stood at the top of the viewing tower.

Afterwards we drove on, going down and down along the switchback road leaving the snow far behind. Finally we reached the bottom of the pass and headed for Hetauda, a busy town in the lowlands, to search for bread. It was late in the day so there was little about and what we did buy was costly and tasted fousty. We then drove west along a dirt road, under reconstruction, until we found a suitable place to park for the night.

The next morning, New Years Eve, there was no water to wash the dishes, or ourselves, as the tank was empty. Fortunately there was just enough for tea. A group of locals hung around watching us pack up. We were soon on our way, enjoying the scenery of lush green vegetation and delightful thatched houses. The road was rough and frequently corrugated, like we'd experienced in Africa, so we were jostled about in our seats. There were huge teams of men labouring on the new road as we drove along trying to find the turn to Chitwan National Park. The uneven, muddy track was slick and slippery and at one point the Land-Rover had to ford the river. Near to the outskirts of the park there were several simple village houses with many people and domestic animals about. The forest became denser the further we drove into the park.

It was possible to stay at the Elephant Camp Hotel, but pricey! So we continued on to the riverbank where, pleasingly, we could park for free. A number of overlanders were already there with their Land-Rovers.

Two Australians and an Irish fella, who worked for Tearfund in Bangladesh, had ridden in on bicycles. I found out that my teenage heartthrob, Cliff Richard, had staged concerts in Britain to raise funds for that aid organization.

After lunch we took a late-afternoon stroll down to the river, where we sat on a fallen tree trunk. Either side of us tall elephant grass swayed in the breeze, framed by the dense green forest and the snow-peaked Himalayas away in the distance. A variety of birds flitted around and we saw several stunning kingfishers adorned with turquoise, brown and white feathers. Many working elephants waded across the river, guided by their trainers, as they carried small logs in their trunks.

We relaxed and enjoyed the warmth of the jungle and listened to the orchestra of chirping crickets, croaking frogs, crackling of foraging in the forest and the trumpeting of elephants, as we bathed in the amber sunset and bade farewell to 1977.

On New Year's Day we were up by seven to go on an elephant safari. We needn't have begun so early as everyone else was laid-back with no rush to get the activity underway. So Alec and I chilled and watched the baby elephants chomping their breakfast: freshly gathered grass and leaves.

At half-past-ten we were introduced to our elephant, which knelt down so we could climb onto its back. We sat on a big sack cushion stuffed with straw and strapped securely onto the elephant's back. The driver sat just behind its huge ears on a piece of hessian and gave directions with his feet. He had remarkable control of the enormous creature, which appeared quite gentle and graceful.

Initially it was a comfortable, stable ride until we went down the riverbank, then it felt strange and unsteady as we were tipped this way and that. The elephant strode across the river and up the other side to follow a narrow track. It swished by the elephant grass, which was so tall we could only just see above it. Startled birds flew out as we rustled on by. Going into the jungle, the elephant ploughed through the undergrowth between the trees. If a branch was blocking the way, the driver hacked it off with his machete and the elephant pulled it down with his trunk and trod it underfoot.

For over an hour we trudged along under a shady green canopy of leaves. Monkeys swung from branch to branch, chattering with excitement. As for big game – well, we did spy a pair of rhinoceros.

The next day, after the morning mist had burned off, we ventured out on a crocodile hunt with five other overlanders. As the bottom of the large canoe was awash, Alec removed the vinyl-upholstered base of the front seats from our Land-Rover for the two of us to sit upon.

We travelled along the river for ninety minutes at a gentle pace, grateful for the skill of the oarsman. The journey took us past the elephant grass and into the heart of the forest. The air was hot and humid and hummed with the sound of flying insects.

The oarsman guided the canoe along a murky inlet stream, and then he stopped and directed us to step out onto the soft, muddy bank and continue along on foot for a couple of miles. With seven of us walking along, trying to tread lightly and talk in whispers, the shy crocodiles kept themselves hidden. Alec did see one slip into the water, but I just saw the wash. A vulnerable baby deer drank water from the edge of the riverbank.

I felt constantly nervy as we took the long and strenuous walk back along the banks to the canoe. Unfortunately our return ride to camp was short lived. The canoe barely moved as the oarsman paddled against the current with the weight of seven passengers. So everyone got out again to walk all the way back to camp. We were partly on the shoreline, fighting our way through the tall, scratchy grass, and occasionally wading through the water on the sandy riverbed.

As Alec and I were keen to leave the national park that afternoon, we forged ahead of the group to where the Land-Rover was parked. Unfortunately it was across on the other side of the river. We waded for most of the way until a boy in a canoe turned up and gave us a ride across the deeper middle section to the far shore.

It was mid-afternoon by the time we'd had lunch and packed our stuff away and the big canoe arrived. Alec paid the man and retrieved our damp seats to refit into the Land-Rover. We drove back along the park track, forded the river and continued to the main dirt road. At Narayanghat we took the ferry, which was a wooden platform rigged across two boats. Having crossed the main river, we were thankful to be driving along a smooth tarmac road for the 100 miles to reach the Nepal/Indian border.

Total distance driven = 30,780 miles

Taj Mahal to the Golden Temple

3rd to 17th January 1978
India

From re-entering India it took us four days to drive almost 500 miles to Agra. En route we stayed in Varanasi, at the familiar campsite, to attend to maintenance and chores and buy fresh food supplies. We enjoyed our dinner at a nearby roadside tea-stall: rice with peas, cauliflower, deep-fried, battered, stuffed tomatoes, curried aubergine, tomato sauce, vegetable chappatis and tea. The owner was as pleased as punch as we tucked into the meal, relishing every morsel. Food with soul!

The animated, rotund owner wore the standard long, cotton, baggy trousers in beige with matching woollen hat, royal-blue shirt with the cuffs rolled back and a sleeveless, long, quilted navy-blue jacket. He took our compliments seriously and asked us to take a photo of him to send from England with an 'Egon Ronay Certificate'. He stood on the earth in front of his tarpaulin-covered shack. His smile and joviality vanished as his neatly trimmed grey moustache portrayed his proud demeanour as the photo was taken. His assistant kept busy cooking more curry for hungry customers who waited patiently, seated on wooden benches at the rustic tables. The aromatic scents of cardamom, ginger, turmeric, saffron and onions enveloped the scene, battling against the petrol fumes of the constant passing traffic, an arm's length away.

Traffic over those days had been a nightmare. You have to experience it to believe it. We passed through towns where there were hundreds of people mingling about amongst the trucks, buses, bullock carts, rickshaws, trishaws and roaming holy cows. Skinny dogs with bleeding, fly-nibbled ears skulked around in the streets. Two dogs fighting over a bone, viciously attacking each other brought their skirmish onto the road and narrowly missed our wheels.

Away from the towns there were many crashed vehicles abandoned on the roadside or even in the road. An upturned heavy lorry lay blocking much of the road with its contents of freshly picked, soft, raw cotton piled beside it. The worst we saw was an overturned petrol tanker. The tank had dislodged and rolled into a field. The cab and truck chassis had tipped onto a wooden cart and smashed it to pieces. The black water buffalo that had been pulling the cart lay dead, still and bloated. It had been there a few days and its stench filled the air. We wondered what had happened to the drivers of the cart and truck.

The next key destination was Agra, first to see the beautiful mausoleum of Itmad-ud-Daulah built with white marble extravagantly inlaid with semi-precious stones. From the mausoleum we went to see Agra Fort with its red sandstone walls surrounding many buildings, palaces, audience rooms, luxurious baths and two white marble mosques. At the teahouse we sipped tea and friendly chipmunks entertained us, as they happily ate biscuit crumbs from my hand.

But the star location of the day was the architectural jewel of the Taj Mahal, with its exotic gardens enhanced with pools and fountains. The reflection of the marble domed structure was mirrored in the long channel of water in its foreground. Alec, along with a host of other mostly Indian tourists, took the standard iconic photo. We ventured along the tree-lined pathway to marvel at the exceptional mausoleum created by master craftsmen. It was commissioned by the Moghul Emperor Shah Jahan and built during the seventeenth century in memory of his favourite wife, Mumtaz Mahal. I touched one of the exquisitely decorated white marble pillars and stroked my fingers across the cold, ultra-smooth, floral mosaic design of inlaid precious and semi-precious gems.

We stayed for quite a while, admiring all that we saw before going to look around the tourist stalls set up outside the Taj Mahal complex. Eventually it was time for us to leave to search for a place to park for the night.

'You come stay at good campsite – I show you.' A young teenager badgered us as he followed Alec and me back to the Land-Rover.

'Come, I show you good place,' he pleaded as he walked sideways just a pace before us, almost blocking our stride.

We had planned to go to the recommended Highwayman campsite, but the lad was amiable enough, so we invited him to ride in the back of the Land-Rover and direct the way.

He successfully led us to Green View campsite and introduced us to the manager, who showed us around. It was a recently opened, small establishment, with a tidy kitchen, the day's Indian newspaper in English available and a cassette recorder playing relaxing background music. It had a new, clean white toilet with a handy can of air freshener too. You could see they were trying to make a go of it and we were glad to stay as the only guests that evening.

The lengthy early-morning call to prayer by the local imam at the nearby mosque, robbed us of three hours of sleep. So we were up early for an easy-going morning, during which I tried making a Genoise cake in the pressure cooker. It was edible, but not a competition winner.

'Alec, have you tried sitting on those lovely new wicker armchairs outside the manager's office?'

'No. Why?'

'Well, I think you should test them.'

Alec walked across and sat down on the attractive high-backed armchair with its strung-webbed seat.

'Very comfortable – aren't they like the chairs we saw at that café the other day?'

'Yes, that's what I thought,' I replied. 'I asked the manager what he'd paid for them.'

'And?'

'Thirteen rupees, only thirteen rupees!' I cheerily announced.

'Why that's just eighty pence – who would make a chair for such a pittance?'

Our folding chairs bought in Sicily were showing signs of wear and tear, so I asked the manager if we could buy two wicker chairs from him. Wonderfully he agreed and would only take what he paid for them: not a rupee more. What a bargain. They nestled nicely together to fit easily in the back of the Land-Rover.

Later that morning we drove west from Agra to see the former capital city of the Moghul Empire – Fatephur Sikri, an impressive complex of red sandstone buildings, including one of the largest mosques in India, Jama Masjid, built in the sixteenth century by Emperor Akbar. As we arrived, the place was throbbing with hundreds of Indians on account of the arrival of British Prime Minister James Callaghan, on an official visit to the country. To the thrill of the audience he left with his small entourage in a helicopter.

From Fatephur Sikri we drove on to the Bharatpur Bird Sanctuary, a half-hour drive west. The warden kindly allowed us to park for the night in the grounds.

The alarm rang at five-thirty and I shut it off quickly. They say the early morning is the best time to observe birds. An hour later we had washed, dressed and eaten breakfast. As we embarked on our venture we saw that we were too early: it was a moonless night, the sun was hidden and the birds were still roosting.

'I feel quite chilly,' I said to Alec as we walked quietly along the barely visible dirt path.

'Me too. Let's go back and fetch our jackets.'

As we approached the Land-Rover we could see another early riser, a peacock, flaunting its feathers. It strutted away from us as we opened the door and grabbed our jackets. Having sorted ourselves out, Alec locked the back door and turned around.

'Shush, Alec, look over there,' I whispered.

'Wow, where did she come from? Quick, give me the camera.'

As I fished around in my cloth bag to pull out the camera, the young spotted deer that had caught our attention walked right up to me and poked its nose into my bag.

I passed the camera to Alec and tentatively stroked the neck of the curious, delightful creature. Alec captured the moment. But we need not have rushed, for this little friend adopted us for the day and walked close to our heels for five hours as we strolled around.

The bird sanctuary was such a restful place to be, with only a few other visitors. Our binoculars enabled us to view many birds in the trees and in the long reeds of marshland by the side of the lake: ducks, geese, flamingoes, storks, cormorants, kingfishers, snakebirds, ibises, eagles etc. An extraordinary time spent close to nature.

We exchanged tranquility for pandemonium as we left the sanctuary after lunch to drive on to Delhi. As we arrived in the evening in the bustling city everyone was leaving work, many on bicycles. A few drivers careered along the wrong side of the road in their cars with their headlights full on, hoping to beat the traffic jam. Crazy!

We parked on the outskirts of Delhi for the night, then entered the city the next day to spend five days at the tourist camp. There I had a cooking jamboree and had a go at making bread in our clay dish oven, and then made two types of jam: banana and apple, and guava. That would keep us going for a while, and worked out at a quarter of the cost of bought jam. We bought a thick, heavy iron frying pan in the market and successfully popped corn as a fun snack to munch on.

Naturally Alec took the opportunity to work on the Land-Rover and, for a change, replaced a broken leaf spring at the front of the vehicle instead of the back.

On a couple of evenings we went along to the Delhi branch of the Children of God. There we were given a warm welcome at their shared dwelling, and more *Mo Letters* were passed on to us. We ate hearty meals whilst the group sang and acted out poignant skits.

Our journey from Delhi to Amritsar spanned over 250 miles along the main highway, a well-surfaced tarmac road across the north Indian plains. The land was extensively farmed and we passed through busy towns and villages along the route. An abundance of fruit and vegetables were for sale.

We stayed for the night outside of Amritsar, but on Monday morning we drove into the city and parked at the railway station. Across the street was the tourist office, our first port of call that day.

'Good morning, sir,' I addressed the amiable young gentleman who manned the orderly office.

'Good morning,' he replied. 'How can I help you?'

'Where can we go to have a vaccination against cholera?'

'Ah, that would be the Government Hospital.'

'Is it far away?'

'No, not at all. You can walk there in ten minutes.'

'In which direction would that be?' Alec asked, pointing to the city map he'd picked up off the counter. The man outlined the route and we left his office and walked to the crossroads. With a precarious dash across the street, we managed to avoid all other road users.

I followed Alec as he consulted the map, and after ten minutes walk we actually arrived at the hospital, a rundown building with a promise of improvements with two new wings being built. It took a while to discover where the vaccination office was, having enquired with half a dozen different people.

We went along a patchy-cream-painted corridor with a shiny, grey concrete floor, to the second door on the right. The door was open and the male nurse, wearing a white medical jacket and a royal-blue Sikh turban, was attending to a patient. We hesitated to say anything and drew back to the side of the corridor wall to wait our turn.

'Next,' the nurse called as the patient left his office.

'Good morning, sir. We need vaccinations against cholera. Can you do this for us?'

'Yes, of course. Do you have your vaccination books?'

I stepped forward and handed him our yellow booklets, before sitting down on the plain wooden chair. Alec stood behind me. The room smelt of surgical spirits. Mr Singh, the nurse, first filled in our booklets and recorded the vaccinations in his ledger. He stamped all the documents with satisfaction. Next he prepared the vaccinations, taking glass syringes and reusable needles. The vaccine looked decidedly cloudy.

'This doesn't look good,' I hissed to Alec, mad with myself for not having brought along the disposable syringes and needles from our Land-Rover.

'I'm very sorry, sir, but I see you don't have disposable syringes.'

'No, this is all that the hospital has. But they're clean. I sterilized them myself this morning,' he stated, trying to reassure me.

Awkward. But I wasn't happy. I wasn't happy at all.

'Alec, we must go back to the Land-Rover to fetch our syringes,' I said as I looked from Alec across to the nurse, who was all ready to proceed. 'I'm sorry but we'll be back soon.'

We walked out of the door, leaving our precious booklets in Mr Singh's safekeeping, as he returned the syringe to the enamel kidney dish and sat down at his desk, bemused.

'Next,' he called.

'Well, that was a fine kettle of fish. How come you didn't bring our syringes?' Alec harped on as we scuttled away, back along the corridor.

'I'm sorry, my mistake,' I admitted. 'But it would be foolish to go ahead.'

On our way back to the railway station car park, we popped into a dispensary and asked about the nature of the cholera vaccine. The pharmacist said it should be a clear liquid, unless it's been subject to a change in temperature, when it will go opaque.

Within half-an-hour we were back in Mr Singh's office. We reported our findings at the dispensary and I handed him two new disposable syringes and needles. He listened to our reasoning and very graciously went to the tired old fridge in the corner of his room and extracted an unopened vial of cholera vaccine, enough for ten vaccinations. He handed it to me for my scrutiny. The liquid was clear and in date and it felt cold.

'Yes, that will do very well. Thank you for your understanding.'

His head swayed from side to side as he prepared the vaccinations again and administered them into our upper arms.

'It will be a fine thing indeed when every person here can have their vaccinations or injections with disposable syringes and needles,' he said.

It took another hour of waiting for the Chief Medical Officer to sign our vaccination certificates before we could leave. On our walk back to the Land-Rover we were able to call at the address of the Children of God team that we'd been given, but no one was there.

Whilst in Amritsar, we visited the memorial to hundreds of Indians massacred by British soldiers in 1919. It happened during a public demonstration in the walled Jallianwala Bagh public garden. It was sobering to look down the well and reflect on the many who had jumped to their deaths as they fled to escape the bullets.

A visit to see Sri Harmandir Sahib, the Golden Temple of the

Sikhs, was a wonder to behold. The holy complex was bordered along each side by continuous, elegant white buildings with arched colonnades facing inwards. There were four grand entrances into the area and a wide path edged the vast pool, in the midst of which stood the striking Golden Temple, reached by a bridge walkway level with the water. We mingled amongst the worshippers as we strolled around the sacred site, observing much.

Near to the temple was a nine-storey octagonal tower. We climbed the steps inside to the balcony at the top, from where we could see kites flying over the city rooftops. Further within the city we explored a fabulous bazaar with so many tempting things to buy. The smart Sikh entrepreneurs set a high standard in business.

As we drove out of Amritsar it was dark, but we ventured on into the countryside and found a place to stop for the night, on a verge by a group of trees.

On the following day we continued to the India/Pakistan border and crossed with no problems at all and we were back in the city of Lahore by lunchtime.

Total distance driven = 31,872 miles

Highs and Lows

18th to 24th January 1978
Pakistan – Iran

Whilst staying in the grounds of the Salvation Army building in Lahore once again, we chatted with many of the overlanders who had travelled to the city in a variety of vehicles: a general post office van, a Morris Minor, a Mini, a converted ambulance and even a 'dolly-wagon' as Alec referred to one old-fashioned campervan.

Driving in the latter was an interesting pair, a brother and sister travelling together. Mr Burton was of average height and clean-shaven, with a full head of brown hair, which belied the fact that he was sixty-five years old. He was dressed in a blue and green plaid, short-sleeved shirt, with a knitted waistcoat, long grey trousers and black, leather, lace-up shoes. His sister, a few inches taller and six years older than him, was dressed in a white and green, floral, cotton dress, a dark-green cardigan plus sturdy brown shoes. Her snowy-white, long hair was swept up in a tidy bun, emphasizing her chubby, round face and twinkling blue eyes.

Alec chatted to Mr Burton about vehicles and they exchanged stories of challenges experienced on their journeys, whilst Miss

Burton invited me into their pale-yellow mobile home and put the kettle on. I felt like I was in a pensioner's cottage. It had large windows either side of the back that allowed daylight to flood the interior. The mustard-yellow crimplene curtains hung on runners and were tied back with olive-green velveteen cord.

When she opened the fridge the interior looked the same as if she were in a stationary home in England. Leftovers were kept uncovered on dainty floral tea plates. Fresh fruit and vegetables were in the bottom drawer. Five eggs of varying sizes, with feathers and all, were safely lodged in an egg rack. Miss Burton took out the small china milk jug that matched the sugar bowl already on the fold-down table. She opened a packet of biscuits and placed a few on a pretty gold-rimmed plate. Four cups and saucers with teaspoons were set on the table. The kettle boiled and tea was made in a stainless-steel teapot, covered with a pale-pink, knitted teacosy. Miss Burton called the men in to sit with us on the yellow-crimplene-covered cushioned seats. The interior was significantly roomier to our Land-Rover. Sipping tea and dunking Rich Tea biscuits, we listened to their travel tales.

Originally they were in business together, and after twenty years they sold everything and went around the world. They stopped at St. Kitts Island in the Caribbean, where they established a sugar cane plantation, hiring local labourers. After some years they continued on their travels, touring America, Canada and then back to England. The brother worked for a further fifteen years before retiring. Next they went on a three-month trip around Morocco and later set out on their current two-year trip to India and back. What remarkable siblings.

The day was moving on and we needed to be out and about exploring Lahore. First a visit to see the grand Badshahi Mosque with its elaborate red sandstone façade decorated with a marble inlay of floral and geometric designs. Three huge, white-marble, embellished domes of the mosque could be seen above the outer high walls.

Taller minarets of sandstone, each stood at the four outer corners of the perimeter wall that surrounded the inner mosque. It was built during the reign of Moghal Emperor Aurangzeb in 1671. The mosque was located opposite the striking Fort of Lahore, which unfortunately was not open to tourists that day.

Walking on through the old city, the streets were narrow. You needed to be on your toes and keep your wits about you to avoid being run down by a passing tonga. (A tonga was a two-wheeled, canopied wooden cart pulled by a horse, providing the local taxi service.) Uncovered manholes were also ready to swallow you up, should you put a foot wrong.

At Kashmiri Bazaar we meandered along the maze of shops that overflowed with stock: plastic wares, suitcases and bags, fabrics and shoes, in abundance. I wondered who bought all that stuff. How did the shop owners make enough money to cover their costs and a salary to live on? There was a street where every shop, one after the other, was selling brass and chrome cooking pots. In another street all the stores sold electrical goods, televisions and radios.

From a succession of food traders, I bought twelve pounds of milk powder in plastic bags, six pounds of oats, a pound and a half of peanut butter, a pound of toffees, six eggs and half-a-pound of butter. With the cooler weather it was possible to keep butter in the Land-Rover without it turning to oil. The candyman's stall was a delight to behold, with handmade sweets in a rainbow of colours, displayed in pyramids on trays.

Laden with goods, it was dark by the time we looked for an auto-rickshaw, but our journey was cut short when its motor conked out. Alec hailed another and we returned to the campsite hungry for our supper, followed by Bible study and bed.

'Have you planned the route ahead?' I asked Alec the next morning as we ate homemade chapattis for breakfast with delicious butter and my homemade jam.

'Well yes, it's all new terrain as we will be travelling south towards Quetta.'

'So we'll be avoiding Afghanistan altogether?' I queried.

'Yes, the more southerly route west along here will take us directly from Pakistan into Iran,' said Alec as he pointed the route out on the map.

'I wonder how much snow we'll be travelling through?' I asked.

'That remains to be seen. We'll take one day at a time and deal with any challenging road and weather conditions as we come across them.'

It took three days to drive to Quetta via Multan, Sukkar, Shikarpur and Jacobabad. The terrain changed from flat farmland, growing sugar cane and corn, to flat desert plains with stubbles of dry brown vegetation. Thankfully the roads were wider with less traffic and fewer people and animals to contend with. Much of the route followed alongside the railway track and it was terrific seeing the magnificent steam engines pulling along the passenger carriages or freight wagons. TOOT – TOOT! The smoke billowed out of their tall funnels, creating black clouds that floated in the sky, trailing behind the trains as they forged ahead to their next destinations.

Our meals continued to be regular and tasty, with stops at roadside cafés and time to cook a satisfying dinner in the evening like beef curry, dumplings and potatoes. I also successfully baked a pineapple upside-down cake in our clay dish oven.

The journey took us onwards into the rugged range of the barren copper-and-russet-toned hills of the Bolan Pass in Baluchistan, the western province of Pakistan.

On the Sunday morning, three days after leaving Lahore, we were all ready to drive on when there was a major problem with the seal between the engine water pump and the cylinder head. It had been dribbling during the previous twenty-four hours, but as Alec started the engine that morning it dramatically sprayed water from under the bonnet onto the wings.

'Darn it, I'd hoped we'd reach Quetta before the seal burst,' Alec sighed.

'Can you fix it?' I asked.

'Not without a replacement seal, and can you believe it, we have a seal and gasket for every part of the engine, but not that one!'

'Well, what will you do?'

'Good question! I'll take it to pieces and see what I can come up with,' Alec said hopefully.

For three hours Alec worked outside in the bitter cold. He masterfully reshaped a rubber seal from our drinking water purifier spares, to replace the perished one in the engine.

I made peanut butter chapatti butties and mugs of tea to keep us warm.

'Here goes.' Alec switched on the engine, and then climbed out of the Land-Rover to check the exposed modified seal.

Thumbs up!

'Hurray!' I clapped enthusiastically and gave him a kiss. 'Well done, Alec, you're a star mechanic and improviser.'

The seal held: not a drop of water to be seen anywhere around the engine. Alec pulled down the heavy bonnet with satisfaction. He packed away the tools and I the kitchen items. We were eager to leave that remote, wild location in the Bolan Pass for it was no place to linger.

Twenty-seven miles further on we arrived at the modern town of Quetta. It was quite different to other towns we had visited with its orderly, clean streets and calm traffic. The shops were more enclosed and only handcart stalls were outside along the streets, which was just as well as it was bitterly cold.

I bought two aerogrammes from the post office, and then we found a charming tearoom like what you'd find back in England, with smart wooden tables with curved-back wooden chairs. We sat near to the big window to watch the world go by, as we drank tea from fine china teacups and wrote our letters. Alec wrote one to his former boss at the British Antarctic Survey office in Cambridge, England. He asked him if he would provide a reference for any Twin Otter aircraft maintenance job that Alec hoped to be offered when we returned home. My aerogramme to Dad, our base manager, was on a practical note too, asking if he could arrange for our medical insurance to be extended. Naturally I gave him and Mum an update on what we'd been doing since I last wrote in Lahore.

I looked up from my writing and saw two disabled men whose legs were amputated mid-thigh, pass by the window. They were warmly dressed and each sat on tiny wooden boxes that were set on four wheels. The men propelled themselves along with their mittened hands, scooting along the paved road, a precarious venture that gave them a degree of independence to be admired, but surely there could be a better way.

After an hour in the tearoom we returned to the post office to mail the letters and then drove south out of Quetta. We passed a sign – 'London 5,886 miles'. It felt curiously heartwarming to see the name of our capital city emblazoned in the outback of a former part of the British Empire. It was as if the ties with our homeland were not totally discarded by the authorities there.

Talking of authorities, we were not far out of Quetta when we were halted at a customs post. The smart uniformed officer took our vehicle papers and passports for documentation into his roadside office. All was in order and Alec was given permission to drive on. The uneven road took us out of the hills and down into the wilderness of a vast desert region, where nomads dwelt in their tents. As dusk fell they shepherded their flocks of sheep and herded their camels back to camp.

We parked for the night beside the sand banks not far from the railway track and I cooked dinner and baked a fruitcake. A steam train trundled along, the illuminated carriages highlighted the silhouettes of passengers travelling towards Iran.

Tika ti ka, Tika ti ka, Tika ti ka, Tika ti ka.

The night was cold so we took advantage of the warmth generated by the cooker and went to bed early. Contented and cosy, we fell asleep.

'What did they want?' I asked Alec as he climbed back into the Land-Rover the next morning. Two bearded, turbaned and warmly dressed men had ridden up the road together on a single bicycle to speak with Alec. He was in the midst of doing his daily 'pre-flight' check of the Land-Rover. They shook hands and greeted Alec before cycling off down the road back towards Quetta.

'Oh nothing, as far as I could make out. Seems they just stopped by to see if all was well.'

'Maybe they thought we had broken down as you had the bonnet up.'

'Could be,' Alec agreed. 'Are you finished clearing up yet? We've a long journey today and we need to get going soon if we want to reach the border by this evening.'

'All right, all right, hold your horses. I just need to empty the washing-up bowl outside and pull the roof down,' I declared.

Alec had already climbed into the driving seat and turned on the engine, champing at the bit.

As it was, our journey of over 250 miles to the border took us through barren desert with mountains away in the distance. The sandy ground turned to a gravel plateau, mile upon mile of nothingness. Tiny villages were few and far between. How did anyone survive in such desolate terrain?

We came across a parked Land-Rover and a Ford Transit van. Twenty Dutch overlanders had been travelling together for four months. They had been to Nepal and then to Goa in southern India and they hoped to reach the Netherlands in three weeks. The tour leader and his right-hand man, a mechanic, were trying to fix burntout wires in the Land-Rover's engine compartment. Meanwhile everyone else was milling around, looking travel weary. There was not much we could do, so we made haste and drove on while there was still light.

We had tested the fruitcake at lunchtime. It was a bit burnt on the bottom, but otherwise edible. For supper that night I boiled potatoes, reconstituted a meat bar with onions and peas, and stewed fruit and cooked milk pasta for dessert. It had been an unusually plain day, just travelling from A to B. I felt rather travel weary myself. It was almost a year since we had set out on our adventure and now it had become a normal way of life.

'You're looking glum, Jan. What's wrong?' Alec remarked as he looked up from perusing a map of Iran.

'Oh, I don't know. Today's been long and monotonous, it's cold and my feet are freezing.'

'So you don't feel like you're in a movie right now?'

'No, they miss out the humdrum bits.'

'Well, tomorrow we can look forward to a possible tense scene going through the Iranian customs.'

'Oh yes, that could be nail-biting stuff,' I said in jest, hoping for an easy passage into Shah Mohammad Reza Pahlavi's oil-rich kingdom.

Alec cuddled up real close that night, warming my bones and driving the blues away from my mind.

The next day showed promise: the sun had shown up and I was feeling warm and even overdressed in my jeans and toasty sweater. It was just a ten-mile drive to the Pakistan border control. The customs officer scouted the Land-Rover for drugs, banged on the bodywork and looked underneath. He tried to cadge a packet of razor blades before he documented the vehicle details. The passport official duly stamped our passports to prove that we had left the country and we were given a gate pass to go under the raised barrier – out into no-man's land.

To reach the Iran border we travelled a further 75 miles along terrible roads with tortuous corrugations across the flat gravel plateau. Whenever Alec could, he drove off-road where the surface was smoother, but it proved time consuming as he snaked between the coarse shrubs, aware that they could become tangled in the wheels.

The Iranian border post was a collection of smart buildings with the railway track running between. A train had just pulled in and the passengers alighted to have their documentation and baggage checked. We parked the Land-Rover alongside a few other vehicles and were directed to the quarantine office, a huge, empty room painted green. An olive-skinned man in a white clinical jacket vetted our vaccination certificates, passed them back and nodded for us to go. No extra jabs for us, thank goodness.

Next to the passport office, where the officials wore smart uniforms with big, peaked caps. The lapels on their jacket shoulders were adorned with the gold braid of rank, to give weight to their self-importance, as they delighted in being in control. Our passports were found to be in order and stamped accordingly to show we had permission to be in Iran.

But it was not the quarantine or passport officers that made us a touch edgy – it was the customs officers.

A bearded young man dressed in a navy-blue suit came across to the Land-Rover, looked it up and down and said, 'I'm off to eat my lunch now. Drive your vehicle over there and park across the pit. While I'm away you can empty every part of this vehicle. I will inspect it thoroughly on my return.'

Alec followed his orders and positioned the Land-Rover over the pit for a full inspection. The wind cut across the vast countryside, which was empty and desolate apart from the train, a few vehicles and the buildings. As it blew, it covered everything in its path with a layer of dust.

'Our things will get filthy if we get them all out now,' I said to Alec. 'I dare say his lunch break will be a leisurely one. We could be waiting a couple of hours.'

'Well, we know that we're not hiding any drugs or weapons. Let's pray the Lord will work it out and we'll just empty the roof box.'

I placed our plastic tablecloth on the earth as Alec climbed up onto the bonnet and stood on the spare wheel to unpadlock and unlatch the box. Item by item he passed the contents of our wooden storage box down to me. Our possessions were displayed for all to see, just like a jumble sale.

It was early afternoon and three longhaired white youths were having their personal things removed from their backpacks and checked by another customs guy at a long table under an awning. He was rough and clumsy and a camera dropped to the ground. The owner picked it up and checked for damage. I wondered how it would be when the other customs officer looked through our things.

An hour later he showed up, looking bleary eyed after his lunch and nap. He muttered to us that we had not removed everything. We said nothing. Just let him get on with his job, poking through the cupboards, beneath the bench seat, under the bonnet and then down the steps into the pit to examine under the chassis. Next he climbed up onto the spare wheel on the bonnet and looked into the empty roof box and then riffled through its contents back down on the ground.

'What's this here?' he asked, tapping the wood frame along the roof.

'It's an elevating roof,' Alec replied.

'Show me.'

Alec unlatched the exterior catches whilst I climbed inside the Land-Rover and pushed the roof up into place. The officer climbed in for the second time and swept the back of his hand all over the insulating fabric of the curved aluminium surface. He checked on top of our worktop, running his fingers along the channel at the back. He found nothing suspicious and nonchalantly left and moved on to check the next vehicle.

I packed away the things he'd removed from the kitchen

cupboards, whilst Alec went into the customs office to complete the documentation with the Chief Officer.

It took a while to repack the roof box, as it was a jigsaw puzzle fitting everything in. We wound our watches back an hour. We were glad to gain the extra time to drive that afternoon far away from the border officials into Iran.

'Phew, that wasn't so bad after all,' Alec remarked.

'Thank God. That siesta did him wonders.' I smiled.

Total distance driven = 33,055 miles

Catching Up

25th January to 8th February 1978
Iran

Bukan, Iran
8th February 1978

Dear Mum, Dad, Margaret, Tony and Janet,

Well, here we are back in Iran. Hope you received the letter that we sent from Lahore. Can you believe it's one year since we left England? We're often thinking of all our friends and family at home and overseas. Jan's last count of how many postcards we've sent since being away is 150, and that excludes all those sent to you and her folks.

Thanks for your letter, which we collected in Esfahan. Also had letters from Jan's parents, and Nigel and Helen in Vienna. Pity we didn't get your Christmas card and letter in Kathmandu.

Mum, I thought I remembered you saying, that you didn't

want to be secretary for the local branch of the Women's Institute again. You're easily persuaded and you love it really! How are the birds in the aviary coping with the winter this year, Dad?

Give our congratulations to Cliff and Monica on their new baby girl. My old school buddy was a godsend. Do you remember just before we left your place, when the Land-Rover had a serious oil leak from the crankshaft and Cliff replaced the seal? What a major job that was. He saved the day.

Talking of babies, Nigel and Helen in Vienna wrote and told us great news: they're expecting their third child. They also warned us to stay well away from any contact with the Children of God. It's a cult! Apparently the leader of the organization, David Brandt Berg, alias Moses David, encourages all sorts of sexual practices to promote his take on Christianity. He communicates to his followers via those Mo Letters we've been collecting since Kathmandu. It's scary to think how easily we could have been sucked in and how many young people are. Needless to say we made a fire and burned the Mo Letters.

You say you have wintry weather; well, it's none too warm for us now. Every morning for the last ten days we've woken to find Jack Frost has been painting on the windows and all the metalwork inside the Land-Rover sparkles. But we've never been cold at night with our duvet and a blanket.

From the Pakistan/Iran border to Zahedan, Bam, Kerman, Yazd and Esfahan we've driven along paved roads through endless desert, often gravel plains with a few dry, brittle shrubs here and there.

At Esfahan, an interesting and pleasant town, we stayed at a smart campsite. It had the luxury of hot showers. We took care of all the necessary maintenance and chores and afterwards had a restful day or two there. Jan took the opportunity to repair my pyjamas.

Petrol here is only twenty-six pence a gallon, so we're able to fill up our fuel tanks for a song. This oil-rich country shows off its wealth in its smart, modern town buildings, smooth tarmac roads with the benefit of actual pavements and even ornamental roundabouts. There are many more privately owned cars and trucks and fewer men loaf about on street corners with nothing to do. We've visited a number of historical sites here and seen many Iranian tourists taking photos of one another on their day out. This is unusual to see the locals with cameras and gives a sense of western influence and modernity with personally organised leisure time, in contrast to the unrelenting working lifestyle of the nomadic and farming communities we saw in Asia.

The other day we visited the remains of Persepolis. Seven years before it was the 2,500th anniversary of the Persian Empire, so the wide road that led us to the site was flanked with the still standing flagpoles and streetlights, which seemed totally out of place in the remote desert location. A campsite of Middle-Eastern-style tents remained in the grounds. Apparently leaders of foreign states had been accommodated there during the celebration.

According to our tourist leaflet, Darius the First founded Persepolis in 518 BC. It was primarily built as a spectacular showcase centre for receptions and festivals of the Achaemenid Persian Dynasty. Unfortunately my namesake, Alexander the Great, came along in 330 BC and set fire to Persepolis. What remains of the original edifice is the best we've seen for grandeur. Stories were told through carved stone figures of warriors, citizens, animals and transport of the day, on the walls along the stately stairways. There were huge columns and the ruins of what must have been magnificent buildings. Breathtaking workmanship. It's hard to imagine how it was built – what ingenuity of engineering skills and of painstakingly detailed sculpting, and the sheer hard labour of many, many people.

On to Shiraz, where we visited two mosques with dazzling interiors of mirror work and stained glass windows that threw a rainbow of colours onto the mirrors. West to Kazerun, through the hills to Behbahan, passed the oil and gas fields across miles and miles of flat terrain. Jumbo orange flames burned off gas in the distance and plumes of black smoke rose high in the sky. Along the road going east came lorry after lorry all transporting giant metal pipes. We must have seen miles of pipeline going past. Next we came to the hectic industrial town of Ahvaz where the teeming traffic was chaotic, so we were glad to leave after changing money at the bank.

At Shush, previously known as Susa, we saw the ruins of the palace mentioned in the Biblical book of Esther. We also visited the shrine of the prophet Daniel, where his green marble tomb was housed in a mirror-embellished room. Before entering we removed our shoes and Jan was given a cloth to cover her hair. There were many pilgrims crowding in, who threw thousands of rials within the framework around the tomb, which they kissed and caressed.

On our journey today we stopped at a transport café for lunch. In pleasant, clean surroundings we were served a delicious meal of beef kebab on a plate of white rice, with a big dollop of creamy butter, a scoop of thick yogurt and a sprinkle of mild spices. Enjoyed with a chapatti and fine-tasting black tea. It was a memorable meal.

We plan to be back in England around 1st April after visiting friends. We have an invitation to spend several days with Nigel and Helen in Vienna, then my mate Bob from army days insists we spend Easter with him and his now fiancée Sabine, near Frankfurt. You should send your next letters to POSTE RESTANTE, IZMIR, TURKEY by 12th February, or as soon as you receive this letter.

See you all soon.

Love Alec and Jan

xxxxx

Total distance driven = 35,255 miles

Toil and Trouble in Turkey

9th to 13th February 1978
Turkey

Our adventures on our return into Turkey were tinged with trouble. What with the cold and snowy weather, we needed to keep focused on gaining ground going west. Then to top it all, a devil of a guy showed up one day and gave us the heebie-jeebies.

The border crossing from Iran into Turkey went as smooth as silk. The customs officer just had a quick look amongst the things in the back and then sent us on our way. Shepherd boys were busy tending their sheep on the snow-covered hills by delivering hay on small sledges. We weren't sure where those lads lived, as there were few houses about. When they gave signals requesting cigarettes and we had none to give, we expected a backlash of anger, but they just waved us on.

The road was variable from compacted snow to slippery, slushy mud. As we drove through a snow-covered mountain range, down into valleys and through gorges, we followed the course of a river. The road went right alongside the riverbank and at other times high above with a cliff drop directly down to the water. Frequently Alec had to avoid rocks that had fallen down onto the track.

We drove steadily down a steep incline to a bridge, crossed the river and continued on slowly for another forty-five minutes until we stopped at a barrier across the road. The local gendarme informed us that the road ahead was blocked and we'd have to backtrack thirty-five miles and head in the direction of Van. It was getting late in the day so we made haste and were able to reach the bridge and park in front of the local public workers' dwelling.

A middle-aged man came out to see what was up and we tried to communicate that we needed to be there for the night. It wasn't until we showed him the back of the Land-Rover where we would sleep that he understood and was willing for us to stay. As I fixed dinner there was a knock on the door and the man and his young friend invited us for tea.

Later we went into their humble house, into a simple room lit by an oil lamp and heated by a blazing wood burner. We had to keep moving our chairs back when the heat became unbearable. Then, with a never-ending supply of hot, sweet black tea, we were completely coddled. Our cheery hosts eagerly looked at and discussed between themselves the maps and brochures that Alec had brought along. It was a pleasant end to a tiring day.

A blast of cold air hit us when we eventually left their place to plod through the deep snow the short distance back to our chilly Land-Rover for the night.

We made an early start the next morning. It was six-thirty when we bade farewell to the workmen and drove across the bridge to ascend the road heading east towards Van. It was blowing a blizzard. The fresh snow was thick on the road and Alec drove extremely carefully in four-wheel drive. It was a narrow track that climbed through the hills with a cliff face to our left and a sheer drop to our right. Icy-cold cobalt-blue water flowed furiously in the river down below.

After only three miles the situation became treacherous as the road became steeper and the wheels on the Land-Rover wouldn't grip. The heavy vehicle stopped climbing upwards, but instead slid to the right. The wheels were turning forwards, but we were slipping backwards. Alec had to bring all his driving skills into action and hold her steady. We held our breath and sent arrow prayers heavenwards.

It was impossible to go forward, so Alec changed into reverse gear and slid and coerced our Land-Rover, slowly, slowly, down the hill. Miraculously, we arrived safely back at the bridge. Alec then had sufficient room to manoeuvre the vehicle around and drive across to the previous night's camp. We parked thankfully and breathed a sigh of relief.

I put the kettle on as we took time to weigh up the situation. For inspiration Alec picked up the Bible to read that day's study, which was about Moses leading the Israelites across the wilderness. We prayed to God to give us an answer to our predicament.

'We could be here for weeks,' Alec pondered.

'Well, at least we're safe,' I encouraged, 'and have plenty of food, warm clothes and fuel for the cooker.'

So there we were, quietly sat drinking tea and recovering from the horrendous fright as we waited for an answer.

'Snow chains! That's what we need, snow chains!' Alec suddenly exclaimed, thumping his clenched fist on the bulkhead. 'IDIOT! Why, oh why don't we have chains? What was I thinking?'

At that same moment there was a knock at the door. The young workman stood there with another man to see why we had returned. They too suggested snow chains.

On checking the map Alec estimated it was about five miles uphill to the nearest town of Hakkāri. We donned our warmest clothes and covered up with our waterproof jackets and trousers, woolly hats, scarves, gloves and boots. With the Land-Rover securely locked, we left it under the watchful eye of the workmen and set off at a steady pace to trudge through the snow. It was still snowing but the wind had dropped.

WOOF-WOOF-WOOF!

I jumped as a big, wolf-like dog bounded towards us. It didn't know whether to bite us or lick us, as it growled and wagged its tail at the same time. Carefully we left its territory and were glad it didn't follow us as we continued up the steep road.

A passing lorry driver took pity and stopped to give us a ride. We rode in the open back of the lorry, chilled by the rush of cold air as we travelled the last mile into town.

Hakkāri had an assortment of shops, a tourist hotel, several banks and market stalls that sold fresh fruit and vegetables. We went in search of auto supplies and a pleasant young man tagged onto us. Apparently during the summer tourist season he would assist visitors to the area. Unfortunately as we arrived at midday all the shops and banks were closed, so our man about town treated us to tea. Our presence in one of the two teahouses drew the attention and custom of the local men, as we brought a little interest on another snowy, wintry day.

We about gave up hope of ever buying snow chains as we waited and waited for the shops to open. At four our patience was rewarded when we tracked down a store that could sell us a set of snow chains for forty pounds. We gulped at the price, but needs must, so Alec changed a few traveller's cheques at the bank and we made our purchase. We were soon on our way out of town, walking on the slippery, snow-packed road, knowing that the night was drawing in and we had a long way to go down the hill.

After a mile, a pick-up truck pulled alongside us and offered to take us down to the bridge. We were thankful for the ride, but unsure if we were in a local taxi or not, so Alec prepared to pay him as we arrived at the bottom of the hill.

'*Zwei hundert lira*,' the driver said, speaking German, a commonly used language in Turkey.

'Two hundred lira!' Alec exclaimed, not believing the charge could be six pounds for such a short ride.

'*Ja, zwei hundert lira.*' He wasn't joking as he sneeringly repeated the sum.

We climbed out of the cab and Alec checked his pockets to see how much we had. The driver got out too and walked around to our side of his truck. I felt threatened by his aggressive stance.

Alec could only rustle up sixty-five lira and he offered this to the greedy man.

The driver grabbed the money, raised his clenched fist and shouted, '*Zwei hundert!*'

As I looked up I realized that his mates had arrived, their vehicles strewn alongside the truck. They gathered around and urged him on. Alec's eyes and mine met fearfully, as we had no idea where this sinister situation was heading. There was not a friendly face in sight and daylight was slipping away.

'Help!' I cried out silently as warm tears washed over my cold, flushed cheeks.

Alec continued to search for any money he might have missed. As he checked once again inside his jacket and under his thick knitted jumper, he discovered something in his shirt pocket. He pulled out two American one-dollar bills neatly folded together. He passed them to the driver, who examined the green bills, turning them this way and that and smoothing them flat. Bizarrely he kept only one dollar and returned the second to Alec.

The driver and the men slapped each other's backs and muttered with great satisfaction before returning to their vehicles and driving off.

We stood shaken and dumbfounded at what could have transpired had it not been for the power of the American dollar. The sum total of the dollar and the sixty-five lira the driver had already received was only eighty-five lira, less than half the amount that he'd demanded.

'Thank God for America,' Alec said as we began the final part of our walk across the bridge to the Land-Rover.

It was not long before we were welcomed into the workmen's house again. We sat by their cosy fire, drinking piping-hot tea as we related the terrible tale. Through the aid of pen and paper we conversed and discovered that we should only have paid twenty-five lira for the ride from town.

The next morning we were up early again. After breakfast, Alec drove the wheels onto the snow chains and fastened them tightly with bungees. We bade farewell to the workmen before driving again eastwards up the steep hill out of the valley. Thankfully the snow chains proved their worth as they gripped the snow and took us safely along. Every so often Alec would stop to check the chains, and when the bungees broke he made big rubber bands out of an old inner tube. On reaching the main road, we turned left towards Van, and at lunchtime Alec removed the chains, as the route was no longer snowbound.

We drove high in the mountains where the terrain was bleak and frozen. We arrived at Lake Van to see stunning scenery of deep-blue water surrounded by a winter wonderland of snowy hills down to the shore. A marvellous camping spot, although very close to the road so that when trucks went by they sounded their horns. In fact three individual truck drivers stopped to warn us that it was going to snow and it would become very cold. 'Why not go on to the next town and stay in a warm hotel?' they suggested. We assured them we were well aware of the conditions and would be okay.

As we were running low on water I took a saucepan full of fresh snow and melted it to make lots of hot drinks. For supper that evening I made a meat pie with carrots, followed by milk pasta and fruit. We were in bed by ten-thirty and were soon sound asleep.

Suddenly, at midnight, we were woken by the sound of a vehicle pulling up close by. Doors opened and closed and we heard voices of men approaching. Alec tried to open the window but it was jammed with ice, so he cautiously opened the back door.

Two armed soldiers had come to warn us of bandits. It was unsafe to stay there overnight and we must go to their guard base. We were sorely miffed, but this was not the time and place to insist on staying. After all, they had the guns!

So they waited whilst Alec half-dressed himself and climbed into the driver's seat to follow their escort. Meanwhile I knelt on the bed and kept my arms around our kitchen stuff on top of the work surface to prevent it flying everywhere. Fortunately it was not a long drive and once parked up, we were left in peace to sleep the rest of the night away.

It was indeed a very cold night, the coldest we had experienced; even the water in the kettle froze solid and the windows were glazed with artistic patterns. The route the next day to Tatvan and then Bitlis took us over snow-damaged, potholed tarmac roads and mucky mud tracks that sprayed brown slush up onto the Land-Rover.

But the roads improved as we left the snowy hills behind to drive beside undulating farmland where green blades of crops were sprouting through the tilled, dark earth. Donkeys were hard at work carrying heavy loads of branches for their owners. A welcoming, warm, sunny day drew the women out of their little mud houses. They were dressed in bright, colourful, long dresses and bloomers with white, flowing scarves covering their heads. Their appearance brightened our day with the hope of spring.

We drove via Diyarbakir and headed out onto the open plains going westwards. By the end of the day we'd driven 280 miles and found a quiet place to camp for the night by an abandoned military tank. For supper we had cheese omelette and kidney beans with bread and butter followed by apple crumble and custard. Bedtime.

Midnight madness revisited when we were rudely awoken by soldiers who whacked the back corners of our Land-Rover with their bayonet, 'at the ready' machine guns. They insisted we were in danger of bandits and must go to the safety of the gendarme post. It was a nerve-wracking ride following the armoured jeep in front, with another tailgating behind. We had no idea how far we had to go and we were dressed for bed and not for gallivanting in the chill of the night. Thirty miles later we arrived to find nowhere flat to park so we settled on a slope facing upwards at a tilt.

The following day we drove to Urfa where we bought the obligatory third-party car insurance. On to the country market town of Birecik, which stood on a hill by the Euphrates River. The terrain of rolling hills led to flat areas of cultivated land, and the earth changed shades from dark brown to orange and a rich red. Olive trees, apple trees and grape vines were still hibernating from the winter.

We continued on to Gaziantep, and then went south to Kilis, right next to the Syrian border. The road passed many Turkish lookout posts and vast military barracks. With the Syrian hills to our left and the snow-capped mountains of Turkey to the right, the scenery was delightful in the gentle, late-afternoon sunlight. Not wishing to be disturbed again that night, we approached a gendarme post and asked where we could park. They directed us to park just beyond the perimeter fence and later offered us a glass of tea.

Total distance driven = 35,439 miles

On the Tourist Trail

14th to 23rd February 1978
Turkey

Çanakkale, Turkey
23rd February 1978

Dear Mum, Dad, David, Paul and Joanne,

Thanks for the three letters we received from you in Izmir, including the registered letter. We were grateful to hear that Air Associates are enquiring on Alec's behalf for jobs when we return to England. Thanks, Dad, for sorting all our documents out; we were really pleased to find the Green Card had arrived safely.

We are both so looking forward to coming home and seeing you all. Thanks for saving a Christmas pudding for us to enjoy with our first Sunday roast dinner, which you've promised to cook on our return. If all goes well, we'll be sailing from the Hook of Holland on Friday night, 31st March, arriving in Harwich on

Saturday 1st April. We may call in to see the Great Aunts at Clacton-on-Sea on the way to Brentwood.

Since the letter I sent from Iran we have had quite the adventure driving along a southerly route through Turkey. After leaving the snow-covered hills of the east we were glad to find the sun and signs of spring in the picturesque countryside in the west. We are now in the land of olive trees and lemon, grapefruit and orange groves.

It was interesting to visit Antakya, which was built near to the ruins of Antioch where followers of Jesus Christ were first called Christians. The city bazaar was excellent with its range of inviting food stalls. They sold most things loose out of sacks, like flour, couscous, dry beans, lentils, wheat, sugar etc. If you wanted to buy cheese, they let you have a sample to taste and decide which sort you prefer. We bought some soft white cheese that had matured in a goatskin. The blackened portion scooped out of the leg is so strong it makes Gorgonzola taste like Primula. It's delicious sprinkled on spaghetti bolognaise.

Our latest achievement with food is with Alec making thick natural yogurt, using dried milk powder. He makes two pints at a time and we eat it with fresh fruit for dessert.

We saw a small wooden barrel of a sticky, brown, sweet substance, which the stall owner said tasted delicious spread on buttered bread. We dipped a finger into the goo and licked it clean. Yummy! Purchase made first, then we called in at the local tourist office to ask what we'd bought and discovered it was extract of raisin. You can try some when we get home.

So from Antakya to Iskenderun, on to Adana and then to the coastal town of Tarsus where St. Paul was born and Anthony met Cleopatra. Talk about history coming alive. Turkey is full of ruins and evidence of a bygone age. We visited Cennet and Cehennem, two caverns known as heaven and hell. The former was easy to descend into, but the latter was inaccessible. Alec went into a well, down a spiral staircase, to see the stalactites and stalagmites. Pretty spooky!

The ancient Roman amphitheatre of Aspendos, which could have seated twenty thousand people in its heyday, proved a great place to do the washing. Alec discovered an accessible tap on the outer wall of a closed café – closed because it isn't the tourist season right now. After days of solid rain, on that day at Aspendos it was scorching hot so the clothes soon dried. Alec took the opportunity to wash the dirty Land-Rover too. Nobody seemed to mind.

We drove just beyond Antalya and camped on the beach for a couple of days. It was so peaceful there we felt like staying for a week, but the weather was not so promising once again. On the Sunday many locals came for picnics and barbecues. A little girl gave me a bunch of yellow anemones and a lady gave us a dozen oranges. Alec changed the gear fluid and mended a puncture whilst we were there.

On Monday we drove back into Antalya and had an enjoyable walk around the delightful harbour and town. We sat drinking a glass of tea at a café by the waterfront and ate freshly baked pretzels. The water was so clear you could see the fish swimming about.

We called in at the hot springs of Pamukkale near Denizli, an amazing place of vast, white mineral steps down the side of a hill, with pools of warm water. The day was bitterly cold, so I wasn't about to undress and take a dip, but rather pulled my Chilean wool poncho close around me and we left.

We also visited the ruins of Ephesus and the lovely, friendly town of Selcuk where Alec managed to sell our jerry cans, as we no longer need them. Then we went north to Izmir to collect our letters from Poste Restante. It was even colder that day, so we had to bundle up and wear our hats, scarves and gloves as well.

After visiting the ruins of Pergamon near Bergama we drove

along a coastal road to find a place to park by the beach. We had an interesting evening when two men turned up in a delivery van and parked alongside us. They were very friendly Turkish men who insisted we join them for supper. So there we were, Alec and I, sitting in the back of their van, which was stacked with three thousand litres of wine. We ate mutton cooked in olive oil with green vegetables, spring onions and radish, enjoyed with fresh ekmek, the local bread, and a glass or two of wine!

Conversation was limited to the little German they and Alec knew, but they made it clear they were not at ease for us to stay for the night at the beach. They insisted we follow them to Ayvalik and we agreed – to keep them happy. We parked by the harbour, and then the oldest man took us across to the nearest restaurant to drink tea. Such generosity!

So today we are in Çanakkale parked on a high area of ground, an old cannon site, watching a flotilla of ships moving to and fro along the stretch of water known as the Dardanelles, between Asia and Europe. Earlier, when we were in town to buy the ferry tickets to make our way on to Greece, we heard a cacophony of noise being made by a four-man band playing drums, clarinet and violin. They heralded the arrival of four 'fighting' double-humped camels adorned in regal tasseled blankets, complete with jingling bells. I guess the fight was to take place later in the day.

So this is the last letter I'll be writing to you all. The next that you'll hear from us will be when we talk face to face. Can't wait!

So take care. See you soon.

Lots of love,

Alec and Janice.

xxxxx

Total distance driven = 37,312 miles

Homeward Bound

24th February to 22nd March 1978
Greece – former Yugoslavia – Austria – Germany
– Holland – England

At our first seaside village in Greece we called by a grocery store and were welcomed by the owner with a glass of brandy. That certainly warmed our cockles on the fresh, wintry morning as we browsed around the shop. We bought the essentials – butter, olives, cheese and wine – then were directed to the bakery to buy delicious sesame bread. The traditional village of quaint white cottages with red-tiled roofs was flanked on either side along the coast by new holiday homes of all shapes, sizes and states of completion. One villa masqueraded as a flying saucer.

The road took us inland through the hilly countryside, past many villages, but we were seeking our own private beach campsite and persistently took any road we thought would take us closer to the sea. En route to Kassandra, we saw a sign to 'Sani Beach Camping' and followed the road through a pine forest to the site, which was unfortunately closed for the winter. Then we had a right merry-go-round trying to find our way out along the dirt tracks, which soon turned to mud. Eventually we left the forest and drove by cultivated fields down towards a lovely, isolated, sandy beach, where the sea gently lapped the shore. We made camp while the bright-orange sky mellowed as the sun slipped behind Mount Olympus just across the water.

Having located a prime beach hideaway, the next day we took advantage of the chance to relax and sat out on our Indian bamboo armchairs. There was a chill in the air so Alec made a fire with some driftwood that he'd gathered. A little black mongrel dog was walking by and it came and sat with us for a while, enjoying the warmth of the fire.

We took the opportunity to study further of Paul's travels in Turkey and Greece. It was remarkable how often places we were reading about in the Bible had coincided exactly with where we were travelling at that stage of our journey.

During the day many small boats sailed by. It was a shame the water was too cold to take a dip, but to be by the water, to smell the salty air and to hear the wash of the waves was bliss. We tucked into hot pancakes cooked in the frying pan over the open fire.

The evening drew to a close as we drank a mug of coffee and played Scrabble as the fire died down. Three fisherman walked by in their thigh-high boots, carrying glowing lanterns. We watched the sky being painted with changing golden hues as the sun slowly said goodnight.

From tranquil beach to hectic modern city: we entered Thessaloniki the next day, our first western metropolis since leaving Vienna six months before. High-rise flats and offices, fancy shop windows, fashionable clothing and furnishings all on show. As we walked along the high street we looked like scruffy country bumpkins alongside the expensively, elegantly dressed city slickers.

At the huge supermarket, shelves were stacked full of the same items packaged in different wrappings, promoting why you should buy this brand or that. The hustle and bustle of shoppers, who jumped the queue at the checkout, disturbed us, as they raced on to their next engagement. We left without making a purchase, then discovered a small, quiet corner shop down the road and found just what we were looking for: a culinary souvenir – three kilos of plump green olives sealed in a large, screw-top, yellow, plastic container.

From Greece we drove into Yugoslavia, having convinced the border patrol that we were not hiding any drugs, no not even under the bed. The road to Skopje followed the contour of hills, down into valleys and through many tunnels. The roads at first were in good order, then deteriorated to potholed tarmac or cobbled roads that juddered the Land-Rover as the wheels drove over. Many wooden carts were going along, pulled by fine, well-fed horses with shiny coats and long, flowing manes. They clip-clopped along the roads while being overtaken by a wide variety of cars, from family saloons to expensive Lamborghinis. As we drove by rolling plains of cultivated land, farmers were working with horses and cows as well as using tractors. White snowdrops and yellow primroses decorated the grass verges.

We spent a day in Belgrade, this time wearing our best clothes as we left the Land-Rover parked in Republique Square and moseyed along one of the main streets, Marsala Tita. The city gents and ladies were dressed in leather coats or jackets as they popped in and out of the modern shops where eye-catching displays of goods were on sale. We ventured into a five-storey department store where they sold practically everything. There were colossal stacks of goods, the majority made in Yugoslavia. The food floor was truly amazing with every type of cheese imaginable, smoked meats and sausages, freshly baked bread, bottles of locally produced wines, tinned foods and live fish, which they would kill on the spot after you made your choice. The strong smells struggled for dominance, creating a tangible but invisible cloud.

Grateful for the fresh, crisp air as we walked out into the street, we soon found ourselves following a crowd of people walking into a rather grand Church. The fragrance of incense and multiple burning candles filled the atmosphere. The worshippers kissed a candle before lighting the wick. As they walked around the sanctuary they would stop before a gilded icon of a saint and press their lips to the painting and then go on to the next one.

Feeling hungry, we left to search for some tasty food. Our noses led us to a busy restaurant for a scrumptious beef burek, a sweet apple strudel and a glass of beer each.

We took a walk through the city park along with many locals to see the boats and barges at the confluence of the Rivers Danube and Sava. The Belgrade Fortress was strategically built to overlook the two rivers and it housed a military museum with cannon and tanks displayed outside on the grass.

Our days of sightseeing were drawing to a close. By now it was early March and our minds and hearts were set towards England. But we still had to make a few promised visits to friends on our way back.

After five days travelling through Yugoslavia we crossed into Austria and headed through the Alps towards Vienna on modern, well-maintained highways. The temperature dropped as we climbed upwards to the Semmering Pass. The pine-forested mountainsides were draped in snow. Skiers of all ages whizzed down the mountain ski-slopes, and then hopped on a chair lift to go up to the top again. The picturesque alpine houses supported a thick layer of heavy snow on their steep roofs.

Nigel and Helen had reminded us every time they wrote that we should visit on our way back, so we were very surprised to find they were not at home when we arrived in Vienna. I phoned at a call box, but no one answered. We drove around to their home at four, but no one was in. Maybe they were out for a walk and Nigel was at work? We waited until half-past-five but no one came. We drove to Nigel's office, but the lights were off and no one was there. We called at a corner shop for bread and yogurt and went back to their home – no one.

As we were standing waiting and wondering what to do – the landlord showed up. He informed us that Helen's father had died suddenly, hence the family were away in England. Their absence was not of their choosing, but we were cheered when the landlord kindly checked their mailbox for us and found two letters from our parents. We thanked him and drove off to the woods to the car park at Bellevue, the abandoned restaurant where we had first encountered Nigel. It was raining.

We had a cup of tea to soothe our disappointment over our absent friends as we opened our letters.

'Wow, Alec, listen to what Dad's written,' I chirped up. 'Air Associates have had a good response for job prospects and Brymon Airways in Plymouth, Devon, want to interview you.'

'That's great news,' Alec replied, 'and the Southwest will be a fresh new area to explore when we settle back in England.'

Within a couple of days of driving on the autobahns from Austria into Germany we arrived in Offenbach, near Frankfurt, at Bob and Sabine's. Having welcomed us on our outward journey over a year before, they were thrilled to have us back again to stay for a ten-day holiday at their flat. While Bob, an aircraft engineer, was out working at the airport and Sabine was teaching at school, they let us have the freedom of their home to relax. Good food, bubble baths, lazing around reading, window-shopping in the city, a visit to the pub and an outing to the bowling alley – it was an opportunity to re-orientate ourselves to the norm.

On 21st March 1978 we left their home to drive to England. It was probably the worst day for weather of our whole trip as we battled snow, hailstorms, high winds and driving rain. The windscreen wipers did their best to keep up, but it was a struggle. The drive amongst the heavy traffic on the autobahn was a real challenge for Alec, as vehicles thundered along past our well-travelled Land-Rover.

We knew we were driving through Holland as we passed by canals with houseboats anchored and windmills, their sails battered by the gales. No one was out and about cycling!

We arrived at the Hook of Holland to book a place on the 11 p.m. crossing to Harwich, Essex. We were surprised not to drive onto the Dutch ferry. Instead our Land-Rover went on its own adventure when it was lifted high into the air by a crane and lowered onto the rocking deck. The crossing was rough, we slept restlessly and I felt extremely seasick at one stage.

Morning came and the weather had calmed down. We went to the washrooms to freshen up and were ready to disembark by seven. Our Land-Rover was the first to be lifted by crane from the deck onto dear old Blighty. As we drove to the customs declaration station, we were prepared to declare all. The jolly friendly officer was only interested in my necklace from Cameroon, in case I could grow marijuana plants from the seed beads!

It was a short drive into town and we arrived before the banks were open. Alec only had seventy pence in his pocket and we were almost out of fuel. Fortunately there was a cosy café open and we had enough to buy two cups of tea and two Welsh rarebits.

The bank opened at half-past-nine. We changed money, bought fuel and were soon back en route, glad to be driving on the left.

Our first call was to visit my Great Aunts at Clacton-on-Sea, three quaint, elderly spinsters who could have stepped right out of a storybook – Alice, Glad and Maude. They were always interested in our travels and welcomed our visit.

Then we stopped at Latchingdon, to visit my dearest friend Rosslyn and her husband Brian and daughter Laura. While we had been away there was a new addition to the family, Gavin, one of a number of babies born to various cousins and friends during our absence. It was wonderful to meet the little one and I wondered how long it would be before we were expecting.

Each mile we drove, we were closer to home. We hadn't phoned my folks and they were not expecting us for another week. I can't tell you how excited I felt to be seeing them again. Tony, Betty, David and Paul Howes, plus Joanne: my very own family. It would be a while before we could see Alec's folks, Minion, Marjorie, Margaret and Tony and our lovely niece Janet, but that would be another day to anticipate with great joy.

We rolled into Brentwood, turned right at Wilson's Corner, drove down the Ongar Road to Larkins Playing Fields, turned right again into Windsor Road and pulled up outside our family home. I jumped out and skipped to the front door as Alec locked our trusty Land-Rover. I rang the bell and heard someone approaching in the hallway. The door opened and there stood my Mum.

'Janice!' she cried as she reached her hands out to me. With a kiss on my cheek she called to Dad.

'Tony – put the kettle on. They're home!'

Total distance driven = 39,583 miles through 29 countries in Europe, Africa and Asia.

After

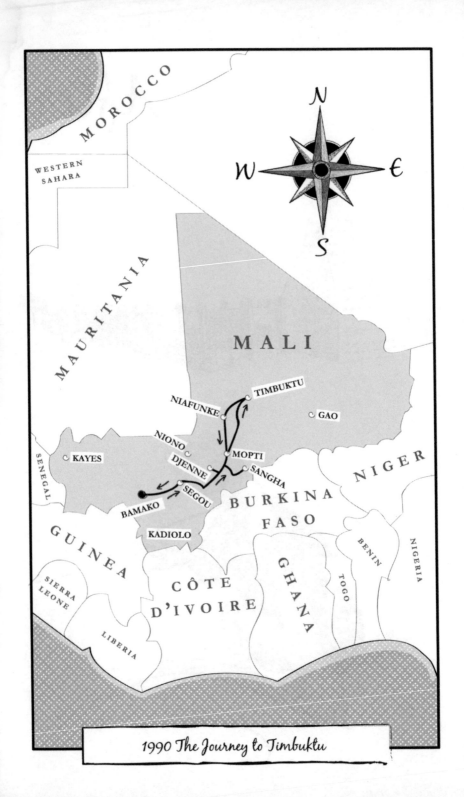

1990 The Journey to Timbuktu

Onwards We Travel

Twelve years later whilst living in Mali,
we took an adventurous trip with our four children,
Esther (11), Heidi (9), Charles (4), Maria (2),
and Enoch, our Malian co-worker.

Alec & Jan Forman,
Mission Aviation Fellowship,
Bamako, Mali, West Africa.
7th July 1990

Dear Mum and Dad,

The long-awaited trip to Timbuktu, the mysterious desert city, has taken place! The journey was over 1,200 miles there and back again. Each member of the family has many tales to tell of such a trip. Here are just a few.

A water pump, pipes, people and baggage were loaded into the vehicle before we set off around eight in the morning for the eight-hour drive to Djenné. We arrived mid-afternoon in time for the weekly market, where for Esther the most interesting part was the horse and cart park – some horses lazily munching hay in their nosebags, others being harnessed, many setting out for home, pulling gaily painted wooden carts loaded down with whole families and their market purchases. Jan enjoyed re-visiting Djenné, her first time since 1977 during our Land-Rover trip. Little has changed since.

The next evening found us at Sangha in Dogon country, a collection of villages perched on top of the Bandiagara escarpment. Maria had fun sitting up high on my shoulders as we all took an early-morning guided tour down the rocky path. We saw the caves of the ancient Telem people high under the ridge of the escarpment. The legend goes that the Telem used levitation to access their homes. Lower down the rusty-red cliff, we visited the camouflaged mud villages.

Mopti was to be our departure point as we set course for the north, but first we had to go on a ferry across the River Niger. Charles was very excited, as it had been his preoccupation for several days. 'When do we go on the boat, Dad?' he would frequently ask.

On reaching the other side, the track became imprecise with many false trails, but Enoch and I remembered between us the direction to go, as we entered the true Sahel with its sandy terrain and scattered thorn bushes. Late in the afternoon we arrived at Diré, to stay with Don and Sue and their four children, Stacie, Steve, Lindsey and Lesley. Our children were antsy to be out of the vehicle to play and make new friends. That night was spent sleeping on beds set up on the flat mud roof, under the stars – magical.

The next morning Rally arrived at the house to be our guide to a Bella Tuareg village some six miles from town, going along donkey tracks. We arrived at a group of grass-mat huts where I was to survey the possibility of digging a well. The water would be used for drinking and household needs and Rally had hopes of having a fenced-off vegetable garden too. His wife had literally gone mad with starvation a few months before and had needed hospitalization and prayer to stay alive and become sane. To grow vegetables was unusual there in the desert, but it would be a way of increasing food supplies for the family. Life is incredibly hard and at present they use a dug well, but dare not pull too much water as the sides might cave in, destroying their fragile lifeline. But a concrete-lined well would secure water for themselves, their animals and for growing vegetables.

As logistically it will be as easy to dig two wells as one, we will be seeking funds for another. The second well will be at a village of fishermen and their families of the Bozo people group. Their only drinking water is from the river, which is host to any number of diseases. Here is a real opportunity to make a difference in the lives of these people.

Our surveying completed, we then drove further north to Timbuktu and stayed in the mission guesthouse. On the Monday morning, the Pastor of the fledgling Timbuktu Church drove with Enoch and me to an existing new well in the desert, where the pump we had brought from Bamako was to be installed.

We first sat on a dune under a thorn bush with the Chief and elders of the local Bella people and drank tea. On such occasions it's a great temptation to show our western impatience to get on with the task in hand, but it's more important to be willing to sit and drink tea than to show off your efficiency to them.

Over the following five days the pump installation went ahead as planned with a few hold-ups: like waiting a day and a half for a lorry to be repaired that was to bring the gravel; needing to find a source of water to mix the cement when the nearest well dried up after only pulling twenty gallons; then a huge dust storm came through on the last evening so we had to abandon the work and drive back into Timbuktu, before our original tracks were obliterated by the shifting sands. The next morning the task was completed and the pump installed. By midday clean, clear water issued from the pump drawn from one hundred feet below ground.

That evening we had arranged to show the Jesus film at the village that would benefit from the pump, but late afternoon a tremendous wind struck Timbuktu, bringing torrential rain for an hour that threatened to destroy the mud houses. Come early evening the sky had cleared and we drove out to the village. Some forty people gathered to sit on the damp sand dunes under the starlit night. The Pastor narrated the story of Jesus in their Tamashek language prior to the video film being projected in French.

It was good to have the opportunity to also visit the Pastor in his home and meet his family. Heidi especially enjoyed playing with Zaida, their cute Dachshund puppy, and I'm being petitioned to bring back a pair of puppies from the next litter when I return here in November.

Amongst many other memories, I remember how the Lord had a hand in arranging our return route. This trip being with the family, I very much wanted to minimize any dangers in travel. On our way up in mid-June we had crossed Lake Débo when it was dry, but after the rains this was a risky route as the lake could have flooded.

We returned to Diré, to stay overnight and enjoy once again Sue's delicious home cooking: chicken with biscuits and gravy. Then everyone was up early the following morning, as I planned to leave at six to try to make the twelve-hour drive to the tarmac road at Niono before dark. But, just as we were about to leave, I discovered a slow puncture on a front wheel. It took an hour to repair, before setting off on bush roads to a village near to Niafunké. There we had to choose the route to Niono or take the route to Mopti. As we were asking the locals the way to Niono, a UNICEF vehicle driven by a Malian came alongside. He said he was driving to Mopti, as it was the shorter distance to the tarmac road. So we went in convoy with him and didn't even get our tyres wet, arriving in Mopti around four in the afternoon.

We slept on the roof of a guesthouse until three in the morning, when the heavens opened. Quickly we scrambled off and went down the steps to keep dry inside. The storm lasted for five hours as it swept across Mali. If we had gone the other way as planned, we could have been stuck in a sea of mud and it would have taken days to reach Niono. Surely God allowed that puncture to delay us, in order that we would meet another 'Angel' that day?

Thankful, to have arrived home safe and sound.

With lots of love from
Alec, Janice,
Esther, Heidi, Charles and Maria
xxxxxx

Appendix

Useful Information for the Reader

QUICK CONVERTER

1 mile = 1.61 kilometres
1 kilometre = 0.62 miles

1 UK gallon = 1.20 US gallon
1 UK gallon = 4.55 litres
1 litre = 1.76 pints
1 pint = 0.57 litres
1 quart = 1.14 litres

1 pound = 0.45 kilograms
1 kilogram = 2.20 pounds

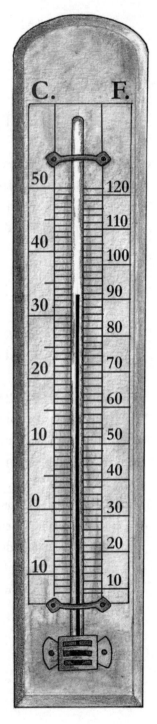

FAMILY TREE AS OF 1977

Minion & Marjorie Forman had two children, Alec & Margaret.
Margaret had one child Janet and was married to Tony Snaith.
Tony & Betty Howes had three children, David, Janice & Paul.
Alec Forman married Janice Howes on 5th April 1974.

CURIOUS FACTS

At age 16 years Alec walked the Pennine Way - 256 miles.
At age 16 years Jan led the Brentwood Drum Majorettes.

Foreman Glacier (69°18′S 71°22′W Coordinates: 69°18′S 71°22′W) is a glacier flowing south-southeast from the Havre Mountains into Palestrina Glacier, in the northern portion of Alexander Island, Antarctica. It was surveyed by the British Antarctic Survey (BAS), 1975–76, and was named by the UK Antarctic Place-Names Committee in 1980 after David Alexander Foreman, a BAS aircraft mechanic at Adelaide Station, 1973–76.[1]
http://en.wikipedia.org/wiki/Foreman_Glacier
(NB. There may be a spelling error in Forman,
but we're delighted anyway!)

WHAT IS A LEAF SPRING?

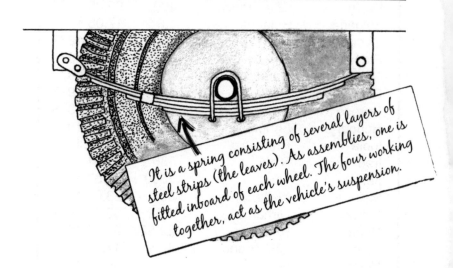

It is a spring consisting of several layers of steel strips (the leaves). As assemblies, one is fitted inboard of each wheel. The four working together, act as the vehicle's suspension.

We diligently kept records of every penny we exchanged or spent. Over the 403 days of the trip we spent on average £10 a day.

EXCHANGE RATES
FOR ONE POUND STERLING

COUNTRY	CURRENCY	£1	DATE
Afghanistan	Afghanis	77	15.09.1977
Algeria	Dinars	6.75	27.02.1977
Austria	Shillings	27.66	19.07.1977
Benin	CFA Francs	400	09.05.1977
Bulgaria	Bulgarian Lev	1.6	17.08.1977
Cameroon	CFA Francs	400	28.04.1977
France	Francs	8	14.02.1977
Germany	Deutsch Marks	3.8	20.07.1977
Ghana	Cedis	5	14.05.1977
Greece	Drachmas	68	26.02.1978
Hungary	Forints	33	06.08.1977
India	Rupees	15	14.10.1977
Iran	Rials	136.2	25.01.1978
Italy	Lire	1500	05.07.1977
Mali	Mali Francs	800	28.05.1977
Morocco	Dirhams	7.62	30.02.1977
Nepal	Rupees	22.52	05.12.1977
Niger	CFA Francs	400	17.03.1977
Nigeria	Naira	1	04.04.1977
Pakistan	Rupees	18.5	17.01.1978
Rumania	Lei	20.5	10.08.1977
Spain	Pesetas	113	30.02.1977
Togo	CFA Francs	400	11.05.1977
Tunis	Dinar	0.72	16.06.1977
Turkey	Lira	30.3	24.08.1977
Upper Volta	CFA Francs	400	22.05.1977
Yugoslavia	Dinars	34.9	02.03.1978

	A page from our many records...					
27/8	60 Multivites - Istanbul	L	27-00		–	90
29/8	Cap - Tarakli	L	30-00	£1	– 00	*
31/8	Turkish coffee maker-Ankara	L	30-00	£1	– 00	*
1/9	Petrol for cooker- Aksaray	L	13-00		–	43
2/9	Peg doll from Derinkuyu	L	15-00		–	50 *
3/9	2 Turkish cups+ saucers Urgup	L	40-00	£1	– 33	*
3/9	Nomadic carpet-Kayseri	L	1,000-00	£33	– 00	*
5/9	3 litres B/P oil -Erzurum	L	60-00	£2	– 00	
5/9	Air pressure gauge " Tehran	L	40-00	£1	– 33	
9/9	Air mail env+paper-postcards	R	90			73
10/9	Bridgestone tyre-Sply-Tehran	R	3,330	£27	– 15p	
10/9	Newspaper -Tehran	R	10			08
11/9	New tyre fitted -Amol	R	50			41
12/9	Petrol for cooker-Shahpahad	R	18			13
14/9	Washing-up liquid-Mashad	R	46			37
14/9	9 us gallon eng oil 2uogall Gear	R	2,500	20		37
15/9	2 litres petrol cooker-Taibad	R	16			13
22/9	Gift to our patient-Laghcaran	A	100		1	30
26/9	Horse-riding -Bande Amir	A	100		1	30
30/9	2 litres petrol-cooker Bamyan	A	17			22
1/10	Notebook, batteries, pencils, crayons	A	54			70
2/10	2 grass baskets - Kabul	A	70			91
2/10	2 toilet rolls - "	A	52			67
2/10	100 Razor blades - Kabul	A	200		2	60
2/10	Springs+repair- tube change Kabul	A	755		9	80
					108	38

List of equipment and

CLOTHES

ALEC	JAN
blue anorak	red anorak
waterproof jacket and trousers	waterproof jacket & trousers
2 pairs jeans	2 pairs jeans
FID* jumper	FID* jumper
red velour jumper	red velour jumper
blue velour shirt	yellow velour jumper
blue/white check shirt	green velour jumper
purple check long sleeved shirt	african patterned blouse
brown check long sleeved shirt	cheese-cloth cream blouse
short sleeved shirts x 2	cream & brown trimmed vest
khaki shirt	blue velour shirt
smart trousers	tie-dye green top & skirt
underpants	red & white knitted hat
socks, heavy & lighter pairs	shorts
leather boots	long green skirt
Wellington boots	embroidered long red skirt
sandals	nursing uniforms x 2
shoes	knickers
maroon polo-necked jumper	bras
shorts	socks, heavy & lighter pairs
FID* plaid warm shirts	tights
scarf yellow	sandals
hat	lace-up shoes
swimming trunks	bikini
jungle hat	boots
red & white Arabian headdress	red & white Arabian headdress
overalls	cream & brown cardigan
ties x 2	gloves
belts	chiffon scarves
gloves	brown & white Chilean poncho

*Falkland Island Dependant Survey = Alec's from Antarctica

380

supplies for the trip...

PERSONAL ITEMS

toothpaste
after-shave lotion
Eskamel anti-spot
tweezers
emery board
handkerchiefs
nail brush
sun-tan oil
toothbrushes x 4
tampons
hand cream

nail scissors
hair grips
razor & blades
talcum powder
bars of soap
deodorant
perfume
lip salve
nail clippers
hair cutting scissors
shampoo

hair brush
comb
2 watches
jewellery
make-up
hand mirror
money belts
passport pouches
sun glasses

TRAVEL DOCUMENTS & USEFUL BOOKS

passports with visas
UK drivers licenses
international drivers licenses
UK cheque book
Carnets de Passage for vehicle
camping carnet
travellers cheques
cash in various currencies
accounts book
log books and diaries
receipts for cameras etc.
french/english dictionary
spare passport photographs
Bartholomew Maps: Europe & Asia
Michelin Map 153 Africa North &
West

vaccination booklets with
inoculations against:
small pox, yellow fever, polio,
gamma-globulin for hepatitis,
diptheria/pertussis/tetanus,
cholera, typhoid.
photocopies of professional &
educational certificates
insurances: personal, baggage,
medical & vehicle

MEDICAL SUPPLIES

contraceptive pills
sterile paraffin gauze
aspirin
Stemetil
potassium–
permanganate
calamine lotion
spasmo-cibalgin
slow sodium
Piriton
bandage kit
cicatrin powder
insect repellant
hydrogen peroxide
paracetamol

Anusol
Paludrine
Tyrosets
ampicillin
gentian violet
Eurax
scissors
thermometer
Whitfield's Oint.
Dettol
magnesium sulphate
Deep Heat Balm
Avloclor
Synalar cream
tetracycline

Gellusil
syringes/needles
cotton wool
Kurafid book
Pink healing oint.
laxative tablets
mercurochrome
eye ointment
multivitamins
tooth tincture
elastic bandage
plasters
Mimm's meds book
Midwifery book

HOUSEHOLD SUPPLIES

sleeping bags x 2
pillows x 2
pillow cases x 4
duvet with cover
green fleece blanket
nylon fitted bottom sheet
mosquito net
mini-electrical fan
washing powder
tea towels
j-cloths
washing-up liquid
Vim scouring powder

disinfectant
Milton fluid
clothes line, rack & pegs
coathangers
hand brush
saddle soap
sponge
sealed lid bucket/washing
enamel bowl
spare shoe laces
small sweeping brush
scouring pads
Swarfiga cleaning gel

whistling kettle
lemon squeezer
egg cups x 2
enamel pudding bowl
chemical toilet
water pump
charcoal water purifier
plastic jerry cans for water
water connector plumbing
Primus petrol stove 1 burner
Primus paraffin stove 2 burner
spares for cookers
large plastic storage boxes
small plastic storage boxes
mugs x 2
large plates x 2
tea plates x 2
soup bowls x 2
forks x 2
knives x 2
spoons x 2
teaspoons x 2
rolling pin
wooden-spoon
tablespoon
plastic washing-up bowl
wash-bag
toilet fluid
kitchen mini scales
soap dish
lemon slice squeezer
battery hand mixer
coloured towels
toilet rolls x 20
funnel

candles
matches
plastic seals for tins
muslin cloth
fire extinguisher
cruet set
tin opener
FID* knife & sharpener
sieve
small ladle
aluminium foil
grater
sharp knife
bread knife
vegetable knife
bottle opener
corkscrew
nest of saucepans
saucepan handle grip
pressure cooker
measuring jug
biscuit barrel
garbage bags
rags
teapot
fish slice
tea strainer
stainless steel serving dish
flannels
Thermos flask

FOOD

Ryvitas
Oxo cubes
baked beans
BAS* treats
bread mix
semolina
marmalade
saccharin
rice
dried yeast
salt
black pepper
curry powder
herbs
honey
jams
arrowroot
spaghetti
vinegar
lentils
currants
sultanas
jellies
sugar
flour
cookery books

cooking oil
margarine
Alpen
Horlicks
porridge oats
tins of: evaporated
milk, rice pudding,
cheese, soup,
pilchards, sardines,
meat.
packets of soup:
chicken, minestrone,
scotch broth, tomato,
mushroom, ox-tail.
dried food:
milk, carrots, fish,
pears, peaches,
meat blocks, egg
powder, sliced onions,
garden peas, peppers,
potato flakes,
tomatoes,
mushrooms,
mixed vegetables,
apple flakes, prunes,
cabbage, apricots.

tea bags 900
boiled sweets
vanilla essence
vegetable broth
peppermint tea
brown sugar
peach whirl
Marmite
paprika
spices
bicarbonate of soda
peanuts
butterscotch whirl
lemonade powder
lemon squeeze
glucose
compo biscuits
pearl barley
mustard
haricot beans
Ovaltine
bolognaise flavour
Angel Delight
blancmange
custard powder
jars of paste

MISCELLANEOUS SUPPLIES

penknives x 2
still camera
flash for camera
camera haze filter
batteries for cameras
cine camera
protective camera bag

silica-gel crystal sachets
films
binoculars
compass
sellotape
brown shopping bag
swiss cow horn

white-out

pack of cards

dice

Scrabble

<u>trading goods</u>: marbles, necklaces, safety pins.

rubber torch with batteries

felt-tip pens

pocket magnifier

plastic bags

Army New Testament

tambourine

pencils & sharpener

eraser

safety pins

nylon string

elastic bands

Parker pens & refills

smoke flares

hot water bottle

hair rollers

Penlite & batteries

drawing pins

nursing scissors

steel measuring tape

airmail envelopes

writing pad

sewing kit

photos of family etc.

graph paper

ruler & divider

address book

radio/cassette recorder

blank postcards

carbon paper

key rings

alarm clock

mile measure for map

Solitaire

coloured pencils

two-man tent

stapler & staples

LANDROVER SPARES & TOOLS

clutch

fuel pump

e-metal

plugs & bulbs

inner tubes

oil & fuel filters

sand ladders

bungees

engine oil

winch rope

shovel

brakes

shock absorber

coil

fan belt

puncture repair kit

gaskets

light rubber spares

transmission oil

brake fluid

tool box

hydraulic bottle jack

tyre levers

Acknowledgements

Four years ago when I began the project of writing our story I never knew who would step up and support me with this venture. I am grateful to Howard, with TeachBeyond, for giving me the freedom to focus on writing this book. My thanks to Helen, Bo, Heidi, Mary Beth, Maria, Susannah, Maysie, Tomas, Myrna, Elva and Drew, who willingly gave of their valuable time to read the text at different stages in the process. Your valuable critique and wise counsel enabled me to develop and take a hold of the thousands of words that tumbled from my mind as I tapped into our travel diaries and letters.

Additional thanks to those professionals who have used their expertise and skills to complete the publication of this book to such a high standard: David B, Charlie, Morwenna, Ally, Jeremy, Rosie, Naomi and Sarah. Special thanks to John, for the time you devoted to the voice recording of our reading extracts from the book.

While there have been readers of the manuscript, there have also been listeners. Those who have gathered around our dining table for a meal and have graciously listened to my reading a chapter or two. A larger audience listened to me read a few pages during Dinner & Dialogue at The Art Factory. Thanks for all your valuable encouraging reviews. I'm also grateful for the ladies at CBSI and the folk at ACB who have patiently supported me in this venture.

Thanks to friends in Germany, Mali and Moldova who have shown enthusiastic interest in the book. Hopefully it will be a possibility one day to have it translated into your languages.

Many thanks to all of you who followed the progress of the completing stages of this book since January 2013, through our Facebook page, 'Operation Publish'. It has been a joy to gather so many known and unknown supporters around the world, as we have shared extracts from the text and scores of our travel photographs.

Acknowledgements

You have been a great motivation for me to keep going and now that you have the completed book, may it be a jolly good read.

Thanks to our family and many supporting friends who have faithfully backed us up through thick and thin, as we returned from this epic journey in 1978 to continue on the greatest adventure of all. We welcome interaction and your comments through our webpage
www.strangerslikeangels.com

A special mention has to go to the 'Operation Publish' team who went the extra mile. This has been a Forman family project as each one of our children has come alongside me to contribute their talents in significant ways to make this book happen.

You are the Star team of whom I am very proud indeed.

Esther – designed the cover, created the illustrations, maps and other artistic elements.

Heidi – my personal assistant, constant encourager, avid proofreader and creative advisor.

Charles – marketing advisor, social media and webpage instigator, promotional trailer.

Rebekah – team psychologist who stood by when the tears fell and I was stuck for the right words.

Maria – scanned over one thousand of our travel slides and edited and presented the photos.

And to my extraordinary husband Alec, without whom this story would not have happened. He is the love of my life and as this book is published in 2014 we will celebrate forty years of marriage.

Janice Barbara Forman